THE WORLD OF ULYSSES S. GRANT

SERIES EDITORS

John F. Marszalek & Timothy B. Smith

TIMOTHY B. SMITH

THE DECISION WAS ALWAYS MY OWN

ULYSSES S. GRANT AND THE VICKSBURG CAMPAIGN

Southern Illinois University Press
Carbondale

Southern Illinois University Press
www.siupress.com

Printed in the United States of America

21 20 19 18 4 3 2 1

Jacket illustrations: *top*, "Siege of Vicksburg," cropped (Library of Congress; original print by L. Prang and Company, July 5, 1888); *center*, "U. S. Grant, Lt. Gen. U.S.A.," colorized (Library of Congress; original photograph by E. and H. T. Anthony, circa 1862–64); *bottom*, map showing the siege of Vicksburg (USGenWeb Archives).

Library of Congress Cataloging-in-Publication Data
Names: Smith, Timothy B., 1974– author.
Title: The decision was always my own : Ulysses S. Grant and the Vicksburg Campaign / Timothy B. Smith.
Description: Carbondale : Southern Illinois University Press, 2018. | Series: The world of Ulysses S. Grant | Includes bibliographical references and index.
Identifiers: LCCN 2017040510 | ISBN 9780809336661 (cloth : alk. paper) | ISBN 9780809336678 (e-book)
Subjects: LCSH: Vicksburg (Miss.)—History—Siege, 1863. | Grant, Ulysses S. (Ulysses Simpson), 1822–1885—Military leadership.
Classification: LCC E475.27 .S69 2018 | DDC 973.7/344—dc23
LC record available at https://lccn.loc.gov/2017040510

Printed on recycled paper. ♻

This paper meets the requirements of ANSI/NISO Z39.48-1992 (Permanence of Paper) ∞

To Danny and Mark

CONTENTS

MAPS

PREFACE

"I never held a council of war in my life," Ulysses S. Grant noted long after the Civil War. Certainly, on several occasions he had gathered his officers together, such as at Fort Henry in preparation to attack Fort Donelson and then at Vicksburg in formulating a response to John C. Pemberton's capitulation inquiries. At other times, he met with smaller groups of officers such as John McClernand and Lew Wallace at Fort Donelson, William Sherman at Shiloh, and a host of general officers at Chattanooga and throughout the Virginia campaign. But these meetings never took on the aura of a true council of war, and he noted that while he always listened to the "interesting and constant stream of talk" about headquarters and frequently conferred with his generals, he always made the ultimate choice himself. "The decision was always my own," Grant declared.[1]

Decisions are at the center of military operations. At no time are military pieces wound up like toy soldiers and allowed to play out battles and campaigns with no overall guidance. In fact, it is no coincidence that the modern army's nine principles of war are closely wound around decisions, intending as they do to help commanders at all levels make the best possible choices at any given time amid the fog of war. Of course, the frightening part is that battles, wars, and sometimes nations often hinge on the effects of decisions both great and sometimes small, made by leaders on all scales of the military hierarchy. An entire nation's existence can, and has, hinged at times on the results of a military leader's wise or poor decision.

There is no greater operation of the American Civil War in which to examine key decisions than Ulysses S. Grant's Vicksburg Campaign. Grant made numerous decisions in the nearly nine-month-long operation. Some had greater repercussions than others, but the overall flow of decisions indicates not only the complexity of the campaign but also its decisive nature. Adding to the fact that the campaign itself was an amazing feat, it was played out upon a huge chessboard, much larger than most western campaigns and certainly dwarfing operations in the east. Making the campaign even more amazing was that Grant rendered many nontraditional decisions, which went against the accepted theories of war, supply, and operations as well as against the chief thinkers of the day, such as Henry Halleck who, of course, was Grant's superior. Yet Grant pulled off the victory, and he did so in compelling fashion if not according to strictly accepted military protocol.

Grant's most important decisions can be boiled down to a few, and these choices literally determined victory or defeat. Accordingly, it is logical to organize a book that examines Grant in the Vicksburg campaign around those key decisions. The eight chapters will cover eight of the most important decisions Grant made: to begin operations against Vicksburg, to make the campaign a one-push effort with himself in command, to begin active operations around the city itself, ultimately to go below and sweep toward Vicksburg from the south, to march east of Vicksburg and cut the railroad before attacking the citadel, to assault Vicksburg in an attempt to end the campaign quickly, to lay siege once assault failed, and finally to parole the Confederate garrison rather than send them to prison camps. Each of the eight chapters revolves around one key decision, and in that sense this book is somewhat akin, in a more military than autobiographical manner, to President George W. Bush's famous memoir, *Decision Points*.[2]

Collectively, these are the decisions that made up the most brilliant, complex, decisive, and lengthy (just beating out Grant's own Petersburg effort) campaign of the war, and arguably one of the most impressive in all of history. And the focus has to be on Grant himself, as he was without a doubt the central agent of change. What was already a difficult undertaking would have been exponentially more challenging under a different commander, mainly because Grant was so willing to throw the protocol of contemporary military theory, and also outright orders for that matter, to the wind and take chances no one else dared hardly to even discuss. There has not been a modern, academic study of Grant's decision-making process at Vicksburg until now, and this study offers plenty of lessons and clues about Grant's command style.

The lessons that emerge from studying Grant's decisions within the Vicksburg campaign are indeed important, so this book will attempt to provide more than just a narrative of the operations and Grant's activities. One indication of Grant's ability can be seen in the extreme military complexity of the Vicksburg campaign. Not just a normal set-piece encounter where armies met each other on the battlefield after a period of maneuver, the Vicksburg campaign was a nine-month operation set on a terrain of over 250 miles from north to south by 150 miles east to west (as compared to the *entire* Eastern Theater's size of approximately 100 by 100 miles). Ample railroad and river transportation routes in this area added to the complexity. The command of troops on campaign and in garrison over the area as well as the coordination of the navy's arm in the operations similarly took decisive actions. In this campaign, Grant illustrated what a talented general he was while at the same time displaying none of the butcherism for which he has been so unfairly maligned. If there was ever a campaign of finesse and maneuver, it was Vicksburg.

Another major indication of Grant's ability was his adaptability. Hardly any of the campaign, once finished, looked the same as Grant had envisioned nine months earlier. While other commanders became confused when carefully laid plans did not work out, Grant simply kept moving and changing his approach if not his final goal. Grant tried to reach Vicksburg a total of six times before a final effort succeeded, and even that was strewn with modifications and adjustments to the plan, whether it was altering the landing spot to Bruinsburg, moving against Jackson itself, or laying siege to the city instead of gaining it by assault. Grant proved that he could think on his feet and wield his powerful army in different ways than originally planned.

Yet Grant had much more to do than command his army's military activities. Another major intent of this book is to illustrate just what a burden the administration of his department and army was and how much of Grant's time was taken up with mundane administrative correspondence even amid the military operations. Normal logistics of feeding and equipping both man and beast for military tasks was enough to worry anyone, but on such a large geographic scale it was that much more difficult. Added in were political and societal issues such as dealing with contrabands, Southern civilians, and trade.

Many of the administrative issues Grant faced were frequently housed in larger political frameworks. While Grant the military commander not only had to see to military movements and administrative support services, he also had to do it within the context of watching politicians and amid continually rising and falling Northern morale. Many politicians and media personalities were against Grant, especially as the campaign ground along slowly over the early months, but Grant displayed much political acumen, often portrayed wrongly as naïveté. His political cleverness will hopefully help readers understand this great campaign further.

Finally, in addition to the military, administrative, and political complexities of the campaign, Grant's multifarious personal life was also important. He was a family man who loved his wife and children and wanted to see them as often as possible. He also had other relatives, including a father, Jesse Grant, who wanted to profit from his son's position. The fact that his family did not always get along, especially his wife Julia and her father-in-law, added another degree of worry, and that was beyond even the near capture of his wife and child at Holly Springs and his son Fred being on campaign with him and actually receiving a minor wound at Big Black River Bridge. Certainly, Grant's professional duties were extremely complex during this campaign, but his personal and family relations were also in the forefront of his thoughts.

Other clues into Grant's ability also rise out of a study of the general at Vicksburg, such as his frequent attempt to use humor, perhaps as a way of easing the tension of such a complex operation. The time spent on mind-numbing administrative activities is also evident, as Grant apparently could not help but become involved in minutiae perhaps better handled by staff officers (admittedly, Grant frequently complained of a lack of dedicated staff, forcing him to do many jobs himself). Another factor that has been much discussed was his drinking, which appears at times during the campaign. While the old adage "where there is smoke, there is fire" is appropriate, any drinking Grant did, and accounts are mostly all purely speculative and circumstantial, never caused him to stumble militarily or put the army in danger. In that sense, perhaps the role of Grant's guardian staff officer John Rawlins, working as more of a personal friend than subordinate, and certainly that of Julia attest to the importance of Grant's personal life and relationships.

Grant emerged from the Vicksburg campaign as the victor and would go on to even greater heights during the rest of the war and afterward. Still, of all of Grant's actions during the war, Vicksburg, for all the complexities and hardships, was perhaps his finest hour.

With that said, it is unfathomable why few historians have examined Grant himself during this campaign. There have been many good biographies from historians such as William McFeely, Brooks Simpson, Jean Edward Smith, Ron White, and Ron Chernow, and almost equally as many good studies on the Vicksburg campaign, such as those by Michael B. Ballard, Terrence J. Winschel, and, of course, the ultimate three-volume opus by Edwin C. Bearss. Some military biographers have delved deeply into Grant's military career, including the Vicksburg campaign, especially J. F. C. Fuller, Bruce Catton, and Kenneth P. Williams, but monographs dealing with Grant and the Vicksburg campaign itself are infrequent. Ballard's study of Grant during the siege itself is first rate, but obviously it covers only a month and a half of the nine-month campaign. The last time a historian examined Grant at

Vicksburg was back in 1955, when Earl S. Miers wrote *The Web of Victory: Grant at Vicksburg.* It is my hope that this present book will fill such a major gap in modern Grant historiography.

* * *

Many people have aided me in writing this book, including archivists, editors, and publishers who have painstakingly gathered and in many cases published Grant's voluminous correspondence. Several historians read the manuscript, including John F. Marszalek, my coeditor on this Grant series and my mentor and friend. Along with the two readers for Southern Illinois University Press, all provided wonderful feedback and made this book stronger by their efforts.

Working with the staff at Southern Illinois University Press has been a delight, especially editor Sylvia Frank Rodrigue. She not only shepherded this project through its early publishing stages but has also done such a wonderful job on other books in this series, as well as the other books under her care. Judy Verdich, Amy Alsip, and the other staff members at the press also made the process enjoyable and easy.

I am thankful for my God's blessing in life, both temporal and eternal, as well as my family's support, including that of my three girls: Kelly, Mary Kate, and Leah Grace. My parents George and Miriam Smith continue to be my chief fans. I have dedicated this book to my two much older brothers, Danny and Mark. Despite a childhood of them holding me down while the dog licked my face, shooting me with various contraptions such as homemade cannons, and knocking out my two front teeth, among many other kid brother shenanigans, I still love them dearly. Life certainly would not be the same without them, and I am grateful for their presence in my life.

THE DECISION WAS ALWAYS MY OWN

PROLOGUE: THE MILITARY EDUCATION OF ULYSSES S. GRANT

Americans today are well aware of the standard educational system in the United States. Most students go through elementary school in younger years, followed by secondary instruction in middle and high schools. Yet the elementary and secondary educations do not produce graduates who are ready for professional workforces; most who obtain professional status go through, at the least, some type of vocational training, earning associate's degrees or graduating from an institution of higher learning with a bachelor's degree in whatever field they plan to work. Of course, advanced graduate degrees can also be obtained, offering college graduates much more specialized degrees such as MBAs, law degrees, PhDs, or medical degrees. But the four years (normally) of higher education is what most often points students to a chosen field; it is in those four years that students gain their most basic introduction to a specific field of study.

While most military officers certainly go through the same elementary and secondary educations, their higher education is different. Most become involved in military studies either through a reserve officer training program at a major university or through the nation's five service academies. From there, military officers also gain higher graduate degrees either in civilian graduate programs or through the numerous war colleges and schools set up by the military for additional training and study.

Today's modern course of military education is far different from what it was in the past. Ulysses S. Grant represents a case in point. On the surface, he took the standard nineteenth-century path of a military education that built upon civilian elementary and secondary schooling. He then enrolled at West Point and graduated with a commission in the army. Thereafter, he had no chance to study further, simply because most of the additional schooling in war colleges and elsewhere mostly did not emerge until the reforms implemented by Secretary of War Elihu Root after the Spanish American War. As a result, it is a simple matter to trace Grant's "formal" military education, but examination of such "actual" learning takes a much different route. Essentially, Grant learned the most on the battlefield.[1]

Grant attended his local Ohio schools as a youngster but showed little interest in his studies. He worked at the same time he was going to school, and even many years afterward recalled that he still had a particular distaste for that time because "the rod was freely used there, and I was not exempt from its influence." But that elementary education had little or nothing to do with his military education, and in that sense it cannot even be considered part of his military training. Perhaps the only major skill Grant learned prior to West Point that could be translated to his military service was his horsemanship, which in itself was not a military-exclusive learning experience. People of the nineteenth century viewed horses much as modern Americans view automobiles, so Grant's mastering of the equestrian art in childhood is no different than a military Humvee driver mastering the art of driving as a teenager.[2]

Grant's true "elementary" education in military science came at West Point. His years there introduced him to the military basics. Little in Grant's West Point education fitted him for military greatness, however. Thousands of cadets who graduated through the years never remained in the army for any extended period of time or never left a major historical mark. Moreover, because West Point's curriculum at the time under Sylvanus Thayer and Dennis Hart Mahan was heavily geared toward engineering, Grant's education in terms of strategy and tactics was extremely limited. And even what Grant learned that could have prepared him for a future illustrious military career was not well received. Grant later wrote, "I did not take hold of my studies with avidity, in fact I rarely ever read over a lesson the second time during my entire cadetship." He also freely admitted that he spent more time reading novels "than . . . books relating to the course of studies." He was careful to point out, however, that the novels were "not those of a trashy sort."[3]

Yet Grant was able to build on his military education at West Point with a "secondary" education that he earned in the field. Significantly, Grant noted in his memoirs that "every officer, from the highest to the lowest, was educated in his profession, not at West Point necessarily, but in the camp, in garrison, and many of them in Indian wars." It is no coincidence that congressmen, while later establishing national military parks at Civil War battlefields, noted that the preserved sites "would be worth an entire course in textbooks on the strategy of a campaign and battle tactics." It is also no coincidence that on top of all the classroom book learning in today's military schools, there is also a major emphasis on field education, from staff rides for officers to field maneuvers and training for enlisted personnel and officers alike. In Grant's case, his field education came during his years in the regular army after his graduation in 1843. He resigned from the army in 1854, but the years between his graduation and his resignation taught him how to administer military garrisons and conduct actual military maneuvers. The pinnacle of this secondary military education came during his time in the Mexican War, when he learned firsthand what war was all about.[4]

Grant's military academy training was effectively the lead-up to his higher military education, and his four years in the Civil War effectively earned him a "bachelor's degree" in military science. It was here that Grant studied in various field classes to master his major art of command. And, interestingly, Grant's four years in the Civil War can be compared accurately to the standard four years of any college student.

The freshman, or "plebe," year is normally seen as the introductory experience, when wide-eyed freshmen get their first taste of freedom and begin to understand the need for self-control and self-governance. Grant certainly came to realize these things from a military standpoint in his first year of the Civil War from February 1861 to February 1862. It was then that the untried colonel, promoted during this time to brigadier general, famously related his inexperience upon first meeting the enemy, writing in his memoirs that once he and his men approached the Confederates, who subsequently fled, that "my heart resumed its place. It occurred to me at once that [Colonel Thomas] Harris had been as much afraid of me as I had been of him. This was a view of the question I had never taken before; but it was one I never forgot afterwards." The lessons were learned well. In fact, if there was a "rookie of the year" for the Union in that first year, from the formation of the Confederacy to Fort Donelson, it would certainly have been Grant. No other general officer was as successful as he was in terms of battlefield victories and public attention.[5]

Then the sophomore year followed, always the hardest period for a college student. Normally, students evolve from happy-go-lucky freshmen to more serious sophomores when they learn that college is not all fun and games; they realize that they need to buckle down and begin to focus on their declared major. Grant certainly hit a "sophomore slump" in his second year from March 1862 to March 1863. It was then that he learned many lessons, including that the enemy did not always do what he thought they would and that the classes were much more difficult than he had imagined after a year of freshman-level coursework. Grant learned that politics were almost as important as military tactics, that terrain was a major factor in determining victory or defeat, and that his superiors were not always in his corner.

Grant's rough second year was certainly hard on him, but he prevailed even if he produced less success than he had during his first year. He gained the ire of his superiors on numerous occasions, could not get along with several of his subordinate commanders such as William S. Rosecrans, and fumbled through numerous attempts to reach Vicksburg, all while his superiors and politicians were seemingly working against him behind his back. Grant frequently described periods during this year with such remarks as "my position was so embarrassing in fact that I made several applications during the siege to be relieved" and "my position at Corinth, with a nominal command and yet no command, became so unbearable that I asked permission of Halleck to remove my headquarters to Memphis." It was definitely Grant's lowest point during the war.[6]

Fortunately, matters soon turned around. Grant's third year in the war was much like a college student's junior year, when maturity develops and students put determined time and effort into their studies. Normally, the junior year is filled with courses from the student's major. Grant certainly made great gains in professionalization in his junior year from March 1863 to March 1864. It was then that Grant waged a brilliant campaign with major political ramifications at Vicksburg and then infused a morale boost into the operations around Chattanooga in the fall of 1863 and emerged victorious. He incisively noted that during this period "a military education was acquired which no other school could have given."[7]

The senior year is most often when college students take their capstone courses and demonstrate that they have mastered their major satisfactorily enough to be granted a degree. That was certainly true of Grant. His junior year victories had earned him promotion to lieutenant general. He then displayed his mastery of military science in his operations from April 1864 to April 1865 in Virginia, where he fought Robert E. Lee to a standstill and eventually forced the Confederate's surrender, ending the war in Virginia and for all practical purposes elsewhere as well. Grant graduated from a higher institute, if you will, in April 1865—at the head of his class.[8]

If the analogy of comparing Grant's military learning to modern educational patterns is continued, Grant then went on to graduate school and earned a master's degree as postwar commanding general of the army and as interim secretary of war. Of course, the terminal degree in Grant's field of military command, much like the PhD in modern educational circles, was the role of commander in chief as president of the United States.

Grant's military education thus did not take the form we usually imagine. Rather, it was almost a hands-on apprenticeship, except that he taught himself. Without the knowledge of Clausewitzian theory (war is an extension of politics; attack enemy armies instead of gaining geographical points), Grant turned out to be much more Clausewitzian than Jominian (geographical waging of war with secure communication and supply lines), like most soldiers of his era became. That Grant discovered the Clausewitzian way of war from scratch, having never read or studied the famous writer, makes the military education of Ulysses S. Grant all the more remarkable.[9]

Grant's Vicksburg Campaign, running from November 1862 to July 1863, essentially occurred during Grant's "second semester of his sophomore year" and the "first semester of his junior year" of military education. The Grant who made many attempts to reach Vicksburg in the early stages of that campaign was soon replaced by the almost completely metamorphosed Grant of his early junior year. The effect emphasized a boldness in Grant that swayed the path of the war and the nation.

CHAPTER ONE

"I GO FORWARD WITH THE ADVANCE"

"In compliance," Ulysses S. Grant wrote on October 25, 1862, "with General Orders, No. 159, Adjutant General's Office, War Department, the undersigned hereby assumes command of the Department of the Tennessee." It was a short, curt order, but it was one of the major stepping-stones in the improbable rise of the clerk from Galena, Illinois; and it was exactly what Grant needed at this particular low point to allow his career to blossom. Grant had been under his superior's thumb for much of the year-and-a-half-old war, and Henry Halleck had kept a careful watch on the unpolished Illinoisan lest, Halleck feared, he get into a truly drastic situation that might cost the United States the west or perhaps even the war. Grant had almost done just that several times now, in Halleck's estimation, most notably at Fort Donelson and then at Shiloh, but Grant's bold determination not to give up had saved him and his army each time. Halleck had thereafter kept close tabs on Grant, allowing him little leeway for any offensive operations that might lead to another crisis, but now with the elevation to this new command, Grant earned much more liberty. He would definitely use it.[1]

The newfound opportunity was not solely larger geographically, although the size of Grant's command did increase. The new Department of the Tennessee encompassed areas all the way north into Illinois at Cairo and included Forts Henry and Donelson as well as areas in Kentucky and Tennessee west of the Tennessee River. Importantly for future operations, the command also included north Mississippi, although it did not extend as far south as the Gibraltar where everyone knew the next major fight would come—Vicksburg; that area was purposefully left in no man's land between Grant and the Union commander to the south, Nathaniel P. Banks. Whoever got there first would seemingly add that area to his department. When Grant took command on October 25 at Jackson, Tennessee (despite the original orders going out on October 16), he consequently took over a mammoth area of land, much of which was still in Confederate hands.[2]

Beyond control of the greater geographic area, Grant's promotion to departmental command had even larger significance. He had commanded smaller districts earlier in the war, but all of these had been under Halleck's close observation. An opportunity for more authority had come in mid-July when Halleck moved from Tennessee to Washington, DC, at the behest of Abraham Lincoln. Halleck had to have someone to fill his void in the west, but he chose not to give Grant the opportunity at that time. Halleck had commanded all the armies in the west in the Department of the Mississippi, including those under Don Carlos Buell and John Pope in addition to Grant's, but he chose to split the west up into differing sectors as it had been prior to Shiloh. Grant merely continued in his command of the districts of Cairo and West Tennessee, with little more authority and even less independence; Halleck still kept a very close eye on Grant, even from Washington. Grant was still miffed years later when he described the situation in his memoirs: "When General Halleck left to assume the duties of general-in-chief I remained in command of the district of West Tennessee. Practically I became a department commander, but no one was assigned to that position over me and I made my reports direct to the general-in-chief; but I was not assigned to the position of department commander until the 25th of October."[3]

Matters thus changed little as the summer waned and the fall brought many additional challenges. Grant remained encased in west Tennessee, with no authority to act independently and no ability to do so even if he had received the authority. He had far too few troops to mount a major offensive, scattered as they were around the western theater. And some of the troops he had were soon called to other areas as crises emerged, most notably to Kentucky to defend against the Confederate invasion there. Accordingly, little changed from Grant's vantage point, but the entire war was altered for Halleck. With invasions along a thousand-mile front from Maryland to Kentucky and even in west Tennessee—where Grant's troops stopped the enemy at Corinth in early October—Halleck found himself much too busy to watch over every move made by what he considered his crude commander. As a result, Halleck finally promoted Grant to departmental command. With it came authority to act as he deemed fit.[4]

It would take Grant all of one day to start formulating an advance.

I

"You never have suggested to me any plan of operations in this department," Grant wrote Halleck the day after he assumed control of the region. To many generals, that would be tantamount to receiving a mandate for defensive operations, but Grant interpreted it as being no rein on offensive activity. As a result, Grant began to formulate a move and ultimately came to make the first significant decision in what would become the Vicksburg Campaign: to begin offensive operations into Mississippi with the ultimate goal of obtaining the river city and fully opening the Mississippi River and its great valley. "This was a great relief," Grant later wrote, "after the two and a half months of continued defense over a large district of country, and where nearly every citizen was an enemy ready to give information of our every move."[5]

Grant had made a significant decision, to be sure. In fact, it produced his first offensive movement in the west in months, since Grant himself had implemented the movement to Fort Donelson after Fort Henry fell in early February 1862. The later advance up the Tennessee River to Pittsburg Landing had been Halleck's decision, and Charles F. Smith carried it out while Grant was wallowing in Halleck's ire at Fort Henry. The advance on Corinth had been Halleck's as well, with Grant again under the general's thumb and this time even contemplating resignation. Once Halleck broke up his armies after taking Corinth, however, the offensives ended, and the Federals had been strictly on the defensive since the end of May 1862. Indeed, the westward movement to Memphis was to solidify recently obtained territory and to hold the rail line. Don Carlos Buell's movement eastward toward Chattanooga had a similar goal. Observing the Federals' Jominian, garrison-style mentality, the Confederates quickly went on the offensive, forcing Grant and company to parry their threats into late October.[6]

Grant's decision to begin operations against Vicksburg did not come without much thought, however. He did not even have the required numbers of troops compared to the amount of current territory he was tasked with holding. Grant had earlier reported to Halleck that he had a grand total of 48,500 men strung from Illinois to Mississippi and from Memphis eastward guarding railroads and newly acquired territory. He had organized this force into four divisions: William T. Sherman's at Memphis, Stephen A. Hurlbut's at Jackson, Charles S. Hamilton's at Corinth, and Thomas A. Davies's in the rearward areas at Columbus, Kentucky. Moreover, Grant had recently called for reinforcements "to keep up the confidence of our men as well as to give sufficient strength to meet the enemy."[7]

Such defensive-mindedness vanished when Grant took the larger departmental command, and he began to formulate a plan that could see him use the troops he had to go on the offensive. Grant notified Halleck in his October 26 letter that, at present, "I can do nothing but defend my positions, and I do not feel at liberty to abandon any of them without first consulting you." Perhaps Grant was letting Halleck know that he was merely conferring with him, but Grant then took the safe route and gave a recommendation as to how an offensive could be started. He suggested abandoning all the rail lines around Corinth, "to all points of the compass," and opening the Memphis and Ohio, thereby allowing him to concentrate his troops at Grand Junction on the Mississippi Central Railroad. Only a few troops would be needed to maintain Memphis, for which he asked for reinforcements. His plan was simple: "I think I would be able to move down the Mississippi Central road and cause the evacuation of Vicksburg." He added that he would also "be able to capture or destroy all the boats in the Yazoo River." It was a bold plan, but Grant was a bold commander who had been held back for far too long.[8]

The plan was actually simple. Grant would utilize one of only two ways to approach the highly defensible Vicksburg area from the north. Because of the wide Mississippi Delta that stretched inland on both sides of the river from Memphis to Vicksburg, the Confederates were not able to defend any place from river traffic north of Vicksburg once Memphis fell in early June 1862; "[Vicksburg] occupied the first high ground coming close to the river below Memphis," Grant explained. Consequently, a river approach was one option, but it also included difficulties. One was the need to travel by boat and to keep the troops onboard for long periods of time. There were few if any places to camp an army except the narrow levees between Memphis and Vicksburg, so a move by water would have to be quick and decisive or else it would bog down and the soldiers' health would rapidly deteriorate in the wet and constricted area. Added to that, travel by river would require the aid of the navy as well as vast numbers of transports to move the troops and keep them fed. As large as operations at Forts Henry and Donelson and even the movement to Shiloh and Corinth had been, they would pale in comparison to the much larger area that Grant was now proposing to cover; just keeping the men, horses, and vessels fed during the campaign would be an enormous task so many miles into Mississippi. Finally, finding a place to land and attack Vicksburg would be even more difficult. The Confederates had fortified all the high ground along the Mississippi River at Vicksburg, so a direct assault up almost three-hundred-foot bluffs was not possible. A movement up the Yazoo River just north of Vicksburg would offer access to the high ground east of the city, but the Confederates likewise had those areas covered, particularly at Haynes' and Snyder's Bluffs. Getting to Vicksburg via the Mississippi River was a difficult undertaking to say the least.[9]

Grant opted for the other route that lay on the high ground east of the delta. The Mississippi Central Railroad ran in the hills just east of the lowland, from Grand Junction, Tennessee, south through Holly Springs, Oxford,

Grenada, and on to Canton, where it joined the New Orleans, Jackson, and Great Northern Railroad and moved on to Jackson and eventually New Orleans. Grant could move down this railroad, using it to supply his forces, and threaten Vicksburg from the east, potentially causing the city's evacuation without even coming close to it. If necessary, he could follow the hills south along the railroad and emerge east of the city on the high ground so difficult to access from the Mississippi River.[10]

While there were great possibilities with this route, there were also problems. The Confederates could be counted on to harass the lone, thin supply line, perhaps even raiding in the rear and destroying bridges and thus cutting off Grant's troops. Grant admitted as much, writing in mid-November that "as the enemy falls back he increases in strength by gathering up his rail-road garrisons whilst I am weakened by leaving behind protection to my avenues of supply." Likewise, several broad rivers such as the Coldwater, Tallahatchie, Yocona, and Yalobusha cut horizontally across the area between La Grange and Grenada deep in Mississippi. Each ran perpendicular to Grant's proposed axis of advance, and the Confederates could be expected to defend every crossing. Gone were the good old days in west Tennessee when the rivers (Mississippi, Tennessee, and Cumberland) ran parallel with the Union advances and allowed them to drive deep into Southern territory on the backs of the navy. It was only past Grenada that the rivers turned and again offered help to invading Federals, running relatively north-south toward Vicksburg. In fact, emerging at Grenada would put an invading army on the high ridge between the Yazoo and Big Black Rivers, which incidentally was the same basic ridge on which Vicksburg sat.[11]

Grant mulled all these options in the days after he took formal command of the department. He wavered at times, reflecting on numerous rumors of Confederate attacks that had so stirred up the area earlier in October. "The rebel army is again moving, probably on Corinth," Grant wrote Halleck late that month. With so many phantom Confederates apparently everywhere, one of his staff officers wrote, "The general has abandoned all idea of the expedition." Perhaps no reply from Halleck in the few days after his call for an advance was also a dampening factor. Grant was also cautious because of some of the leadership problems in his army, although he had a core group of protégés that he trusted. He had confidence in James B. McPherson, William T. Sherman, Charles S. Hamilton, and others, writing that these subordinate officers were "worth more each than a Brigade of troops under such commanders as some that have been promoted." Grant had forged a bond with

Sherman at Shiloh, but he was also very high on McPherson, whom he had brought quickly up the ranks despite opposition to his hasty rise. McPherson was so close to Grant that Grant's wife, Julia, sewed the general's stars on his uniform coat herself. "He is now second in command with the army in the field and should his name be brought up and be rejected I would feel the loss more than taking a division from me," Grant wrote. "He is worth more than a division of men in his present position, particularly as his successor to the command of a wing would be such a person as would leave me to look after that command direct, in addition to my duties with the whole." Sherman agreed as to McPherson's worth, writing that McPherson "is as good an officer as I am—is younger, and has a better temper." Indeed, one historian has argued that Grant used his two favorite subordinates' temperaments brilliantly: when an effort called for harshness, he sent Sherman; when it called for finesse, he used McPherson. With that said, Grant also considered some other commanders to be problems: "I am sorry to say it, but I would regard it as particularly unfortunate to have either [John A.] McClernand or [Lew] Wallace sent to me. The latter I could manage if he had less rank, but the former is unmanageable and incompetent."[12]

II

Despite the staff officer's statement that Grant had backed away from the idea of an advance, it was never far from Grant's mind. On November 1 he issued orders that "it will be necessary to send forward the regimental trains." He also issued orders for the headquarters to move; staff officer John Rawlins wrote on November 5, "Move every thing belonging to Hd Qrs including Printing Office Press to this place where Hd Qrs of the Dept will for the present be established." Grant was moving forward.[13]

Halleck gave his tacit approval very soon after learning of Grant's preparations and embryonic movements. With all the talk of Confederate attacks, Halleck soon began to flow reinforcements to Grant as well. The results were monumental. While the arrival of troops was to allow Grant to hold what he had, Grant turned the reinforcements into the ability to advance, and thus resurrected his old plan for an invasion deep into Mississippi. By November 1 he ordered Hamilton at Corinth to move westward to Grand Junction with three divisions. After a formal review, Grant also ordered McPherson at Bolivar to move to the same point. Grant himself planned to move south from Jackson and join them. Halleck soon became caught up in the offensive talk and approved Grant's plan, writing, "I hope for an active campaign on the Mississippi this fall."[14]

In actuality, Grant had more on his mind than just moving with Hamilton and McPherson. With many troops now pouring into Memphis as well, Grant could use the extra strength to cover his right as he advanced. To Sherman in Memphis he wrote of his plan: "I go forward with the advance; will push on to Grenada if possible, opening railroad and telegraph as we advance." To make the operation even more forceful, Grant told Sherman that "if you hear of my forces passing Holly Springs, and can put a force on the railroad to repair it, start toward Grenada, repairing the road as the troops advance." Opening the Mississippi and Tennessee Railroad from Memphis to Grenada would allow for more leeway in supplying the expedition, especially once all neared Grenada, where the Mississippi and Tennessee joined the Mississippi Central. At the least, Grant noted, Sherman would "attract attention in that direction."[15]

Sherman's part in the plan developed over the course of the next several days and soon became an integral part of the operation. It was so important that Grant wanted to meet Sherman face to face to discuss the advance, although chances of Grant getting to Memphis or Sherman coming eastward, considering the breaks in the east-west railroads, were slim. Grant decided that the easiest route each of them could take was actually north, Grant by rail on the functional Mobile and Ohio and Sherman by river. "We were but forty-seven miles apart, yet the most expeditious way for us to meet was for me to take the rail to Columbus and Sherman a steamer for the same place." The two transportation routes met at Columbus, Kentucky, and it was there that both generals met in mid-November. It was also there that Grant informed Sherman that his "ultimate object was to capture Vicksburg."[16]

Grant had also been pleading with Samuel Curtis in Helena, Arkansas, to start a column eastward into Mississippi, to perhaps rendezvous at Grenada as well. Curtis was not in Grant's department and could not be ordered to move, but Grant did have Halleck's backing and Halleck ordered it, the move ultimately being made by one of Curtis's subordinates, Alvin P. Hovey. As a result, it was hoped that Federal troops would soon approach Grenada from three directions, with Grant even asking the navy to support Hovey's movement, putting the Union armies in great position to threaten if not take Grenada. In addition, Grant ordered cavalry then in Corinth to cover his left; that body moved south along the Mobile and Ohio Railroad to Tupelo, creating havoc east of Grant's planned route. Grant was not certain whether any of these moves would work, because he was still learning to function in

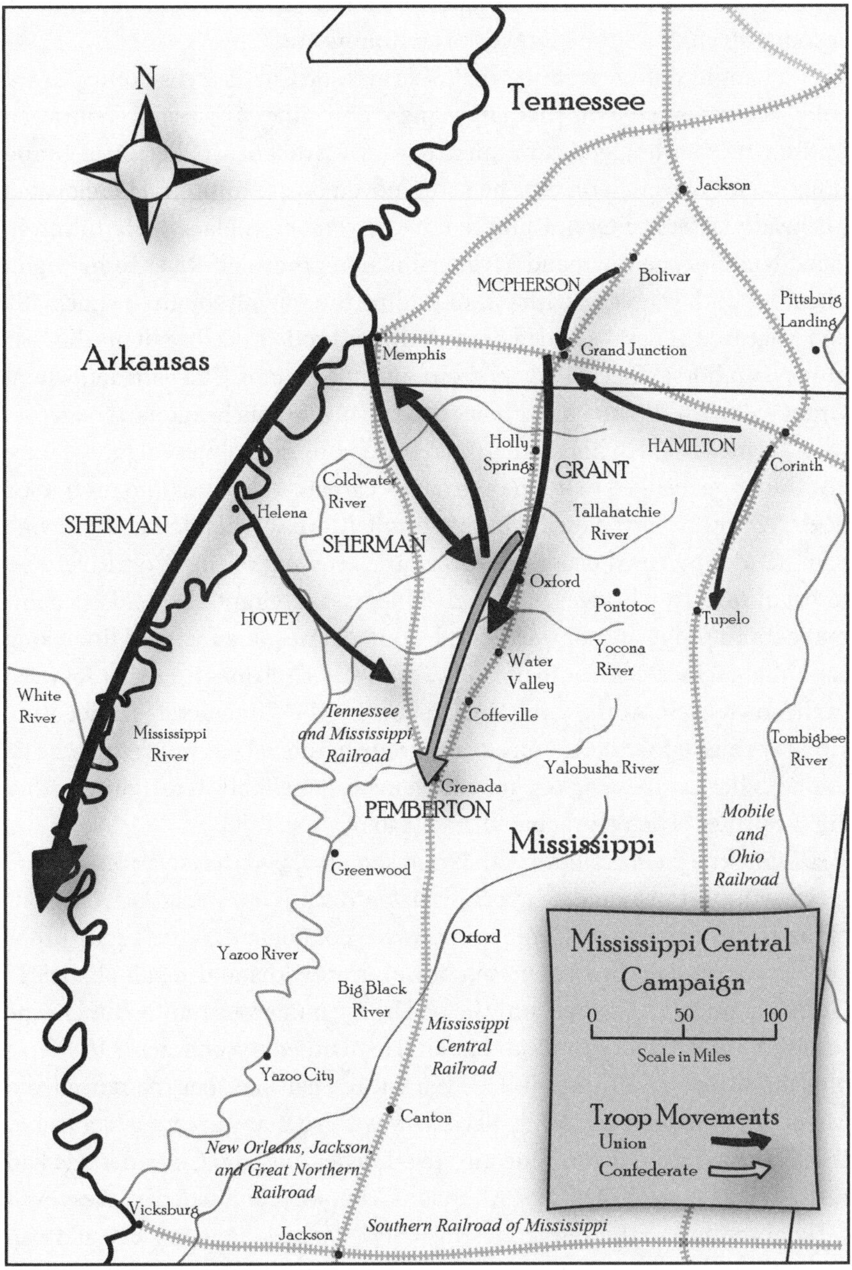

N
Tennessee
Arkansas
Mississippi
Jackson
Bolivar
MCPHERSON
Pittsburg Landing
Memphis
Grand Junction
HAMILTON
Corinth
Holly Springs
GRANT
Coldwater River
Helena
SHERMAN
SHERMAN
Tallahatchie River
Oxford
Pontotoc
Tupelo
HOVEY
Water Valley
Yocona River
White River
Mississippi River
Coffeville
Tennessee and Mississippi Railroad
Tombigbee River
Yalobusha River
Grenada
PEMBERTON
Mobile and Ohio Railroad
Greenwood
Oxford
Yazoo River
Big Black River
Mississippi Central Railroad
Yazoo City
Canton
New Orleans, Jackson, and Great Northern Railroad
Vicksburg
Jackson
Southern Railroad of Mississippi
Mississippi Central Campaign
0 50 100
Scale in Miles
Troop Movements
Union
Confederate

such a large area of operations. He told Hamilton that Sherman was operating "under certain contingencies, depending on certain information he may receive." He added, "We cannot calculate on his co-operation, however, on account of length of time it takes to communicate."[17]

If he could not be certain what Sherman or Curtis were doing, Grant could at least oversee the main movement down the Mississippi Central. In Jackson, he coordinated Hamilton's arrival with that of McPherson at Grand Junction on November 2, but he soon moved onsite himself. He relocated his headquarters to Grand Junction by November 4, placing Hamilton in camp south of the town and McPherson along the Wolf River to his right. The ride south was easy, with Grant leading the way, although the normally good-natured general scolded an orderly who rode too close upon the rear of his own horse's heels. War correspondent Sylvanus Cadwallader, whom Grant evidently trusted and allowed to travel with his headquarters, wrote that "Grant turned in his saddle and rebuked him sharply, saying there were few things he disliked more than to have a careless rider run onto his horse's heels." Grant nevertheless had the movement well in hand, and each wing commander received orders to secure the crossing of the Wolf River and to begin repairing bridges and roads if necessary. Grant also told his commanders to probe ahead; they found Confederates in a fortified line along the Tallahatchie River south of Holly Springs, with elements farther forward in the town itself. At the same time, reports of the Confederates evacuating Holly Springs upon the Union advance only hardened Grant's resolve, as he told McPherson to bring on "no engagement but simply ascertain whether Holly Springs is being evacuated, and if so occupy it."[18]

Despite the good results so far, Grant soon stopped the advance. "We are now having wet weather," he wrote his sister Mary; "I have a big Army in front of me as well as bad roads." Yet Grant was as confident as ever: "I shall probably give a good account of myself however notwithstanding all obsticles." Grant's confidence was certainly helped by the numerous reinforcements he received, some twenty thousand in all. He planned to send many to Memphis but utilize most himself. He even wrote Sherman that the move from Memphis would not be totally necessary with so many arriving troops but that Sherman should continue anyway if he learned the Confederates had really evacuated Holly Springs. Although Grant was confident of success even without the bulk of the new troops, he wisely stopped the advance to allow all to gather. He wrote Sherman, "I will not move from here under a week or ten days," although he added, "I have already been re-enforced to such an extent that I feel no doubt of the result if I should advance now, but as so many are coming it is more prudent perhaps to avail myself of our whole strength."[19]

In the meantime, Grant ordered division-sized reconnaissances to probe to the south. Isaac F. Quinby's division of Hamilton's command and Jacob Lauman's of McPherson's did so on November 8, reaching and crossing the Coldwater River and skirmishing lightly with Confederate cavalry. They returned the next day, having gained valuable information on the evacuation of Holly Springs and the major Confederate line along the Tallahatchie River near Abbeville. In the ensuing days, more reconnaissances went out, with much of the skirmishing being done by Colonel Albert L. Lee and his 7th Kansas Cavalry, which entered Holly Springs on November 13. Meanwhile, the railroad was repaired southward to Davis's Mill, with work thereafter progressing even farther.[20]

Perhaps prompted by Halleck's constant urging of "do not go too far," Grant only resumed his major advance south in late November. He wrote a cousin that he had only made a "slight advance" and that "it is useless for me to pursue further until my reinforcements come up and are in hand." Those reinforcements were soon in Memphis, and he had by this time been in communication with Sherman, who was about ready to move. Thus, an across-the-board advance occurred, with Grant himself moving his headquarters down to Holly Springs by November 29. The telegraph was likewise repaired and extended, allowing Grant to remain informed and to communicate quickly with the outside world. The troops could also receive and store supplies now that the railroad to the Coldwater River had been repaired, and two hundred thousand rations were gathered at that point. Another eight hundred thousand were kept in reserve at La Grange. Soon, Josiah W. Bissell's engineer regiment also arrived to repair the railroad all the way to Holly Springs.[21]

With Holly Springs under Federal control, Grant's next focus was to get through the fortified Confederate line south of the Tallahatchie River. The river was so high that he confessed, "Crossing would have been impossible in the presence of an enemy." And the enemy was present. Grant decided to turn the line, with Hovey's forces from Arkansas outflanking the Confederate Tallahatchie line and Grant's own cavalry moving eastward to a crossing point farther up the river. Both actions evidently caused the Confederate commander John C. Pemberton to pull back. It was an anticlimactic success for Grant where all had seen danger, but Grant, for all intents and purposes, was doing just fine without the limelight of a major battle.[22]

By December 2, the Confederate line along the Tallahatchie River was indeed evacuated in a rush; Grant correctly assumed the primary reason was the fear of Curtis's supposed diversion inland from the Mississippi River. The cavalry followed as best it could despite the terrible weather that had hit and the Confederate destruction of major bridges; Grant noted, "Some of the cavalry swam the river." Grant soon moved his headquarters south of the Tallahatchie River to Abbeville and learned that Sherman and his force from Memphis, three divisions having marched on parallel roads until they reached the Tallahatchie, were only a few miles to the west at Wyatt. Sherman described the river he reached on November 22 as "a bold, deep stream." He added, "I have four boats in the river, and a kind of raft made of the two halves of the ferry-boat, which was a good large one, cut in two." Sherman could also see smoke at Oxford just a few miles to the south, prompting him to believe that the Confederates had withdrawn south of the Yocona River. He also informed Grant of rumors that Panola was in Federal hands, making Sherman wonder if Curtis had indeed sent troops across the river.[23]

Despite rain that set in around December 1, Grant had so maneuvered his forces as to have Sherman, near College Hill, on the right, McPherson in the center, and Hamilton on the left, designating them each as wings of his army. Meanwhile, Grant's forces occupied Oxford, taking over the state university, which war correspondent Cadwallader noted was "a sort of literary center for the state." The Federal arrival also drove a Confederate hospital south. The main depot for the army was also moved south, all the way to Holly Springs, from which most supplies would be drawn and quickly dispersed via the continually repaired railroad. Significantly, Grant was also finding plenty of supplies in the countryside, writing, "I am entirely subsisting our animals upon the country through which we pass and as far as practicable subsisting the troops also." Even so, the railroad was soon repaired all the way to Oxford, where Grant moved his headquarters by December 4. Yet because of the rain and the slow repair of the railroad, Grant chose once more on December 6 to halt and allow his men to go into camp and obtain as many supplies as they could in the area. Only a short move forward to the Yocona River four days later resulted in any advance, although Grant sent cavalry as far forward as Water Valley and Coffeeville to try to save as many railroad bridges as possible. The advances netted many prisoners and news of Confederate retreat, and Grant allowed some Confederates from border states "to take the oath and go home." Eventually, some of McPherson's troops moved nearly twenty miles beyond Oxford, but all forward movement was then halted as Grant stopped and pondered his possibilities.[24]

III

Grant made his headquarters in the Oxford home of one of the University of Mississippi's board of trustees, James Brown. He also found the home of former secretary of the interior and now Confederate colonel Jacob Thompson, whose cotton Grant confiscated. He wrote Secretary of War Edwin M. Stanton that Thompson "left this place as our troops entered." He continued, "I have directed that his fine residence be used as a Hospital for our Soldiers," and added, "should I succeed in finding personal property of his that can be made use of by the Army I will appropriate it for such purpose." Grant sent Stanton "letter books containing the [secretary's] private and official correspondence," which Grant explained "show the treasonable character of at least a portion of the Cabinet of the late Administration if evidence of this kind is necessary to convict them."[25]

While at Oxford, Grant also took his time and mulled over his future options. With rumors emerging of a political effort to allow John A. McClernand to raise an army for a new effort down the Mississippi River to capture Vicksburg, Grant had to keep political as well as military concerns in mind. Accordingly, he exhibited a slow and methodical pace; when he wrote Julia, then at Holly Springs, he noted, "I did intend moving Hd Quarters south to Springdale to-day but as it looks so much like rain and there is no special necessity for it I will not move until Monday or Teusday next." Meanwhile, he wrote to Samuel Curtis, "My mind is not fully made up as to the best method of capturing Vicksburg." In his mind, he still had two options, one of which was staying on the current course. He knew he could quickly "have the railroad completed to Grenada and a supply of provisions thrown in there. From that point Jackson, Miss., could be reached without the use of roads. Jackson once in our possession would insure the capitulation of Vicksburg."[26]

The other option still nagged at him, however, especially with the McClernand rumors growing each week. This option necessitated sending a large force down the river itself to take Vicksburg. While this seemed plausible, and Grant certainly knew by experience the details of invading along rivers, Halleck seemed to be the main supporter of this choice. As early as November 23, Halleck had asked Grant how many troops could be sent down the river to Vicksburg while still being able to hold Corinth and west Tennessee. Grant replied, wondering if formal orders to move down the river were coming. In fact, he asked pointedly, "Must I countermand the orders for this [present] movement?"[27]

Halleck's note no doubt irritated Grant, interfering as it did from a thousand miles away in what he considered a great plan. But Grant was growing more and more accustomed to outside sniping, as he wrote his sister Mary in December, expressing some of his innermost thoughts about his position.

> For a conciencious person, and I profess to be one, this is a most slavish life. I may be envied by ambitious persons but I in turn envy the person who can transact his daily business and retire to a quiet home without a feeling of responsibility for the morrow. Taking my whole Department there are an immence number of lives staked upon my judgement and acts. I am extended now like a Peninsula into an enemies country with a large Army depending for their daily bread upon keeping open a line of rail-road runing one hundred & ninety miles through an enemy's country, or at least through territory occupied by a people terribly embittered and hostile to us. With all this I suffer the mortification of seeing myself attacked right and left by people at home professing patriotism and love of country who never heard the whistle of a hostile bullet. I pitty them and a nation dependent upon such for its existence[.] I am thankful however that although such people make a great noise the masses are not like them.[28]

Halleck fortunately did not force a countermand, but several factors began to come together in Grant's mind to allow for the possibility of utilizing both options, including the relative ease with which he was moving through Mississippi and the quick retreats of the Confederates at each river they defended. Another factor was the order that Grant was to assume command of at least some of the trans-Mississippi troops under Samuel Curtis that were on the east side of the Mississippi River. Grant did not know exactly how many troops that entailed, but he realized it must be substantial given the quick retreat the Confederates made from the Tallahatchie line. Grant also worried about his own supply lines, writing Halleck that "with my present force it would not be safe to go beyond Grenada and attempt to hold present lines of communication." Indeed, he asked Halleck, "How far south would you like me to go?" Perhaps most importantly, Grant was beginning to receive steady reports now, at times through newspapers, of the scheme John A. McClernand had devised of raising his own army and moving down the Mississippi River to take Vicksburg. Grant informed Sherman of these "mysterious rumors of McClernand's command" as early as mid-November, and later quipped, "Two commanders on the same field are always one too many."[29]

Grant decided to utilize both routes, but he would not personally lead an effort down the Mississippi River, preferring to continue on his own course through central Mississippi. He chose Sherman to lead the Mississippi River expedition, and Grant again wanted to talk to him in person. He sent Sherman a note on December 8: "I wish you would come over this evening and stay to-night, or come in the morning." He ended the letter with another "come over and we will talk this matter over." Sherman rode the short distance from College Hill to Oxford, where he found Grant set up in spacious quarters. Sherman wrote that "we discussed every possible chance." On the way back, Sherman rode through the university, the kind of place he was certainly accustomed to, having been a former educator himself. The school had suffered little to no damage during the occupation, although the university's leadership was quite unreceptive. Others in Oxford were not so fortunate. Cadwallader reported that "our advanced cavalry upon entering . . . and getting hold of some liquor, behaved scandalously and robbed the people right and left of everything they fancied."[30]

Taking all the factors together and discussing it with Sherman, Grant soon implemented his two-pronged offensive: "to effect a landing above Vicksburg, probably a short distance up the Yazoo, and have them co-operate with the gunboats, whilst I move south with the remainder of my forces from here." With more and more reinforcements arriving at Memphis, Grant had ample troops to send on both ventures, so the problem of command was what concerned him most. At one point he wavered, even asking Halleck, "Do you want me to command the expedition on Vicksburg or shall I send Sherman?" Before Halleck could answer he had evidently decided firmly to send Sherman, and Halleck agreed the next day, writing, "Sherman would be my choice as the chief under you." Grant ultimately sent Sherman and one of Sherman's three divisions back to Memphis on December 8 to lead the effort down the river "and thus secure Vicksburg and State of Mississippi." Once in Memphis, Sherman would take command of many of the arriving troops John McClernand was indeed raising in Illinois, Ohio, and Indiana. He was also to pick up some of Curtis's troops at Helena on the way down the river and to coordinate the effort with Flag Officer David Dixon Porter, who was predisposed not to trust West Pointers but was soon won over by both Grant and Sherman. Porter even alerted Grant to some of the details of the McClernand affair. Sherman had to hurry, as Grant informed him, because McClernand outranked Sherman and if the politician suddenly showed up, Grant would have to make other arrangements. Halleck had even vaguely warned that "the President may insist upon designating a separate commander," and McClernand had written earlier that "he expects to go forward in a few days." Certainly, McClernand would not be allowed to lead the effort if Grant could help it, and he wrote that "the enterprise would be much safer in charge of the latter [Sherman]." Moreover, if Sherman could actually capture Vicksburg this winter, then the whole reason McClernand had to claim a command would be removed; as historian Michael B. Ballard has said, "If Grant could take Vicksburg, the McClernand problem would be solved."[31]

So the plan was set, but not everyone was enthused. Some of Grant's officers prevailed on Julia Grant to talk to the general, arguing that he was too nice and was letting Sherman have all the glory while he simply held the enemy in place. By extension, of course, they feared Sherman's subordinates would also get all the glory. "We are looking after our own laurels as well," the officers confessed, "and we all chafe under this." They continued, "We want you to tell the General he is too unselfish, but if there is a chance, we young men would like to add a few leaves to our wreaths." Grant simply responded to Julia, "We will hope that Sherman will be successful and, in that case, he will be entitled to the credit."[32]

Sherman made his way back to Memphis quickly with one of his divisions under Morgan L. Smith, leaving the divisions commanded by James W. Denver and Jacob G. Lauman (transferred from McPherson) with Grant. He quickly began his movements southward with Morgan Smith's and two newly organized divisions under Andrew Jackson Smith and George W. Morgan. He picked up Frederick Steele's division at Helena as well. Because of the need to hurry, Sherman noted, "The preparations [and departure] were necessarily hasty in the extreme." His orders were to move down the Mississippi to the Yazoo River and steam up the latter waterway a short distance so that he could then move onto the heights east of Vicksburg. If Sherman could take those, Vicksburg would be doomed. Meanwhile, Grant would keep the pressure on Pemberton near Grenada with a slow push "so as to keep up the impression of a continuous move." Grant even informed Sherman that he would move his headquarters soon to Coffeeville and talked of moving his base of supplies to the Yazoo River once he progressed farther south. Either way, by the river or overland to Jackson, a confident Grant could see the end drawing near. He wrote Halleck, "I have not the slightest apprehension of a reverse from present appearances."[33]

But Grant could at times be too overconfident. Just seven months before, almost to the date, he had used very similar language to inform Halleck that all appeared safe. The date was April 5, 1862.

IV

Even while Grant was conducting an invasion deep into hostile territory, as department commander he also had numerous administrative and personal issues behind the lines to oversee. This was the largest command he had ever held, and with it came a correspondingly larger set of bureaucratic work. Some of it was minor, but several issues required continual oversight. Some, as a matter of fact, would cause Grant many headaches. In reflecting on his rise in prominence, Grant displayed some of his non-egotistic side in late October: "It is a great annoyance to gain rank and command enough to attract public attention. I have found it so and would now really prefer some little command where public attention would not be attracted towards me."[34]

Although Grant was a major military commander and a growing luminary, this did not mean he completely turned his back on his personal affairs. Granted, he depended on his wife Julia to care for the children and the family's personal dealings, but that had been happening for years as Grant had served in far-west posts with the army and then had tried to make a living for the family in more recent years. Grant and Julia had four children: daughter Nellie born in 1855 and three sons, Fred, Buck, and Jesse born in 1850, 1852, and 1858 respectively. One of the reasons Grant had resigned from the army in 1854 was because he missed his family so much. Although he was now commanding a huge army in the field, Mississippi was far less distant than Oregon had been, so Grant took the opportunity when he could to have his family with him. "I have written Julia to come down here and spend a short time," he wrote to his sister from Jackson in October before starting south. "It will probably be but a short time that she can stay but so long as I remain here this will be a pleasant place for her." Illustrating the desire to see his children as well, he added, "If the children have not already been sent to Covington[, Kentucky,] I told her to bring them with her." Even upon beginning the move south in early November, one staff officer wrote another who was moving to rejoin Grant, "The Genl says for Mrs Grant to come with you." The children remained with their grandmother, and Grant wrote his sister Mary: "Tell the children to learn their lessons, mind their grandma and be good children. I should like very much to see them. To me they are all obedient and good. I may be partial but they seem to me to be children to be proud of."[35]

Grant also had to endure squabbling between his overreaching father and Julia, who had joined Grant at La Grange. The general wrote in November that he received an irritating letter from Jesse Grant: "I am only sorry your letter, and all that come from you speaks so condescendingly of every thing Julia says, writes or thinks. You without probably being aware of it are so prejudiced against her that she could not please you. This is not pleasing to me." Later in the campaign, Grant actually scolded both Julia and his father; to Julia he wrote, "I wrote you a letter the other day that I know made you feel badly. It was hard for me to do because I love you but then I thought it would bring you to reflect." Perhaps more troubling was news of son Fred's illness; Grant described the lad as "a big stout looking boy but he is not healthy." Grant laid much of the problem on Fred's mental makeup, adding that "the difference that has always been made between him and the other children has had a very bad influence on him. He is sensitive and notices these things. I hope no distinction will be made and he will in time recover from his diffidence caused by being scolded so much." Grant prescribed cod-liver oil for the boy: "A table spoonful three times a day."[36]

Grant likewise looked after his broader kin and military familial responsibilities. He frequently wrote his father and sisters and even wrote letters to more distant kin. He promised to look into getting a choice assignment for a cousin's nephew, and when an Iowa relative visited, Grant wrote Grenville Dodge at Corinth: "Mr. Hudson is a cousin of mine on a visit to see and learn all he can of the scenes made memorable and sad within the last year. . . . Attention paid Mr. Hudson I will regard as a personal favor to myself." Grant also continuously wrote letters, at times even to Abraham Lincoln himself, requesting new staff members and promotions for those already in his military family as well as other favored officers such as cavalryman T. Lyle Dickey, engineer Frederick Prime, and regular officer George A. Williams. He informed Washington in late October, for example, that "there are now two vacancies on my Staff," and asked that John Rawlins be promoted. Grant could at times also write letters against certain individuals, such as the one he sent to his supportive congressman from Galena, Elihu Washburne. "Knowing that you were fully engaged," Grant wrote in November, "I have not troubled you with a letter. I write now a little on selfish grounds. I see from the papers that L[eonard] Swett is to be called near the President in some capacity." Grant candidly wrote, "I believe him to be one of my bitterest enemies" because Swett had become angry when Grant would not show him business favoritism at Cairo earlier in the war.[37]

Most of Grant's correspondence was more official in nature, from sending mundane reports of the Iuka and Corinth battles to communicating with Confederate commander John C. Pemberton about prisoners and supplies forwarded within Union lines to Confederates wounded at Iuka. He also found time to order a new uniform: "You will please make and forward to me a complete suit—coat vest and pants—including Major General's shoulder straps. Make the vest of dark blue cloth." Some of the official correspondence grew somewhat bitter; he quickly tired of Pemberton's threatening tone, writing, "I will state here that this is the third communication from you to Gen. Sherman and myself since the present advance commenced that has been threatening in tone. . . . On my part I shall carry on this war humanely and do what I conceive to be my duty regardless of threats and most certainly without making any."[38]

Another case in point was his happiness to be rid of William S. Rosecrans, who was transferred to command the Army of the Cumberland. Grant and Rosecrans had tangled over several issues such as the fight at Iuka and the pursuit after Corinth, and Grant had not been impressed. Their letters grew increasingly bitter over time, with Grant writing at one point about Rosecrans giving special favors for his own command: "This is a mistake." On another occasion, Grant lectured: "My dispatch was but a proper reply to yours of this date and others from you equally objectionable." When Rosecrans was subsequently transferred, it was "greatly to the relief of the general," and one staff officer added, "Who was very mush disappointed in him [Rosecrans]." Julia was with Grant at the time and remembered him rejoicing when he got the message, which he held up: "There is good news, good news. Rosecrans is promoted and ordered to take command of the Army of the Cumberland. I feel so happy." Ironically, Rosecrans's departure left Grant and his commanders with a void, as Rosecrans requested David Stanley go with him to command his cavalry. Grant responded that at present "Stanley is the only general in his division, and I have no one to take his place that can be spared." The void was not just on the command level either. Charles Hamilton, who replaced Rosecrans, wrote Grant that he had a major problem: "Rosecrans carried off the maps that were most needed."[39]

Other minor issues were with lesser rogue officers. In late November Grant ordered the arrest of John C. Van Duzer, who managed the military telegraph in the department. The reason for the arrest was "for disobedience of orders and conduct prejudicial to the interest of the service." Van Duzer thought of his operation as equal to Grant's and balked at the department commander's orders. If it had ended there it would not have been necessarily noteworthy, but War Department officials soon became involved and the secretary of war himself ordered Van Duzer's release from prison. Grant had the last word anyway, ordering: "The release of Van Duzer does not entitle him to interfere with telegraph matter or to remain in this department. He must leave by first train." Grant similarly dealt with other offenders, although actually ordering the release of some after their three-month sentences were fulfilled even though they had not served all of the time in the intended Alton, Illinois, prison.[40]

Another issue became more overblown. A newspaper account described a member of Grant's staff who was involved in whiskey speculation and had accumulated some 750 barrels in all. The swirling rumors of Grant's alleged drunkenness no doubt brought the issue even more to the forefront. "As no member of my staff has ever been engaged since entering the army in any speculation by which to make a dollar I care nothing for the publication," Grant wrote, although he did give an explanation. He stated that he had allowed a Memphis citizen to do so and one of his staff officers had "introduce[d]" him to get the whiskey through regulations. Grant noted that the officer "has never been more than a volunteer aide on my staff."[41]

Of more important concern to Grant than churning rumors was supply of his army deep in Mississippi. Grant requested at least fifteen thousand good rifles for the troops, writing that calibers needed to be standardized throughout brigades. In response, Halleck curtly wrote that "there is a scarcity of first-class arms, and each army must take its proportion of lower classes." Of more concern, the amount of food, equipment, and ammunition (two hundred rounds per man) needed for an army the size of Grant's was enormous, and the need to move it all by one single rail line was dangerous to say the least, especially with too few locomotives and cars. Grant unsuccessfully offered to pay for any new transportation "from funds now on hand from earnings of the road." When Grant shifted his approach to a two-pronged operation, the logistical effort became that much more problematic. Now moving overland as well as on a river, Grant's reinforced army needed many more supplies, and they needed to go in two different directions by two different methods. Vast amounts of fuel were also necessary; the railroads feeding Grant's overland army needed wood for the locomotives, and the vessels on the river needed coal in enormous tonnage. Ultimately, the quartermaster officers Grant depended on had to alert him to the limitations involved. One wrote in December as Grant was contemplating sending Sherman by water to Vicksburg, "We will furnish the transportation you require as rapidly as possible. It cannot be done within the time you mention. Coal is very scarce—must depend principally upon obtaining it from points on the Ohio."[42]

Grant also needed to deal with the local citizenry, another problem inherent in operating deep within enemy territory. Grant had to listen to many people who had all sorts of complaints. He was not lenient with guerillas, ordering, "Where citizens give aid and comfort to these fellows who amuse themselves by firing into them, arrest them." Grant had more sympathy with those caught seemingly innocently by the events; in early November, he ordered that citizens who were lacking the basic supplies should be aided, but "sympathizers with the rebellion" would pay the cost. Grant also ordered that "people not actively engaged in rebellion should not be allowed to suffer from hunger in reach of a country abounding with supplies." Accordingly, those known to be in sympathy with the rebellion would be "assessed in proportion to their relative ability to pay." In other instances, Grant scolded his troops for "the gross acts of vandalism committed by some of the men. . . . Houses have been plundered and burned down, fencing destroyed, and citizens frightened without an inquiry as to their status in this rebellion." Grant even took the extreme measure of stopping pay to divisions until the guilty parties could be found. He ordered that the loss of pay be "assessed to the smallest organization containing the guilty parties," whether it be company, regiment, or even brigade. In one instance, Grant threatened to "disband the whole concern."[43]

In at least one case, Grant took larger measures to find out who was responsible for the mischief. Some Illinois cavalry "straggled from their command whilst out, and went to several houses and pillaged everything they could carry away," including from a Mr. Rodgers's house who "has been a most loyal man from the beginning." Grant informed McPherson that soldiers "frightened his family nearly to death, carried off his daughters jewelry and some small articles, tore up his private papers &c." Grant added, "In talking to each other one of them was called Anthony and one Frank." Grant ordered, "If these men can be identified have them put in irons and brought to trial."[44]

Despite all the worries, Grant kept his sense of humor during the campaigning and administration of his department. On November 26, he wrote Halleck: "Having come across a pair of unmentionables in a deserted house entirely unsuited in dimentions for any member of this army, and thinking that so much material should not be lost in these times when the raw material from which they are manufactured is in such demand, I naturally cast around to think who of my acquainta[nces] they might be of service to. I can think of no one but Col. [George] Thom of your Staff. They are therefore to him respectfully donated, with such remarks in the presentation as you may choose to make." It is not known whether the very diminutive Thom thought the joke was funny.[45]

V

If Grant was finding the mundane administration of his department time consuming, the unexpected episodes that cropped up frequently made Grant even more anxious. Most of them were political in nature, illustrating how climbing the ladder in the military brought not just larger military concerns but difficult political ones as well. Clausewitz famously stated that war is an extension of politics. Grant was a military commander with practically no political experience, so he had to deal with politics as he oversaw the military department, largely under conditions that the Lincoln administration was pressing to impose on Southern states returning to full status within the Union. Lincoln appointed Senator Andrew Johnson as provisional governor of Tennessee, but elections were also slated to allow the people to elect their representatives in congress. Therefore, on December 9, while actually at Oxford, Mississippi, Grant issued a proclamation that an election would be held on December 24 to elect congressmen and "such County and State Officers, as, under the laws of the State of Tennessee, the people were entitled to elect at the time of the breaking out of the rebellion." Grant wanted the civilian authorities to handle the process, but he made his military officers available to step in and appoint needed judges and clerks if necessary. Certainly, the military would oversee the transportation of results to the governor.[46]

Grant also allowed the citizens to begin the process of reintegration back into the United States' economy, a political issue at heart because it worked directly against Confederate nationalism. Sherman had begun trading with citizens around Memphis, and Grant continued that policy, "subject only to Treasury restrictions and such other restrictions as local commanders may deem necessary to preserve good order and discipline." He also allowed Southerners' cotton to be brought in for sale. Deep in the fall harvest season, Confederate citizens had cotton on their hands with nowhere to sell it. Grant's decision to accept it gave them a buyer while at the same time lessening their commitment to the Confederacy. In the most flagrant cases where the citizens were known supporters of the rebellion, Grant simply ordered it to "be taken, if they have any, and sent here to be sold for the benefit of the government." As always, some tried to work the system and Grant soon became miffed that "with all my other trials I have to condend against is added that of speculators whos patriotism is measured by dollars & cents. Country has no value with them compared with money." He showed his frustration with all things in general when he added, "To illucidate this would take quires of paper so I will reserve this for an evenings conversation if I should be so fortunate as to again get home where I can have a day to myself."[47]

Because of his military actions' political overtones, travel was restricted in certain areas during the campaigning, especially around the army. In mid-December, Grant even excluded women and children "from the army in the field," although he noted that authorized females such as nurses, laundresses, and "officers' servants" could remain. As the army continually moved south, however, the restrictions in the rearward areas were lifted, allowing citizens to travel more freely. Grant actually opened travel all the way to Oxford on December 15, noting that "instructions from Washington are to encourage getting Cotton out of the country."[48]

The deeper Grant moved into Mississippi, the more he noticed a change in reaction to the Federals. No longer was the army in Tennessee, where the people were accustomed to military occupation and fighting. The path to Oxford and below was a newly trod area. Grant found it an interesting experience, as he informed Halleck. "The people of Mississippi show more signs of being subdued than any we have heretofore come across. They are very cordial in their reception of the Federal officers, and it seems desirous of having trade resumed." That he had only pierced the upper layers of Mississippi counties was significant, because this was one of the areas where opposition to secession existed in 1861.[49]

A special area of concern for Grant as he moved south was the enormous number of fleeing slaves moving into Federal lines. This was another political issue fraught with potential pitfalls, as evidenced by Lincoln's recent issuance of the preliminary Emancipation Proclamation. Grant informed Halleck in mid-November that "citizens south of us are leaving their homes, and Negroes coming in by wagon loads. What will I do with them?" Slaves who were near enough realized that a dash to Union-occupied areas might mean freedom, or at least no more plantation life. They accordingly began to move north in droves, and it soon became a deluge that the army could not handle. The War Department scolded Grant for trying to send them north, but he could not manage them where they were without some changes; "humanity forbade allowing them to starve," Grant wrote. "Finding that negroes were coming into our lines in great numbers," Grant wrote in a note to Lincoln himself, "and receiving kind or abusive treatment according to the peculiar views of the troops they first came in contact with and not being able to give that personal attention to their care and use the matter demanded I determined to appoint a General Superintendent over the whole subject and give him such Assistants as the duties assigned him might require." Grant's decision to deal with this situation in this way prompted the establishment of "contraband camps" at various sites within his department, all under Chaplain John Eaton Jr., whom he named superintendent of contrabands. The very reluctant Eaton accepted the job and worked out of Grand Junction, but numerous camps housing the refugee slaves were soon located all across the department, the most famous being the model camp at Corinth under Grenville Dodge. At all these camps, the contraband picked the corn and cotton that was ripe in the fields, and military supplies and equipment were, without higher permission, provided for them, causing Grant to quip to Eaton, "I wonder if you ever realized how easily they could have had our heads?" Grant nevertheless marveled, "At once the freedmen became self-sustaining." Illustrating the change of policy from slavery to freedom, Grant authorized that "persons whose Negroes have run off and have cotton yet to pick will be allowed to hire the Negroes in charge of Government here."[50]

While Grant responded positively to this highly politicized racial issue, a situation on another front caused him great anxiety and prompted a misstep on his part. While overseeing the economics of the region and the interaction with the local citizenry as well as with those who came south looking to become involved in the blossoming trade—including his father much to his annoyance—Grant made an especial target of Jewish merchants. In early November he described them as "such an intolerable nuisance that the department must be purged of them." He even issued orders that they be restricted from moving south along the rail lines, but "they may go north and be encouraged in it." Later in December, Grant showed his further disdain for the Jews, writing, "They come in with their carpet-sacks in spite of all that can be done to prevent it. The Jews seem to be a privileged class that can travel everywhere. They will land at any wood-yard on the river and make their way through the country. If not permitted to buy cotton themselves they will act as agents for some one else, who will be at a military post with a Treasury permit to receive cotton and pay it in Treasury notes which the Jew will buy up at an agreed rate, paying gold."[51]

The result was Grant's politically naive and infamous "General Orders, No. 11," dated December 17, which expelled Jews from the department within twenty-four hours and ordered confinement for anyone who did not obey. Grant wrote that the Jews violated "every regulation of trade established by the Treasury Department and also departmental orders." The negative reaction was quick and decisive. Some people wrote directly to President Lincoln, explaining how they felt "greatly insulted and outraged by this inhuman order." Grant soon received a curt note from Halleck that rumors of the order had reached Washington and "if such an order has been issued, it will be immediately revoked." Grant meekly did so, although noting that it was done "by direction of General-in-Chief of the army, at Washington." The political sniping did not end there, as an effort in both houses of Congress to issue the "sternest condemnation" of Grant came forward. Both were tabled, but just barely. Grant's political guardian Elihu Washburne led the defense in the house, arguing that "this resolution censures one of our best generals without a hearing." The senate condemnation was more hostile, writing that the order was "illegal, tyrannical, cruel, and unjust," but Senator Henry Wilson of Massachusetts argued that "we ought not to strike a general in the field, and condemn him unheard."[52]

While Grant appropriately took the blame for the unwise order, there was some mitigation later on when Halleck softened the president's reaction. "It may be proper to give you some explanation of the revocation of your order expelling all Jews from your department," Halleck wrote. "The President has no objection to your expelling traitors and Jew Peddlers, which, I suppose, was the object of your order; but, as it in terms proscribed an entire religious class, some of whom are fighting in our ranks, the President deemed it necessary to revoke it."[53]

Yet if Grant's order expelling the Jews received the most attention from modern historians, it was another behind-the-lines political issue that worried Grant the most. Throughout the fall, Grant had heard rumblings about McClernand organizing a separate force to take Vicksburg. Such a project would be fraught with numerous logistical and command problems. Grant commanded the department that McClernand would have to operate in. Could he be truly independent, or would he be under Grant? That Grant did not like McClernand was enough of an issue, but the egotistical politician threatening to operate independently within Grant's command area was too much for Grant to take. With rumors abounding and the plot becoming clearer, Grant even wrote Halleck, asking, "Am I to understand that I lie still here while an expedition is fitted out from Memphis[?]" Halleck quickly responded that Grant was in command of all troops in his department and he had "permission to fight the enemy where you please."[54]

The root of the problem was a lack of unity of command at the very top of the Federal government. Lincoln and Secretary of War Edwin Stanton encouraged McClernand without talking with the military commanders. Thus, Halleck was out of the loop early and advised Grant to continue his own operations even while Stanton and Lincoln ordered McClernand to raise troops in Indiana, Illinois, and Iowa. McClernand's task, as written by Stanton and endorsed by Lincoln, was to take Vicksburg: "When a sufficient force not required by the operations of General Grant's command shall be raised, an expedition may be organized under General McClernand's command against Vicksburg and to clear the Mississippi River and open navigation to New Orleans." Whether Lincoln and Stanton were using McClernand to get him to recruit heavily is not known, but there was obviously enough wiggle room in the order for Grant to retain his command. After all, when has any commander ever had "sufficient force"? Unfortunately, Lincoln wrote an endorsement on the order giving his approval, and McClernand rode that executive endorsement as far as he could.[55]

McClernand began his work with gusto by meeting with Midwestern governors, thinking he would have the command and reap the glory. He soon began to funnel troops to Memphis. Grant then ordered Sherman south with many of McClernand's recently recruited regiments, and McClernand began to suspect something was not right. He wrote Stanton, "I infer that General Grant claims the right to change their destination, and to control all the troops sent to Columbus and Memphis." Consequently, McClernand requested that he be ordered to Memphis to take command of the artillery, cavalry, and forty regiments of infantry he had sent south. By mid-December, that number had risen to forty-nine regiments, but McClernand was still in Springfield, Illinois, requesting permission to move to Memphis. For the next several days, McClernand peppered the War Department with requests, but Stanton only responded that he assumed Halleck had taken care of his orders. Of course, Halleck liked McClernand no more than Grant did, but he could tolerate Grant because of his West Point background, despite their disagreements. He had no such confidence in McClernand, and no orders emerged either.[56]

The reason McClernand received no orders was because Halleck was scheming to get Grant those very same troops and deprive McClernand of any command. Halleck reminded Grant that he commanded all troops in his department. Grant schemed with him, and it was primarily for that reason that he sent Sherman back to Memphis to take command of the congregated troops and lead them south before McClernand arrived. Sherman did so, beginning the second prong of the December advance, and McClernand was livid when he realized what was happening. He fired off a message to Stanton on December 17: "I believe I have been superseded. Please inquire and let me know whether it is and shall be so." He also telegraphed Lincoln: "I believe I am superseded. Please advise me." Stanton responded innocently that "it surprises me, but I will ascertain and let you know immediately." Later that day, he wrote the best explanation he could: that McClernand had not been superseded and that the orders were merely to send the troops to be organized at Memphis. McClernand had done his part, but now Sherman was organizing the troops—for his own movement down the river. Through some deft manipulation and because Lincoln and Stanton turned their backs on McClernand, the political general had indeed been superseded—at least for now. If he could get to Memphis as soon as possible, however, he might still save his army.[57]

In order to calm down the powerful McClernand, Stanton also told him that Grant's troops were about to be reorganized as well. Whether this was a split-second decision in Washington to throw McClernand a bone is not known, but orders soon came that Grant's troops would be divided into corps, with McClernand, as senior under Grant, commanding what was then labeled as the "First Army Corps." Stanton noted, perhaps to quiet McClernand even more, that the new corps would be "assigned to the operations on the Mississippi under the general supervision of the general commanding the department." That kept the possibility of McClernand's independent command open, but obviously there was nothing as of now to keep Grant from taking command of McClernand's corps.[58]

Grant played his role perfectly, even though it required him to deal with a much heavier administrative workload than he would have liked right in the middle of the Mississippi Central advance. On December 18 he received orders to form the department's troops into four corps, with McClernand commanding the senior organization. Sherman, Hurlbut, and McPherson were to command the other corps, and Grant's orders even alluded to the expedition that was about to leave Memphis. Behind the scenes, Grant was very desirous of Sherman leaving Memphis before McClernand could get there and command the troops; "I was in hopes [that] the expedition would be off by this time," Grant wrote McPherson. There was even some trickery in informing McClernand of his new position; Grant did not send a telegram, as historian Brooks Simpson has shown, but a letter that would take much longer to arrive. Hopefully, in the time that it took a letter to reach McClernand, wherever he was en route to Memphis or even in Illinois, Sherman could take Vicksburg and the crisis would be over. And it almost worked. Unfortunately for McClernand, he did not arrive in time to join the force when Sherman left Memphis on December 20; in fact, McClernand did not even leave Springfield until December 23, having delayed his departure to get married, of all things.[59]

Grant had what he wanted, and all seemed to be progressing well.

CHAPTER TWO

"TO COMMAND THE EXPEDITION DOWN THE RIVER IN PERSON"

Ulysses S. Grant had made a key decision back in October 1862 to begin operations against Vicksburg. Up to mid-December, his efforts had gone well. He had navigated through several potential problems, not the least of which included John A. McClernand and his plans to take a share of Grant's command. He had also been able to expand the campaign by hurrying his favored subordinate Sherman to the command McClernand wanted, thereby opening another front in the advance on Vicksburg. Threatening the Confederate Gibraltar from another direction while at the same time outfoxing McClernand was a favorable situation for Grant.

Grant's own wing of the campaign was going well by mid-December. He had moved south across the Tallahatchie River to Oxford and was in the process of sending large units on reconnaissance across the Yocona River toward Grenada. Indications were that the Confederates would not make a stand at Grenada any more than they had along the other rivers. While he had heard nothing from Sherman, Grant guessed the river advance was also making progress, perhaps even causing alarm in the Confederate high command at Grenada and provoking some of the rearward movement Grant was detecting there. A confident Grant happily wrote his sister on December 15, "My plans are complete for weeks to come and I hope to have them all work out just as planed."[1]

Then matters turned. In mid-December, the dual advance began to hit snags, and a series of near disasters threatened to derail the entire campaign. The Confederates were not defeated yet and were actually responding in several different ways. They shifted troops to meet Sherman's approach toward Vicksburg, and they also sent cavalry raids deep into Union-occupied territory to tear up Grant's supply lines. If that was not enough, John A. McClernand arrived right in the middle of the growing crisis. It was certainly not the way Grant envisioned the development of the campaign, but the adaptable general dealt with each situation as it came.

I

"Forrest is crossing [the] Tennessee at Clifton," the message read. In the midst of all the massive correspondence Grant was handling on top of the military campaign he was conducting, this singularly critical message arrived at Grant's headquarters on December 15. Whether it concerned Grant greatly is not known, as he received many false rumors as well. If these rumors had been true, of more concern would have been reports of larger bodies of cavalry crossing farther north and even Braxton Bragg's army in middle Tennessee heading westward, but the only correct item, that of Nathan Bedford Forrest crossing the Tennessee River, was the part that would cause Grant the most trouble.[2]

The message came from a lower-level officer, Jeremiah C. Sullivan at Jackson, Tennessee, and the essence of the message was correct; Forrest had crossed the river at Clifton and was now in west Tennessee. What he would do and where he would go was anybody's guess, and although Forrest was not at the time the Southern icon he would later become, it was not wise to leave a body of cavalry alone within the department . . . especially with so many vulnerable supply lines.[3]

Grant's response was to use behind-the-line forces to try to neutralize Forrest. Within a few days he had cavalry, some even from the area around Forts Henry and Heiman, following the Confederate raider who was evidently moving westward toward the vulnerable railroads. By December 18 Grant also involved infantry from the nearest large garrison at Corinth. He ordered Grenville Dodge to send all the men he could safely spare to catch Forrest and "drive him east of the Tennessee." By that time, Forrest was nearing Jackson, but Grant tried to keep his attention focused on his forward campaign as well as moving Sherman before McClernand could arrive and entangle the operation. He even intended to move his headquarters farther south on December 20 to Springdale, south of the Yocona River and only a few miles from Water Valley.[4]

If Grant intended to remain focused on the forward movement of both prongs, he was sorely disappointed. Forrest had begun to significantly affect the rearward Federal areas, and no one seemed to be able to catch him. Worse, he was making his way toward the critical rail lines, especially the Mobile and Ohio, along which most of the supplies for the army were drawn from Columbus, Kentucky. Forrest had already wrecked the communications between Grant and Jackson and other points north. Grant became so concerned that on December 19 he ordered a temporary cessation of movement because of the threat to the rear. "There will be no farther advance of our forces until further directions," he notified his commanders.[5]

Grant's decision to forestall any advance was fortuitous, although he no doubt wished to press ahead quickly when he learned that Jefferson Davis himself was at Grenada. Then, Grant's cessation of movement became more of a necessity in hindsight because of the next major jolt he received. On December 19, one of his cavalry commanders reported that a scout had learned that the Confederates were pulling out of the Yalobusha River line, despite its major fortifications, and were heading south. While that good news might serve as a prompt for the advance to resume along the Mississippi Central toward Grenada, it did not bode well for Sherman's effort at Vicksburg. If the Confederates reached Vicksburg before Sherman did, then he could be stopped and potentially counterattacked. Unfortunately, the scout had additional bad news. He also included word of "a column of four regiments of cavalry moving up the Pontotoc road this A.M. northeast." Was it a force to cover the Confederate retreat, or another raid to supplement Forrest's effort farther north?[6]

Ironically, Grant had his own raiders out, including Colonel T. Lyle Dickey's 4th Illinois Cavalry on a raid toward the Mobile and Ohio Railroad near Tupelo. When word reached Grant of the Confederate cavalry movement, he initially perceived that the Confederates were after Dickey. Significantly, they crossed behind the Union cavalry, not bothering with them, and continued north. It did not take Grant long to figure it out. When Dickey returned and informed Grant of his success in breaking the railroad, Grant remained only half interested in his report at first, until Dickey mentioned the Confederates moving north. "Grant was instantly on the alert-inquired particularly as to its appearance-estimated strength-the day and hour of its passage-the particular road it moved on, etc., etc.," recalled correspondent Sylvanus Cadwallader. Without even waiting for Dickey to finish, "but without any intention, probably, of rudeness," Cadwallader recalled, Grant hurried over to the telegraph office and began to send out warnings to all his commands. Grant was so busy sending messages and alerting his commanders that he barely took time to even welcome Julia and little Jess when they arrived in Oxford on December 19. Julia remembered that it was odd for Grant not to meet them at the depot, but they went on to his headquarters where the general simply popped out of the office and chattered: "I am fully occupied. I have only time to kiss you; and Jess, you little rascal, are you glad to see me? I must go back now to my office."[7]

Grant indeed reacted swiftly to this new threat, ordering all cavalry available to the Tallahatchie River at Rocky Ford to try to stop the Confederates' crossing. Nevertheless, the worry could be perceived in a dispatch to one cavalryman: Grant wrote that the Confederates "must be prevented from getting to the railroad in our rear if possible." He also alerted the various commanding officers at Holly Springs, Davis's Mill, Grand Junction, La Grange, and Bolivar that he had sent cavalry to Rocky Ford and to stay alert: "Keep a sharp lookout and defend the road, if attacked, at all hazards." The response from Colonel Robert C. Murphy at Holly Springs did not help his feelings, no doubt: "Where is Rocky Ford you speak of? I found no map here and have none but what I have made of surrounding country that are reliable."[8]

Grant's worst fears emerged as the next few hours played out and his railroad supply lines were devastated; he had thought that "by moving against the enemy and into his unsubdued, or not yet captured, territory, driving their army before us, these lines would nearly hold themselves." Now he was learning differently. Forrest continued to raid northward, fighting small skirmishes but not stopping. He reached his evident goal when he severely broke up the Mobile and Ohio Railroad where it crossed the branches of the Obion River northwest of Jackson. Such destruction cut communication as well as supply for much of the department, and it would take a long time to repair it all.[9]

At the same time, the other raid was also nearing its goal. Despised Confederate commander Earl Van Dorn, who had recently lost the battle at Corinth, had been transferred to the cavalry and led his troopers northward from Grenada to hit Grant's supply lines. The most disastrous outcome of Van Dorn's actions was that he captured Holly Springs on December 20 and ransacked the place; the confused colonel of the 8th Wisconsin, Robert C. Murphy, panicked and provided no defense whatsoever. This was the second time Murphy had acted as such, the first being back at Iuka in September. Grant was disgusted at the colonel and later wrote his cousin, who was still lobbying for an appointment for his nephew, that the "surrender of Holly Springs was the most disgraceful affair that has occurred in the Dept. Col. Murphy had a force of effective and convalescent men of over 2000, and any quantity of cotton bales and brick walls to protect himself. He also had warning the evening before that a large force of rebel Cavalry were moving North to attack the road some where, and again nearly three hours before the attack that they would be upon him at daylight." Grant likewise later wrote of Murphy that the surrender was "most reprehensible and showed either the disloyalty of Colonel Murphy to the cause which he professed to serve, or gross cowardice." At the same time, Grant took up for the men themselves, writing, "The capture was a disgraceful one to the officer commanding but not to the troops under him."[10]

In the wake was destruction; one aftereffect was that Grant had to send paroled Union prisoners north to await exchange. Ironically, it could have been worse; it was by the barest of margins that Van Dorn missed a truly important luminary in Holly Springs. As Grant advanced south from Oxford, planning to soon move his headquarters, he had sent Julia back to Holly Springs for safety; "it is a pleasant place," Grant noted in a letter to his sister Mary, "and she may as well stay there as elsewhere." Julia stayed there during the campaigning and would have been there on December 20 except that she had traveled south to Oxford to visit Grant on December 19. Van Dorn also missed Grant's father, who was in the area, having come down to Holly Springs earlier and then intending to move on to Oxford with Julia.[11]

Despite the safety of his family members, Grant still faced his worst military nightmare with the destruction left behind by the dual raids. He received reports that the enemy was "burning ammunition and stores." Later, more details emerged from Holly Springs, with one cavalryman informing Grant that "every man was taken, supplies of all kinds burned; also 3 locomotives and 40 cars. . . . The town was taken a little after daylight. It was a surprise; not above 40 shots were fired. The rebels took citizens, sutlers, and everybody. They are paroling them. They destroyed everything they could not carry away."[12]

Grant initially sent cavalry to follow Van Dorn's raiders but later also sent infantry and artillery to Holly Springs to hopefully salvage something and capture any enemy they could; he wrote Washington that "I yet hope the enemy will find this a dearly-bought success." Grant also sent the nearest bodies of troops from his invading army, writing Colonel Carroll C. Marsh at Waterford, "I want those fellows caught, if possible, and any support you can give toward it with your infantry and artillery I want you to do it." Even so, Grant was not satisfied with the pursuit, removing Colonel John K. Mizner of his cavalry regiment for failure to properly pursue Van Dorn.[13]

In the meantime, both cavalry raiders moved north toward safety, as Forrest rode into Kentucky, threatening Columbus, before heading back to a crossing at Clifton. Before he could reach the river, however, he was caught and nearly captured at Parker's Crossroads. He managed to get away despite

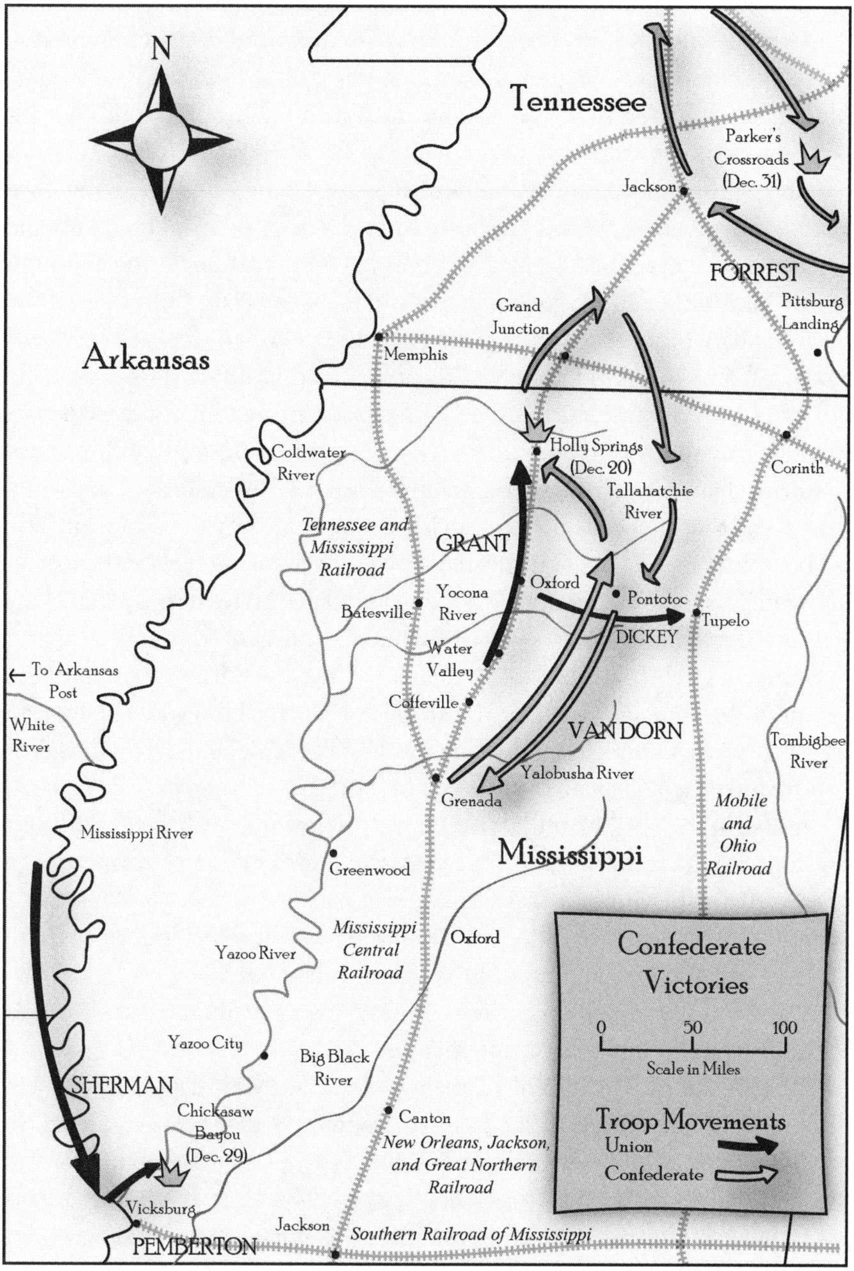

N
Tennessee
Parker's Crossroads (Dec. 31)
Jackson
FORREST
Grand Junction
Pittsburg Landing
Arkansas
Memphis
Coldwater River
Holly Springs (Dec. 20)
Corinth
Tallahatchie River
Tennessee and Mississippi Railroad
GRANT
Oxford
Yocona River
Pontotoc
Batesville
Tupelo
DICKEY
Water Valley
← To Arkansas Post
Coffeeville
White River
VAN DORN
Tombigbee River
Yalobusha River
Grenada
Mobile and Ohio Railroad
Mississippi River
Mississippi
Greenwood
Mississippi Central Railroad
Oxford
Yazoo River
Confederate Victories
0 50 100
Scale in Miles
Yazoo City
Big Black River
SHERMAN
Chickasaw Bayou (Dec. 29)
Canton
New Orleans, Jackson, and Great Northern Railroad
Troop Movements
Union
Confederate
Vicksburg
Jackson
Southern Railroad of Mississippi
PEMBERTON

the Tennessee River rising two feet and several gunboats on patrol at Grant's request to stop the crossing. Van Dorn likewise continued into Tennessee but ultimately made his getaway back to Grenada.[14]

With the news of Holly Springs fresh in his mind and destruction by Forrest evident from the broken communications, Grant mulled his options. McPherson realized that "the cavalry dash into Holly Springs has been a pretty serious affair for us," and a frightened Halleck counseled, "I think no more troops should at present be sent against Vicksburg. I fear you have already too much weakened your own force. Concentrate and hold only the more important points." Grant was coming to the same conclusion and soon decided he must fall back. He ordered McPherson and Hamilton to withdraw to the Tallahatchie line, "The troops retiring by the same route they [had] advanced on." Grant did not give this order out of military necessity, as he did not worry about meeting the Confederate army, which was evidently withdrawing southward even then. In fact, the only real potential threat was to Corinth, and Grant sent two divisions of infantry to reinforce it, knowing Dodge had taken troops north to catch Forrest. Now the primary immediate problem was feeding a concentrated army. With the line evidently broken between him and Columbus and all the accumulated stores destroyed at Holly Springs, Grant had to find a way to feed his thousands of troops. McPherson had already put his men on "three-quarter rations . . . until we ascertain the extent of the damage." To place the army in a safe position while he figured out what to do, Grant thus withdrew north of the Tallahatchie, ordering his commanders to "collect all the cattle fit for beef they can and corn-meal from the mills. Destroy all the mills within reach of you and the bridges after you are done using them." To clear his front even more and forestall any chance of a Confederate counterattack, he also sent cavalry south toward Grenada, ordering them to destroy "thoroughly on your return all bridges on railroad and wagon roads and all mills on the line of your march."[15]

Grant was not giving up entirely. Despite the destruction of the bridges to the south and Grant's assertion that "we are done using them," he was not totally abandoning the idea of advancing along the Mississippi Central. He wrote that "if the rebels get such a check as to leave the road in a condition to be repaired in one week I shall hold the line of the Tallahatchie for the present." He even informed his chief quartermaster in St. Louis not to send his requested locomotives yet, because he was not sure where they would be needed: "They may be required at Memphis Columbus or Vicksburg The particular point not yet determined." Soon, the picture became clearer. Grant wrote on December 26 that "the road north of Trenton is worse than at first reported," and he came to the conclusion that further movement was impossible. He sent a brief note to Sherman notifying him that, because of the raids, "farther advance by this route is perfectly impracticable." Sherman, it seemed, was on his own.[16]

II

Problems had compounded problems, but it was only about to get worse as a series of near disasters threatened to doom the entire operation. One of the major troubles that grew more significant as the days passed was the ability to feed the army, including the horses and mules. With all hope of supply gone, for at least a time, Grant opted to take what he needed from the local area. "Up to this time," Grant later wrote, "it had been regarded as an axiom in war that large bodies of troops must operate from a base of supplies which they always covered and guarded in all forward movements." But Grant was coming to learn that it did not always have to be the case. His correspondence from the time bears this out. He wrote one of his subordinates, "Instruct all your post commanders to collect all the forage, beef cattle, and fat hogs in their vicinity belonging to secessionists, and have them issued by the commissary and quartermaster. Send some forage and cattle to Corinth immediately, or as soon as possible; they are out of rations." Later, he wrote, "You had better collect all the bacon and meat from the secessionists in town to use in case of emergency. If they don't like the association of Yankees, let them move south among their friends." Grant summarized it all in a note to Washington: "For 15 miles east and west of the railroad, from Coffeeville to La Grange, nearly everything for the subsistence of man or beast has been appropriated for the use of our army." He later summed up the effect in his memoirs, writing, "Our loss of supplies was great at Holly Springs, but it was more than compensated for by those taken from the country and by the lesson taught."[17]

The effect on the citizens was obvious. Grant later described in his memoirs how

> the news of the capture of Holly Springs and the destruction of our supplies caused much rejoicing among the people remaining in Oxford. They came with broad smiles on their faces, indicating intense joy, to ask what I was going to do now without anything for my soldiers to eat. I told them that I was not disturbed; that I had already sent troops and wagons to collect all the food and forage they could

> find for fifteen miles on each side of the road. Countenances soon changed, and so did the inquiry. The next was, "What are we to do?" My response was that we had endeavored to feed ourselves from our own northern resources while visiting them; but their friends in gray had been uncivil enough to destroy what we had brought along, and it could not be expected that men, with arms in their hands, would starve in the midst of plenty. I advised them to emigrate east, or west, fifteen miles and assist in eating up what we left.[18]

Grant also made decisions about his larger lines of supply, opting to use the Memphis and Charleston Railroad from Memphis as his chief avenue. "Fearing that damages to the railroad north to Columbus will take several weeks to repair, I have directed the opening of the Memphis road," he wrote in late December. But that could only alleviate some of his problems, especially while the railroad was being repaired mainly around Moscow. "We may find it necessary to send the wagons back to get a second load of supplies," he surmised. Then, even as the railroad was under repair, more trouble developed, causing Grant to take a firmer stance. The main culprit proved not to be more Confederate cavalry raids but sabotaging local citizens. McPherson wrote Grant, "The citizens generally don't know anything, and when they do are not to be trusted, unless corroborated from other sources."[19]

Grant responded firmly concerning the citizens, adding to the growing harshness of the Union position toward Confederate civilians. "Some citizens of Memphis were overheard to say that there was a determination that we should not run the Memphis and Charleston Railroad," Grant wrote Hurlbut, "that it will be easier to interrupt that and force us to move the army to Memphis for supplies than to come here to fight the main army." He continued firmly, "It is my determination to run the road as long as we require it, and if necessary I will remove every family and every species of personal property between the Hatchie and Coldwater Rivers. I will also move south every family in Memphis of doubtful loyalty, whether they have taken the oath of allegiance or not, if it is necessary for our security, and you can so notify them." He also threatened further, "For every raid or attempted raid by guerrillas upon the road I want ten families of the most noted secessionists sent south." Even so, there was a limit to what Grant would do, illustrating what he deemed honorable warfare and outright treachery: "If the enemy, with his regularly-organized forces, attack us I do not propose to punish non-combatant citizens for it; but these guerillas receive support and countenance from this class of citizens, and by their acts will bring punishment upon all." He ordered, "Give notice to the citizens on the road to Memphis that if necessary to secure the railroad every family and every vestige of property, except land itself, between the Hatchie and the Coldwater will be removed out of these limits. Arrest and parole all citizens between eighteen and fifty years of age."[20]

With so much trouble on the Memphis and Charleston Railroad, Grant still looked to reopen the Mobile and Ohio to Columbus as well. He noted, "I have no idea of keeping open the Memphis road except for temporary purposes," although that was the reality for the time being. In order to make sure that this problem did not happen again, Grant ordered that "stockades must be built at every military post or station."[21]

And if the raids, the withdrawal, and other problems concerning feeding the army were not enough, there was another issue: John A. McClernand. Grant had been able to sidestep McClernand's command of the expedition down the Mississippi River toward Vicksburg by hurrying Sherman's troops south before McClernand arrived. Ironically, the Confederate raids that broke his communications actually aided Grant, delaying messages he had sent to McClernand. Still, the politician was certain to arrive shortly, and who knew what he would do. When McClernand arrived at Memphis from Illinois on December 28 he immediately sent two staff officers to Holly Springs to contact Grant. In doing so, he took all the power he could, providing Grant with copies of all official papers giving him the command, including "the order of the Secretary of War recognizing the Mississippi expedition and assigning me to the command of it." McClernand also added, "The President's endorsement thereon manifests the interest he feels in the expedition." McClernand also forwarded orders that stated once again that he was to command the expedition, but under Grant's "general command." Accordingly, McClernand asked for "your instructions in the premises, and that you will be kind enough to afford me every proper facility in reaching my command." In short, McClernand was telling Grant that he had been placed in command of the advance on Vicksburg by the secretary of war and the president himself, that he intended to exercise that command, and that he expected to have no trouble from Grant.[22]

McClernand soon found himself so detached from Grant, even while under his command, that he moved south without orders on December 30 to take charge of Sherman's expedition. In fact, Grant wryly noted the next day that "General McClernand and 49 staff officers chartered the *Tigress* and started for Vicksburg yesterday." It was just another headache that Grant had to deal with, because no one knew what McClernand would do once he arrived at Sherman's position. At the least, he would take command from Sherman, whom he outranked. What he would do then was anybody's guess, but Grant feared the worst.[23]

Yet as bad as it was trying to feed his cut-off army and dealing with the loose cannon McClernand, the most significant difficulty Grant faced as the new year dawned was news from Vicksburg. Original reports indicated Sherman had experienced much success there, even capturing the city. "At Memphis all reports confirm the taking of Vicksburg by Sherman," Grant wrote McPherson from Holly Springs on December 31, "but no particulars can be obtained." There was no victory, of course, and Sherman had not taken Vicksburg. Rather, he had endured a major defeat.[24]

Sherman had sailed down the Mississippi River and up the Yazoo to Chickasaw Bayou, where he debarked his troops and began preparations for an assault. He intended to gain the high ground north and east of Vicksburg, from which a steady supply line could be established and from which an advance on Vicksburg by high and dry land could be made. Unfortunately for Sherman, the Confederates, with interior lines of communication, had been able to move troops to defend the area. Sherman wondered what to do and "listened for days for the sound of his [Grant's] guns in the direction of Yazoo City." Hearing nothing, he still decided to attack. Historian Edwin C. Bearss has challenged Sherman's story, arguing that Sherman, while moving downriver at Helena, had actually received word of Van Dorn's raid on Holly Springs.[25]

Whatever the case, Sherman attacked on December 29. Several divisions of his own command and some from Helena made the attack across the flooded bottoms, but they were never able to make a lodgment on the high ground. Sherman suffered severe casualties in the process, nearly two thousand men. He succinctly summed up his operation when he reported, "I reached Vicksburg at the time appointed, landed, assaulted, and failed. Re-embarked my command unopposed." When word reached Northern newspapers, they said simply, "Repulse, failure, and bungling."[26]

Grant was oblivious to all this until the rumors began to arrive, first that Sherman had been successful. "Report from the South says Vicksburgh in our possession," he wrote Joseph Webster on December 29. With the good news, Grant even toyed with the idea of pulling his own forces back to "the line of Memphis and Corinth." Then word of a major defeat filtered in; "Vicksburg is ours or Sherman is whipped before this," Grant wrote McPherson. Confirmation broke at Hurlbut's headquarters in Memphis on January 3. Hurlbut wrote Grant, "Sherman has had a bitter fight; . . . our men were driven out with great slaughter." Coming on the heels of the disaster at Fredericksburg a couple of weeks earlier and the less-than-enthusiastic results of the fighting at Stones River just a few days prior, the news of the repulse at Vicksburg only added to the depressed feelings in the North that winter.[27]

If there was any consolation about the defeat, it was that Sherman had been able to wage the fight before McClernand had arrived. Actually, Sherman fought the battle only a day after McClernand had reached Memphis. Had McClernand been on site and in command, Grant feared he would have perhaps lost the entire army to capture or destruction. Grant trusted Sherman but not McClernand and his independent operations. But now McClernand was headed south to take over the command. Surely, he would not make another attempt similar to Sherman's, but it was terribly worrisome to wonder what else he might do.

III

Grant knew that the McClernand issue was as much political as it was military, and the recent defeats would be political fodder for McClernand and anyone else who viewed Grant as a disaster. Thus, Grant turned to his guardian congressman Elihu Washburne, to whom he wrote, "You have always shown such willingness to befriend me." Although the pretense of the letter was a call for the promotion of Surgeon John H. Brinton, Grant actually may have been explaining Sherman's defeat to cover himself. Grant knew he would take a hit politically for the repulse, and he knew McClernand would probably use it to his best advantage. "I am now feeling great anxiety about Vicksburg," Grant wrote, "the last news from there was favorable, but I know that Kirby Smith is on his way to reinforce Johnson. My last advices from there were to the 31st." Grant perhaps overstated the positive nature of the results, having written Halleck at least two days earlier that Sherman had been repulsed. Nevertheless, he let the congressman know that it had been out of his hands and that only others could have changed the dynamic; he particularly noted Nathaniel P. Banks, who was presumably moving north along the river from New Orleans: "If Banks arrived about that time all is well. If he did not Sherman has had a hard time of it." Then he tellingly added, "I could not reinforce from here in time, and too much territory would be exposed by doing it if I could."[28]

The wait to find out what McClernand would do once he reached the Vicksburg vicinity did not take long. Despite the delay in Grant's written orders due to the break in communications, McClernand had left Memphis on December 30 and made his way to Milliken's Bend, Louisiana, where Sherman had taken his troops after the vicious fight at Chickasaw Bayou. There, McClernand began to assume what he perceived to be his rightful place in the Vicksburg expedition.[29]

McClernand first tried to consolidate his position. He fired off a lengthy letter explaining what he had been doing and how he had missed the Vicksburg expedition due to late letters and bad timing. He wrote Secretary of War Edwin M. Stanton bluntly that "either through the intention of the General-in-Chief [Halleck] or a strange occurrence of accidents, the authority of the President and yourself, as evidenced by your acts, has been set at naught, and I have been deprived of the command that had been committed to me." Now in command, he showed no shyness about pressing what he believed to be the best option for reducing Vicksburg: Grant would continue south through Mississippi while his own forces operated on the river approaches. Whether McClernand really believed that this was the best approach or whether he wanted Grant out of his way is not clear, but such a move would certainly solidify McClernand's sole command of the river expedition.[30]

McClernand then turned to taking actual command. He provided Sherman with written documentation of his claim to authority, ironically Grant's December 18 order. On the same day, January 4, he reorganized the forces into two corps, his own styled as the First Corps and Sherman's given the title of Second Corps. Even more insulting to Grant and Sherman, McClernand (who outranked Sherman) turned his corps over to Sherman's junior, Brigadier General George W. Morgan, while McClernand commanded the whole. In another attempt to break from Grant's authority, McClernand then gave the entire army a different name, as if it were not even in Grant's Department of the Tennessee. McClernand named his force the "Army of the Mississippi."[31]

Sherman and his friend Grant still had a way to stop McClernand's total usurpation of power, however. Lincoln has ordered a corps-numbering system and stipulated that Grant should have the Thirteenth, Fifteenth, Sixteenth, and Seventeenth Corps in his army. Sherman referred to his corps as the Fifteenth Corps per Grant's instructions, thus leaving it a part of the Department of the Tennessee. McClernand quickly inquired "by what authority [do] you call the Second Army Corps of the Army of the Mississippi the 'Fifteenth Army Corps.'" Grant quickly informed McClernand of the new corps system arranged by the War Department, making McClernand's own the Thirteenth Corps and Sherman's the Fifteenth. Still, McClernand was in command, and there was little Sherman could do about that. In his general orders outlining the change to his corps, Sherman wrote somewhat snidely,

"A new commander is now here to lead you. He is chosen by the President of the United States, who is charged by our Constitution to maintain and defend it, and he has the undoubted right to select his own agents."[32]

While that specially chosen agent was in tactical command, McClernand also had the authority to act on his own impressions, which was exactly what he did next, much to Grant's chagrin. At the urging of Sherman (who actually thought of it) and perhaps to show his independence, McClernand devised a plan to move his Army of the Mississippi back up the Mississippi River to the Arkansas River, up which stood a Confederate fort at Arkansas Post. McClernand viewed this post as a threat to supply and movement on the Mississippi River, but he perhaps saw it as more of a chance to demonstrate his independence from Grant. For whatever reason, he began to prepare a campaign against the Confederates there, without asking Grant's permission or even advising the departmental commander of his plans until he was well into it. With Sherman's help, McClernand was able to talk Flag Officer David Dixon Porter and the navy into accompanying the army, although Porter detested McClernand and insisted that Sherman command the ground forces.[33]

Grant was unaware of any of McClernand's efforts until January 11. He wrote the day before that "I have not had one word officially from the expedition . . . , and am consequently very much at a loss to know how to proceed." When Grant finally received a message on January 11, ironically the day McClernand captured Arkansas Post, he was livid. Grant immediately fired off a message: "Unless absolutely necessary for the object of your expedition you will abstain from all moves not connected with it." Having put McClernand on notice not to start anything else, he then dealt with the movement to Arkansas Post. "I do not approve of your move on the Post of Arkansas while the other is in abeyance. It will lead to the loss of men without a result. So long as Arkansas cannot re-enforce the enemy east of the river we have no present interest in troubling them. It might answer for some of the purposes you suggest, but certainly not as a military movement looking to the accomplishment of the one great result, the capture of Vicksburg." Grant then turned to exercising his departmental authority: "Unless you are acting under authority not derived from me keep your command where it can soonest be assembled for the renewal of the attack on Vicksburg." Grant deemed Milliken's Bend and Young's Point as the rendezvous point and ordered, "Unless there is some great reason of which I am not advised you will immediately proceed to that point and await the arrival of re-enforcements . . . , keeping me fully advised of your movements." He reiterated the order again on January 14: "I would renew directions already given to keep your force in the Mississippi River at the most suitable point for operating on Vicksburg and cooperating with Gen. Banks should he succeed in reaching that place." Later, he also scolded that "the transports in the river available for moving troops are becoming very limited in consequence of the great number now with you. You will therefore discharge any that are not absolutely necessary for your purposes and order them to report here without delay." Although battling a snowstorm, McClernand and Sherman were back at Milliken's Bend by January 21.[34]

The Arkansas Post affair had major ramifications. Grant always knew that McClernand could be difficult, but his continuing reluctance to come fully under Grant's command was especially aggravating. Although Grant did not know it, McClernand was even then skirting Grant's orders, writing another general, "My orders from Major-General Grant require me to at once go to Napoleon, but I shall delay a day or two in order to threaten Little Rock and Pine Bluff as a diversion in your favor." Moreover, once McClernand received Grant's curt note, he fought back with disdain, writing Grant: "I take the responsibility of the expedition against Post Arkansas, and had anticipated your approval of the complete and signal success which crowned it rather than your condemnation. . . . I accept the consequences of the imputed guilt of using it profitably and successfully upon my own responsibility." As a parting shot, McClernand also reminded Grant that "the officer who, in the present strait of the country, will not assume a proper responsibility to save it is unworthy of public trust."[35]

Grant thus had his army strung out along a wide river and an insubordinate commander who thought he should be in charge. Even worse, that commander had political backing, and McClernand was not afraid to use it. McClernand wrote major politicians such as Illinois governor Richard Yates, but the biggest addressee of course was Abraham Lincoln himself. McClernand told him,

> I believe my success here is gall and wormwood to the clique of West Pointers who have been persecuting me for months. How can you expect success when men controlling the military destinies of the country are more chagrined at the success of your volunteer officers than the very enemy beaten by the latter in battle? Something must be done to take the hand of oppression off citizen soldiers whose zeal for their country has prompted them to take up arms, or all will be lost. Do not let me be clandestinely destroyed, or, what is worse, dishonored, without a hearing.

In an even more flagrant act of insubordination, McClernand asked Lincoln, "How can General Grant at a distance of 400 miles intelligently command the army with me? He cannot do it. It should be made an independent command, as both you and the Secretary of War, as I believe, originally intended."[36]

McClernand had clearly overstated his case, and then he unwisely picked a fight with Halleck as well. Halleck in Washington openly argued for McClernand's removal. Stanton only wrote an extremely vague letter of support for McClernand: "I think you need no new assurance of the sincere desire of the President and myself to oblige you in every particular consistent with the general interest of the service, and I trust that the source of events will be such as will enable the Government to derive the utmost advantage from your patriotism and military skill." No doubt, McClernand was not happy with such a fluff answer, but Lincoln's reply was clear as it could be: "I have too many family controversies (so to speak) already on my hands, to voluntarily, or so long as I can avoid it, take up another. You are now doing well—well for the country, and well for yourself—much better than you could possibly be, if engaged in open war with Gen. Halleck. Allow me to beg, that for your sake, for my sake, & for the country's sake, you give your whole attention to the better work."[37]

IV

With his own campaign stalled, Sherman's defeat obvious, and McClernand's usurpation of power gaining momentum, Grant had many decisions to make. News from elsewhere was hardly better, although he began to hear rumors of a semi-victory in middle Tennessee in the first few days of January. Other rumors were less believable, and Grant actually treated them with humor. He wrote McPherson, "I saw a man who said he had heard somebody else say that some one he had forgotten who, had seen somebody else who had seen a Copy of the Chicago *Times* of the 27th which said that Lee was near Washington Halleck was removed the place offered to McClellan Cabinet dissolved and things generally in confusion." Grant certainly placed little stock in such rumors, adding that he had received a note from Halleck signed "General-in-Chief" just a few days before.[38]

Still, matters were not looking good, especially on his front. Each negative event had been a near disaster in itself, but logistical issues caused Grant the most concern in late December. He still had difficulty feeding his army, as his supply line had been ruptured and was increasingly vulnerable as men worked to restore it. Accordingly, Grant tried to get rid of as many prisoners as possible; he corresponded with Confederates at Grenada about exchange, although some were refused because of smallpox cases. Moreover, his retrograde movement was not positive for morale, both for the soldiers as well as the public. More concerning was Sherman's defeat, although Sherman had stayed in the area, moving his troops to Milliken's Bend. Each of these problems could be overcome with renewed attempts to get to Vicksburg, but relying on McClernand could be fatal. That McClernand moved on his own to Arkansas Post was even more concerning in that it not only showed his determination to act independently but also could have produced a defeat. That McClernand actually achieved a victory was a problem as well, as it convinced him even more that he alone had all the answers.[39]

Amid all this, Grant still had to deal with the mundane issues of everyday administration. Troubles large and small cropped up continuously, and his administrative ability was greatly taxed during this period. For instance, he suddenly received thousands of prisoners who surrendered at Arkansas Post. These began showing up in Memphis in mid-January, and Grant had to do something with them. Grant also tinkered with the organization of his districts, especially around Jackson and Columbus, and forwarded reports from Sherman concerning the Chickasaw Bayou battle. Additionally, Grant had to deal with the local civilians, both loyal and disloyal. For those loyal to the United States, he allowed some trade, although with so much military movement occurring on the Mississippi River he soon stopped all trade south of Memphis. To benefit from some of the trade in other areas, he collected money "for secret-service and hospital fund," establishing $100 permits allowing the purchase of cotton and other trade at military posts.[40]

Grant also defended several citizens, as in the case against the 7th Kansas Cavalry. "In their pursuit of Van Dorn," he said, the cavalry had stopped "to plunder the citizens instead of pursuing the enemy when they were so near them." If it happened again, Grant declared, their colonel was to be arrested and "his regiment dismounted and disarmed." Grant did actually relieve numerous officers during this time, including one from the engineer regiment who was offended at receiving orders from outside the departmental command structure and responded disrespectfully. Grant noted that the regiment was under the "Sup't of the Rail Road, and is no more subject to orders from other commanders than troops of one Division are subject to the orders of their superiors in another division. This however does not justify disrespect." At the same time, Grant was so in need of any and all trained engineers that he had them transferred from their original units to the engineer regiment.[41]

Fashioning a coherent policy for contrabands also taxed Grant's time during this period, even with Eaton in charge of the freed slave camps in the district. "Contraband question becoming a serious one," Grant wrote Halleck in January, "what will I do with surplus Negroes? I authorized an Ohio philanthropist a few days ago to take all that were at Columbus to his State at Government expense. Would like to dispose of more same way."[42]

While he dealt with lower-level issues, including a continual call for the promotion of his favored subordinates, the higher-level problems bore on him the most. There was no doubt that he had overall departmental command, but because Lincoln and Stanton had given McClernand some sort of say in the Mississippi River expedition, the issue was much more complicated. Grant was confident in his ability to handle it all, and in two of the three mobile corps commanders: McPherson, despite his youth, and Sherman, even if he did not always agree with Grant and spoke his mind about it. For example, Sherman backed McClernand on Arkansas Post, writing, "As long as the Post of Arkansas existed on our flank, with boats to ship cannon and men to the mouth of the Arkansas, we would be annoyed beyond measure whilst operating below." Once he learned that his friend Sherman had actually first suggested the Arkansas Post expedition, Grant later tried to wiggle out of his opposition; he wrote in his memoirs, "But when the result was understood I regarded it as very important." Significantly, the contemporary records simply do not bear out this claim. For his part, even when he did not agree, Sherman was loyal and supported Grant fully.[43]

That left McClernand, and in normal circumstances he could be outvoted or outpersuaded. But McClernand outranked Grant's supporters, and if Grant continued on a split campaign, one through Mississippi and one down the river, McClernand would have to command the half that Grant could not physically accompany. That was not acceptable, especially with both Sherman and Admiral Porter begging Grant to take command of the river expedition in person. Grant even commented on "their distrust of McClernand's ability and fitness for so important and intricate an expedition" and actually thought "their distrust was an element of weakness." Grant had to figure out a way to get to Vicksburg and oversee McClernand at the same time.[44]

The logical answer was to consolidate the approach to Vicksburg and for Grant to command it himself. This would keep McClernand from making any more side efforts, and Grant warned the Illinoisan that "the Mississippi River enterprise must take precedence over all others, and any side move made must simply be to protect our flanks and rear." At the same time, Grant had to be careful because of McClernand's position, both because of his political backing and the fact that he was second in command. Fortunately, Grant soon received from Halleck the cover he needed to make such a drastic change: when he reported on January 11 that "General McClernand has fallen back to White River, and gone on a wild-goose chase to the Post of Arkansas," Halleck decisively wrote the next day allowing Grant "to relieve General McClernand from command of the expedition against Vicksburg, giving it to the next in rank or taking it yourself." Staff officer John Rawlins actually made out the order relieving McClernand but Grant chose not to use it at the time.[45]

Thus in mid-January, Grant had to make some firm decisions. He could remain where he was, attempting to restart the overland Mississippi campaign once his supply lines were reestablished, or he could drastically alter the campaign. He chose the latter, one of the main reasons being the presence of John A. McClernand himself. Indeed, McClernand's arrival, Grant later noted, "probably resulted in my ultimately taking command in person." With Halleck's permission to take command, Grant decided to make the Mississippi River the single avenue of approach toward Vicksburg and to command it himself. As such, Grant could keep a firm watch on McClernand.[46]

Grant accordingly began his move back toward the river, ending the detour from major Mississippi River operations that had been in effect since February 1862. Almost all realized that the river was the key thoroughfare, but as early as September 1861 the Confederate bastion at Columbus, Kentucky, had stalled all effort to move south. Grant and company had consequently sidestepped Columbus and moved parallel down the Tennessee River, beginning a campaign that ultimately included Forts Henry and Donelson, Shiloh, and the siege of Corinth. Union victory along the Tennessee River in these crucial engagements had led to the Confederate defenses on the Mississippi River becoming outflanked, including Columbus and Memphis, and had netted Union capture of the river all the way to Memphis. This meant that the Mississippi was now open to Vicksburg, as there were no geographically defensible areas of high ground north of the Vicksburg bluffs.[47]

"I will start for Memphis immediately, and will do everything possible for the capture of Vicksburg," Grant wrote, noting that he was going to "regulate matters. I am told that things are going at loose ends there." Grant made his way west in mid-January, first stopping at La Grange and then moving on to Memphis on January 10. There, he made the firm commitment to the Mississippi River approach, writing McPherson, "It is my present intention to command the expedition down the river in person." The campaign would never be the same.[48]

Grant was taking a gamble. Once he moved the army as far south as Milliken's Bend and Young's Point, he could not move it back northward again. He admitted years later that "the strategic way according to the rule . . . would have been to go back to Memphis; establish that as a base of supplies; fortify it so that the storehouses could be held by a small garrison, and move from there along the line of railroad, repairing as we advanced, to the Yallabusha, or to Jackson, Mississippi." But at this point Grant could not give the appearance of a retreat or a withdrawal, especially at such a politically sensitive time. The fall 1862 elections had not gone well for war supporters, and enlistments were down; Lincoln's Emancipation Proclamation was not popular in some circles, and many were openly forecasting Union defeat. Grant later admitted, "It was my judgment at the time that to make a backward movement as long as that from Vicksburg to Memphis, would be interpreted, by many of those yet full of hope for the preservation of the Union, as a defeat, and that the draft would be resisted, desertions ensue and the power to capture and punish deserters lost. There was nothing left to be done but to go forward to a decisive victory." How to do that was the question: "The problem then became," Grant sighed, "how to secure a landing on high ground east of the Mississippi without an apparent retreat."[49]

Grant was indeed in a ticklish position. He found out just how ticklish it was when he went south to talk to the major commanders, writing Porter that "my design is to get such information from them as I find impossible to get here." Only then, he wrote Halleck, would he "have a better understanding of matters than I now have." While Grant learned much about the military difficulties on this first trip down the river, he mostly got a salvo of anti-McClernand rhetoric. He informed Halleck, "I regard it as my duty to state that I found there was not sufficient confidence felt in General McClernand as a commander, either by the Army or Navy, to insure him success. Of course, all would co-operate to the best of their ability, but still with distrust." In such a position, Grant made plain that "this is a matter I made no inquiries about, but it was forced upon me. As it is my intention to command in person, unless otherwise directed, there is no special necessity of mentioning this matter; but I want you to know that others besides myself agree in the necessity of the course I had already determined upon pursuing." Grant later made his feelings even clearer in another message to Washington: "If General Sherman had been left in command here, such is my confidence in him that I would not have thought my presence necessary. But whether I do General McClernand injustice or not, I have not confidence in his ability as a soldier to conduct an expedition of the magnitude of this one successfully." He added in support, "In this opinion I have no doubt but I am borne out by a majority of the officers of the expedition, though I have not questioned one of them on the subject."[50]

After returning to Memphis and implementing some reorganization, which included officially terminating the overland Mississippi Central Campaign and fashioning his army into the four corps as directed, Grant set out down the river for good, arriving at Napoleon on January 18. He planned to move troops as well, including either Hamilton or Hurlbut (he left the decision up to Hurlbut) with much of the Sixteenth Corps. As Sherman noted, Grant was going "to give his personal supervision to the whole movement."[51]

But even with the decision made, McClernand still caused trouble. Grant learned it would be fifteen days before the force up the Arkansas River would be ready for operations on the Mississippi River. Then, McClernand corresponded with Grant in a haughty manner; Grant later described how "his correspondence with me on the subject was more in the nature of a reprimand than a protest. It was highly insubordinate, but I overlooked it, as I believed, for the good of the service." Then on January 18 McClernand wrote again to complain of another perceived slight against the relative strength of the corps. Grant had sent reinforcements down to the army, some being assigned to Sherman, giving him a few more regiments than McClernand. "I wish to call your attention to this disparity," he wrote, "not doubting in the absence of any good reason to the contrary you will at once equalize the strength of the corps."[52]

More importantly, McClernand seemed to be totally out of touch with reality, at least the reality that Grant and his other chief subordinates saw. McClernand had stated that he was "tired of furnishing brains for the Army of the Tennessee." Grant informed Halleck in late January, "I had a conversation with Admiral Porter, General McClernand, and General Sherman. The former and latter, who have had the best opportunity of studying the enemy's positions and plans agree that the work of reducing Vicksburg is one of time, and will require a large force at the final struggle." The novice McClernand was not in agreement. He still thought that he alone could make quick work of Vicksburg.[53]

Grant "was greatly annoyed by McClernand's insubordinate behavior," one aide later wrote. Staff officers tried to get Grant to remove McClernand or either "give him such a rebuke that he could not effect to misunderstand his position as a subordinate." Grant calmly demurred, telling them, "No, I can't afford to quarrel with a man whom I have to command." But if McClernand kept this up, it was going to be a long campaign. Grant nevertheless tried to remain confident. "I am here looking to Vicksburg and intend to go in person," he wrote his cousin on January 14. "It is now known that Vicksburg is very strongly garrisoned and the fortifications almost impregnigable." Then he added, "I will see however what can be done with them."[54]

CHAPTER THREE

"THE PROBLEM IS A DIFFICULT ONE, BUT I SHALL CERTAINLY SOLVE IT"

"The real work of the campaign and siege of Vicksburg now began," Grant wrote. After making the Mississippi River the primary avenue of advance toward Vicksburg and with himself commanding the expedition, Grant made an easy decision to send McClernand's forces back to the vicinity of Vicksburg at Milliken's Bend and prepare for major operations to capture the hill city. He left no stone unturned. "In view of future operations," he wrote McClernand, "I would suggest that stringent orders be made looking to the saving of all sacks emptied by the army, and placing them in charge of an engineer officer. When it comes to erecting batteries, these sacks will come in play most conveniently." He also wrote of "getting such mining tools as will be required," and of "securing a full supply of all kinds of Ammunition for a long siege."[1]

Indeed, the efforts before were somewhat halfhearted, as Sherman's rapid move was actually motivated more by politics than military strategy—to keep McClernand from commanding the expedition. But now the army was concentrating just north of and opposite the river from Vicksburg, and Grant himself was moving south to take command. He arrived at Young's Point, Louisiana, for good on January 28. This pleased Halleck in Washington, who had written often advising Grant to make the Mississippi River his main focus: "The enemy must be turned by a movement down the river from Memphis as soon as sufficient force can be collected." During the Mississippi Central Campaign, he had also advised that "your main object will be to hold the line from Memphis to Corinth with as small a force as possible, while the largest number possible is thrown upon Vicksburg with the gunboats." At the same time, Halleck was not eager to give too many instructions to a commander a thousand miles away. He added, "You will move your troops as you may deem best to accomplish the great object in view." Grant was much relieved but still recognized the enormity of the task; one of his generals, Cadwallader Washburn, wrote that "he looks well and feels pretty well, but feels that he has got a heavy job on his hands."[2]

A heavy job it was. Just reaching Vicksburg's vicinity was not the challenge; getting to a position from which it could be attacked was: "The problem was to secure a footing upon dry ground on the east side of the river from which troops could operate against Vicksburg." Once there, Grant would have to find a way to approach Vicksburg from the east, which was what his earlier overland campaign had originally intended, and even Sherman's prior efforts were geared toward that goal. That possibility seemed to have ended with Sherman's defeat in December, and an all-out assault up the steep bluffs at the city itself was out of the question, especially with the river "very high and rising." Consequently, the northern and western approaches to the city were not considered possible routes of attack, and the southern sector was just as problematic. To approach from the south, the army would somehow have to first pass below Vicksburg, most likely through the bayous and swamps west of the river. Once there, Grant would have to ferry the river, and the lack of boats between Vicksburg and Port Hudson made that impossible. Even if it were possible, supplying the army south of Vicksburg seemed incomprehensible. Even worse, driving across the Big Black River south of Vicksburg would confine the army into a small triangle of territory where it could not maneuver very well. Yet against all the other insurmountable obstacles to the north and west, that increasingly seemed the only really feasible route. Grant later wrote in his report that "from the moment of taking command in person, I became satisfied that Vicksburg could only be turned from the south side." Turning was one thing; sustaining that turning movement was another.[3]

Accordingly, the only real possibility of outright assaulting the Confederate city was from the east. While the land east of Vicksburg would provide room for movement, getting the army there was another matter. Moving up the Yazoo presented troubles, as did the idea of moving from the south. That was why the overland route through Grenada made so much sense. But the advance was now on the river and could not be recalled without large-scale logistical and morale concerns. Grant would simply have to find a way to get his army on the high, dry ground east of Vicksburg. Sherman summed it up when he wrote, "If possible a larger force should somehow reach the ridge between the [Big] Black and Yazoo, so as to approach from the rear." Grant himself described how "once back of the intrenchments on the crest of the bluffs, the enemy would be compelled to come out and give us an open field fight, or submit to having all his communications cut and be left to starve out." The main communication link Grant described, of course, was the all-important Southern Railroad of Mississippi, which ran eastward from Vicksburg to Jackson and Meridian.[4]

A surprisingly confident Grant quickly set his mind to the effort, but the time of year posed another problem. While the region was much too far south for snow to hamper winter efforts, the wet weather nevertheless muddied roads and swelled rivers. Grant wrote of the "intolerable rains that we have had, and which have filled the swamps and bayous so that they cannot dry up again this winter." An advance by the army anywhere on land was thus unrealistic at this point in January, but Grant had other options, mostly water routes. If the wet weather would hamper marching, Grant could try several routes that would allow the water to aid his efforts, not hinder them. On the other hand, he was fully aware too that it would not be long before the lower latitudes produced high temperatures. "I never enjoyed better health or felt better in my life than since here," Grant wrote Julia once he arrived near Vicksburg. Then he added, "The weather however will soon begin to grow warm and unpleasant." It seemed that Grant had only a small window of opportunity before the weather turned, so he had to be prepared when that chance came.[5]

With only water-borne operations a reality at this point, Grant's splendid relationship with Admiral Porter served him well, with the general even providing help with manning the gunboats. It was a good match, although on one occasion Porter informed Grant that an entire company had "mutinied." Porter continued: "Some one gave them a half barrel of whisky amongst their rations, with which they filled their canteens and regaled the crew of the *Benton*, who are somewhat in a like condition, but more tractable." Porter concluded that "they are pretty drunk now and insensible to reason," so he had them put "in irons."[6]

Grant thus began his waterborne advances in January and would continue through April, first seriously attempting to reach Vicksburg itself by using several long-forgotten bayous, creeks, rivers, and passages. The hope was that Grant and Porter could develop a route through the maze of waterways in the Delta that would allow them to either bypass Vicksburg on the west side of the river through Louisiana or allow him to deposit his army on the high ground east of Vicksburg. Accordingly, Grant initiated four distinct efforts. Minor endeavors also took place with Hurlbut's and Hamilton's troops destroying the railroad in north Mississippi as far as the Tallahatchie River. Success in any one of these might allow Grant to reach Vicksburg, and he enthusiastically approved each plan. Although Grant later wrote in his memoirs that "I, myself, never felt great confidence that any of the experiments resorted to would prove successful," the contemporary records tell a different tale. Grant was extremely hopeful, even excited, over some of the possibilities.[7]

Even so, while Grant was confident of success, his own status as commander of it all was growing more precarious. Hurlbut warned him, "I hope you will sweep out the rabble, especially as I learn that mischief-makers are looking after you, with hopes based upon your downfall." One of the main instigators, of course, was McClernand, who in one of his darkest moments on March 15 even wrote his friend Abraham Lincoln about Grant's alleged drunkenness, describing Grant as "gloriously drunk and in bed sick all next day." Grant later noted in his memoirs that "visitors to the camps went home with dismal stories to relate; Northern papers came back to the soldiers with these stories exaggerated. Because I would not divulge my ultimate plans to visitors, they pronounced me idle, incompetent and unfit to command men in an emergency, and clamored for my removal."[8]

Lincoln had already been under pressure to relieve Grant earlier in the war, but at that time he supposedly answered with, "I can't spare this man; he fights." Still, Washington now determined to keep an eye on Grant by assigning newspaperman Charles A. Dana as a special emissary to his headquarters. Ostensibly there to study pay services, Dana actually was to report to Lincoln and Stanton to "settle their minds as to Grant, about whom at that time there were many doubts, and against whom there was some complaint." For his part, Grant saw through the ruse and welcomed the interloper with open arms. For one thing, Dana reported, "He did not like letter writing, and my daily dispatches to Mr. Stanton relieved him of the necessity of describing every day what was going on in the army." For another, Grant was smart enough to realize that keeping Dana at arm's length would only irritate him, so he adopted the opposite approach. Dana reported that "from the first neither he nor any of his staff or corps commanders evinced any unwillingness to show me the inside of things." It was a classic case of keeping your friends close and your enemies closer, and it worked; Dana soon became an avid supporter of Grant in his messages to Washington.[9]

Grant began his determined activities with high hopes but realistic fears, writing of beginning "the impending struggle in opening the Mississippi River." His health was good, and he told Julia that "the trip, with nothing to bother me, makes me feel well. The living on the boat is very fine and my appetite good." War Department observer Dana reflected that same optimism in a telegram to Stanton: "General Grant is dead sure that he will have the place [Vicksburg] within a fortnight." The cheerfulness was matched by news from elsewhere. "Rosecrans has whipped Bragg badly at Murfreesborough and forced him to fall back," Grant wrote with exaggeration in mid-January. Hopefully, Grant would also soon have similar good news for the American public.[10]

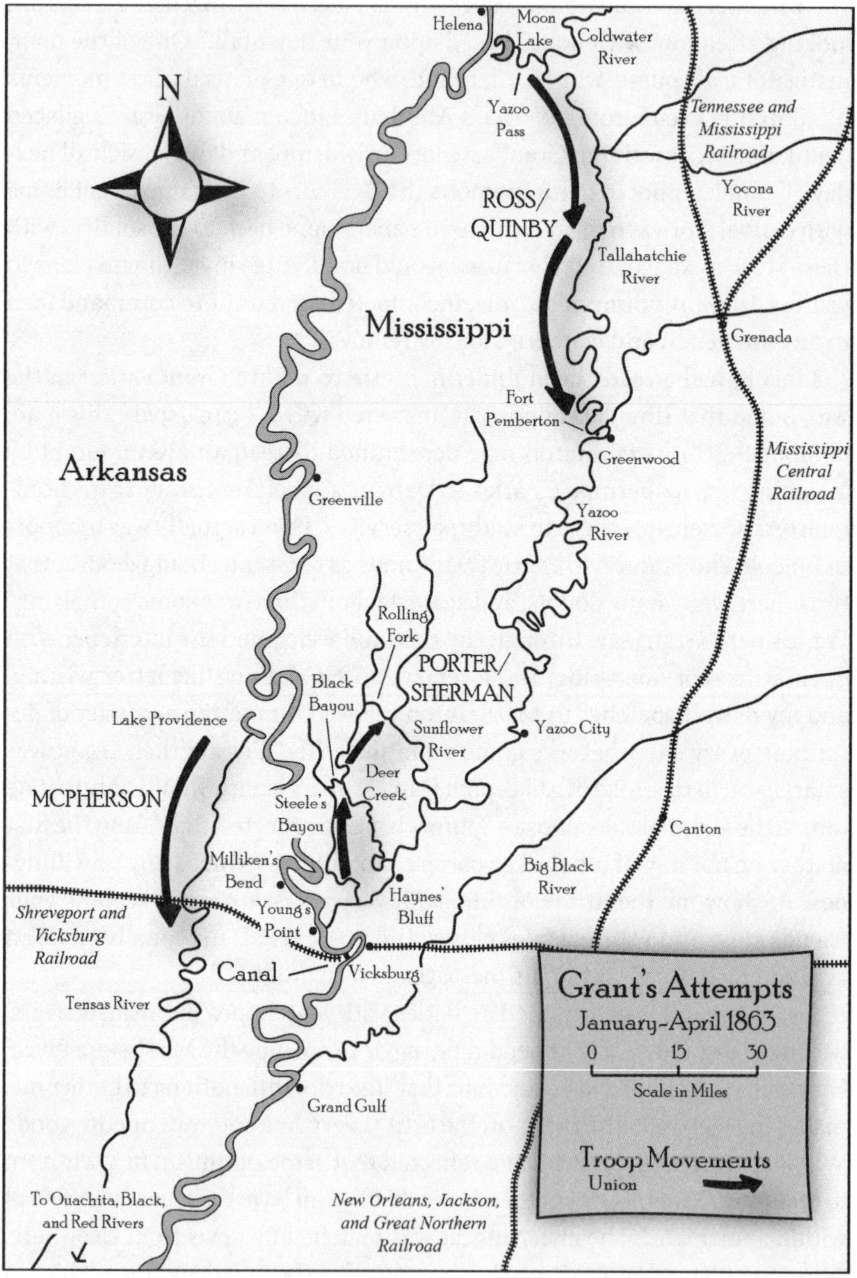
N
Helena
Moon Lake
Coldwater River
Yazoo Pass
Tennessee and Mississippi Railroad
Yocona River
ROSS/ QUINBY
Tallahatchie River
Mississippi
Grenada
Fort Pemberton
Greenwood
Mississippi Central Railroad
Arkansas
Greenville
Yazoo River
Rolling Fork
PORTER/ SHERMAN
Black Bayou
Lake Providence
Sunflower River
Yazoo City
Deer Creek
MCPHERSON
Steele's Bayou
Canton
Milliken's Bend
Big Black River
Haynes' Bluff
Young's Point
Shreveport and Vicksburg Railroad
Canal
Vicksburg
Tensas River
Grant's Attempts
January–April 1863
0 15 30
Scale in Miles
Grand Gulf
Troop Movements
Union
To Ouachita, Black, and Red Rivers
New Orleans, Jackson, and Great Northern Railroad

I

In addition to the quirky terrain features of the delta and three-hundred-foot-high bluffs on which Vicksburg itself sat, nature provided another significant attribute for Vicksburg's defense: the hairpin bend the river made as it passed the city. Flowing south, the river turned quickly to the north before turning sharply south again; Vicksburg sat on the east bank of the southern turn, just south of the hairpin bend. Accordingly, a small peninsula, where the village of De Soto was located, jutted north between the river channels. This bend was significant: not only did steamboats have to slow down to negotiate the massive turn and currents, but Confederates high atop the Vicksburg bluffs also had a clear view of anything coming south on the river long before any boats ever actually approached the city.[11]

Grant still had to find a way to get past Vicksburg without coming under its guns. "I am pushing everything to gain a passage, avoiding Vicksburg," he wrote Halleck on the last day of January. Fortunately, the odd layout of the river also provided some hope for Grant. If the river could be diverted to cut across the base of the peninsula, it would completely bypass Vicksburg and allow for continual naval movement right on past the city. Vicksburg and all its river defenses would in effect be negated, although the Confederates had additional river batteries at Warrenton, just south of Vicksburg, and Grand Gulf even farther south. In any case, the major obstacle would be eliminated.[12]

"I hope the work of changing the channel of the Mississippi is begun," Grant wrote on January 22, "or preparations, at least, being made to begin." The idea of changing the course of the Mississippi River was a mammoth thought, because the river was a mammoth body of water. Yet all knew it could be done, as it had changed course itself many times before. The widespread existence of so many nearby oxbow lakes that once were part of the river channel was testimony itself, but those had been accomplished by nature without the prodding of man. Perhaps man could aid in Mother Nature's work, but no one knew for sure. At any rate, Grant wanted the effort made "and prosecuted day and night until its completion." It became the first concerted attempt by Grant to render Vicksburg useless.

The idea was not new: Union general Thomas Williams had begun construction of the canal when the Federals approached the city from the south in the summer of 1862. Nothing had come of either the canal or the Union presence as the Federals soon retreated. Now that Grant was determined to remove Vicksburg as a factor, he started with this ready-made project. He gave orders as early as January 10 "for the purpose of surveying the ground and determining the practicability of reopening the canal across the tongue of land opposite Vicksburg." He also sent Colonel Josiah W. Bissell of the famous engineer regiment to lend aid. There was some debate over the best place to cut the canal, and there was also discussion of building a new channel farther up, "starting far enough above the old one commenced last summer," Grant wrote, "to receive the stream where it impinges against the shore with the greatest velocity."[13]

McClernand and Sherman quickly detailed troops to restart work on the canal, as many as a thousand men a day. An arriving dredge boat also helped in late February, although it "gave out this afternoon," Grant wrote on March 4. The interest grew even more when Halleck telegraphed to "direct your attention particularly to the canal proposed across the point. The President attaches much importance to this." Grant later wrote in his memoirs that "Mr. Lincoln had navigated the Mississippi in his younger days and understood well its tendency to change its channel, in places, from time to time. He set much store accordingly by this canal." Some alteration of the original canal was allowed to make the channel more acceptable to the river's current and to facilitate its own change of course, but all the work in the muddy slop was hard, resulting in little early success. By January 26, for example, McClernand wrote that "The water flows 3 feet deep in the canal, but gives no evidence of diverting the channel of the river." A dejected Grant informed Julia in February, "We are not much nearer an attack on Vicksburg now apparently than when I first came down, but still as the attack will be made and time is passing we are necessarily coming nearer the great conflict."[14]

Others were coming to the same conclusion. Newspaperman Cadwallader reported that the canal "was standing full of still water, without any current whatever and quite as much inclined to empty itself into the river above Vicksburg as below it." By early February, Sherman was also having second thoughts, writing Samuel Curtis, "Our canal here don't amount to much. It is full of water, but manifests no disposition to change the channel. It is a very small affair, and we can hardly work a barge through it for stumps." Ultimately, Grant called on Hurlbut at Memphis to send "as many able-bodied negro laborers as can be had or spared from Memphis and other portions of your command. They are much needed here for work on the canal." Unfortunately, matters only became worse when in March the river still had not changed its course, but a sudden rise in the water level broke through "the dam across the upper end." Grant later admitted in his report, "The task was much more Herculean than it at first appeared, and was made much more so by the almost continuous rains that fell during the whole of the time this work was prosecuted. The river, too, continued to rise and made a large expenditure of labor necessary to keep the water out of our camps and the canal." Wagons and men could only move on the tops of the levees, which coincidentally was the only place to bury those who died of disease. Wagons and troops moving along the waterlogged levees would sometimes unearth coffins, making it ghastly work for all.[15]

Grant dejectedly noted, "It is exceedingly doubtful if this canal can be made of any practical use, even if completed. The enemy have established a battery of heavy guns opposite the mouth of the canal, completely commanding it for one-half its length." In fact, the army had enough problems just staying above the rising waters: "the continuous rise of the river has kept the army busy to keep out of water," Grant wrote in mid-February, "and much retarded work on the canal." Historian J. F. C. Fuller actually likened Grant to "Noah, [who] looked out upon the waters waiting for them to subside." For that reason, Grant had to find other options: "Some other plan would have to be adopted for getting below Vicksburg with transports." Fortunately, Grant had other ideas and was already moving troops, leaving the almost hopeless canal to paid contrabands. Sherman indicated as much: "But Grant is on two other projects."[16]

II

"By inquiry I learn that Lake Providence, which connects with Red River through Tensas Bayou, Washita [Ouachita] and Black Rivers, is a wide and navigable way through," Grant wrote on January 30. "As some advantage may be gained by opening this [waterway], I have ordered a brigade of troops to be detailed for the purpose, and to be embarked as soon as possible." Thus, even while the canal operations were ongoing, Grant did not put all his hopes there and initiated another effort to get around the Confederate defenses. If successful, it would provide even greater benefit because the outlet for this course, unlike the canal, was the Red River far south of Vicksburg. Movement along this route would also bypass the Warrenton and Grand Gulf defenses as well as inhibit Confederate traffic on the important Red River.[17]

Grant was not sure if this route was feasible for the entire navy and other vessels, but, he wrote, "with this open, a vast foraging district would be opened, and our gunboats of light draft would be enabled to cut off the enemy's commerce with the west bank of the river. I have determined to make the experiment, at all events." He was even more determined once the initial reports came back. Sherman told him, "I have hastily read the reports of the Lake Providence scheme. It is admirable and most worthy a determined prosecution. Cover up the design all you can, and it will fulfill all the conditions of the great problem." Sherman also added, "This little affair of ours here on Vicksburg point is labor lost."[18]

Grant soon put force behind the Lake Providence experiment. He ordered McPherson to send an entire division to work on the effort and for the corps commander to oversee it in person. McPherson, of course, was originally an engineer and was well suited for the work. Grant informed him in early February, "This bids fair to be the most practicable route for turning Vicksburg," and added that "by a little digging, less than one-quarter that had been done across the point before Vicksburg, will connect the Mississippi and lake, and in all probability will wash a channel in a short time." Others thought the scheme worthy as well, with Sherman writing of the route "actually reaching the sea without approaching any bluff or ground easy of defense. This is a magnificent scheme, and, if successful, will be a grand achievement."[19]

McPherson set to work with a will, writing his corps, "Our marching orders have come, and it is for us to respond with promptness and alacrity. We move to capture the stronghold of the rebels in the Valley of the Mississippi." Tangible work progressed for several weeks, with the backbreaking need to remove stumps at the bottom of the lake creating what Grant called "an undertaking of great magnitude." By mid-March McPherson was ready for the levee to be cut, allowing the rushing waters of the river to enter the breach and the lake, raising the level of the water throughout the route. McPherson reported that the levee was finished on March 17 and "the water is flowing in at a tremendous rate, filling up the lake and bayous. We will soon be able to take a good-sized steamer in."[20]

The effort succeeded, to a degree. Grant wrote in late March that the water was sufficient to hold "ordinary Ohio River steamers." Unfortunately, he did not have any of those. He had called for more vessels, but they had not arrived. Most were already in service, notably those east of the Mississippi River engaged in an effort to reach the upper portions of the Yazoo River and the dry high ground east of Vicksburg. "I let the work go on," Grant later wrote, "believing employment was better than idleness for the men."[21]

Geography and water levels eventually played a role in the decision to abandon the Lake Providence effort. In April, the river began to fall, and with it all the smaller rivers and bayous flowing into it. That left many of the formerly waterlogged roadways open to wagon access. Grant noted that "the river commencing about the middle of April to fall rapidly, and the roads becoming passable between Milliken's Bend and New Carthage, made it impracticable and unnecessary to open water communication."[22]

Without steamers to make the trip and with shorter routes becoming feasible, the Lake Providence effort, while successful, was just no longer a worthwhile avenue for transport—especially with other, more promising operations in process.

III

"On the present rise it is barely possible that Yazoo Pass might be turned to good account in aiding our enterprise." So wrote Grant on January 22, even while the canal and Lake Providence efforts were still in their infancy. While Grant hoped to use the canal and roundabout Lake Providence routes to shuttle the naval vessels and infantry south, these were not, by all indications, final solutions to the problem of Vicksburg and the Confederate defenses there. Consequently, Grant had other operations on the east side of the river in mind, hoping that these would provide him access to Vicksburg itself. In fact, Grant wrote that the Yazoo Pass operation would cripple shipping on the Yazoo River, especially Confederate "embryo Gunboats" of "gigantic proportions." Most importantly, it "would enable us to get high ground above Haynes' Bluff, and would turn all the enemy's river batteries."[23]

Yazoo Pass was much lengthier than even the Lake Providence route. The effort began as far north as Helena, Arkansas. On the Mississippi side of the river was a large oxbow lake named Moon Lake, which was a former channel of the river that was now a crescent-shaped body of water. It was wide and navigable, but it was separated from the river by a large levee constructed years earlier by the State of Mississippi to hold back the river and dry out the delta so plantation owners could work its fertile ground. Just a few miles east of Moon Lake was the Coldwater River, which flowed south into the Tallahatchie, which also flowed south and combined with the Yalobusha River to form the Yazoo just west of Grenada at Greenwood. It was the Yazoo that Grant said "is the great object of the expedition to enter." The best way to approach Vicksburg was from the east, and the Yazoo River provided that access, but Confederate defenses near the mouth of the Yazoo River hampered that possibility, as Sherman had discovered in December. Moving up the river from the mouth was therefore impossible, so the idea emerged to outflank the Confederate defenses by coming down the river from its headwaters. Getting a force of gunboats and infantry-laden transports into the Coldwater, Tallahatchie, and then upper Yazoo might provide that possibility.[24]

The trick, of course, was to get from the Mississippi River through Moon Lake and to the Coldwater River. Fortunately for Grant, breaking the levee at Moon Lake would provide much water to work with and would allow easy access. It would be more problematic to get from Moon Lake to the Coldwater River, but there was an old and winding route connecting the two, named Yazoo Pass. Flooding the delta by breaching the levee might put enough water into the pass to float steamboats, although the overgrown pass's condition was anybody's guess. The route had long been navigated by the small vessels of local plantation owners who sent their cotton to market this way, saving them the long trip down the Yazoo to the Mississippi River near Vicksburg. That said, with the building of the levees along the Mississippi it had not been used for years and was probably overgrown by now. Grant later added that upon examination by Federals, the Confederates "have discovered this intention and have fallen timber into the stream."[25]

Nevertheless, Grant wanted the possibilities explored and sent troops to examine the pass on January 29. Rumor indicated that the Confederates had an earthen fortification near the point where the Tallahatchie and Yalobusha Rivers joined to create the Yazoo, but no one knew for sure. Grant was also cognizant of the fact that if the Yalobusha could be reached, gunboats could easily maneuver up it a few miles to Grenada and destroy the railroad bridge over the river, severely hampering Confederate efforts in north Mississippi. Grant especially wanted the railroad bridge destroyed, writing, "Let there be no delay in this matter. Time now is growing important."[26]

Grant's new engineer, James H. Wilson, soon cut the levee. Water rushed through, widening the crevasse and flooding the delta, although it was still only wide enough for smaller vessels. Soon a joint expedition made up of gunboats under Watson Smith and a division of troops under Leonard F. Ross nevertheless began snaking their way through the pass, cutting stumps and limbs to allow the boats through. They quickly hit clear water at the Coldwater River and easily steamed southward to the Tallahatchie until they neared the mouth of the Yalobusha near Greenwood. There, they came upon the rumored Confederate defense, Fort Pemberton.[27]

The boats skirmished with the Confederate guns but could not move forward and began to return to Helena. Grant sent another division under Isaac F. Quinby to try again, this time confident that the flotilla would soon approach Grenada and Yazoo City. He even issued orders for what should happen if the expedition was successful: "The Advance boats should be cautious in approaching Grenada and also Yazoo City looking out for torpedoes. In approaching a town they should notify the inhabitants to surrender and give them but a very short time, say thirty minutes at the outside to make up their minds and not permit them to move their women and children." Meanwhile, Grant heard little of the effort: "my last information from this command was the 17th [of March]," he wrote several days later. "They were at Greenwood, on the Yazoo, a fortified place, and had abandoned all idea of getting past until they could receive additional ordnance stores." It had been worth a try, and Grant still believed "by a prompt movement Yazoo City could have been captured without opposition," but there was no use in worrying over it now, especially when Grant had yet another option.[28]

IV

Grant put a great deal of stock into his next adventure, an option that emerged in mid-March: "I will have Vicksburg this month, or fail in the attempt." This effort east of the Mississippi River to access the Yazoo River north and east of Vicksburg was the brainchild of Admiral David Dixon Porter of the navy, who had first envisioned it as a way of supporting the Yazoo Pass operation by putting naval and land forces on the river behind Fort Pemberton and the Confederate reinforcements. Grant began to see it as another possible option to get his army on the high, dry ground east of Vicksburg for a land campaign. Consequently, when Porter mentioned the idea to Grant and said that he had explored part of the route, Grant was ready to listen, especially with the digging going so slowly west of the river and the Yazoo Pass operation at a standstill.[29]

In mid-March, Grant accompanied Porter on "a reconnaissance some 30 miles up Steele's Bayou. Admiral Porter and myself went in a large gunboat, preceded by four of the old 'turtles,'" the City-class ironclads. Despite the channel being "narrow, very tortuous, and fringed with a very heavy growth of timber," Grant was enthused by what he saw. He was so excited that he gave orders that very day for Sherman to proceed on the route "with a view of effecting a landing with troops on high ground on the east bank of the Yazoo, from which to act against Haynes' Bluff." Grant also left Porter to continue on the route even as he turned back and coordinated infantry support. Grant almost gushed at the possibility "to get all our forces in one place, and . . . [a] firm foothold . . . secured on the side with the enemy."[30]

Like the other attempts, traversing Steele's Bayou would be very difficult. The route ran from Steele's Bayou, which emptied into the Yazoo River near its mouth, through Black Bayou and into Deer Creek. From there the vessels would enter the Rolling Fork and then the Sunflower River, which led back into the Yazoo far north of the Confederate-fortified Haynes' and Snyder's Bluffs. Grant wrote Sherman that "there is but little work to be done in Steele's Bayou, except for about 5 miles midway up the bayou. In this portion many overhanging trees will have to be removed, and should be dragged out of the channel." Of course, Grant had not seen all of the rest of the route, but he ordered Sherman to send a hardy regiment, recommending the 8th Missouri, to cut a way through. Even with the hard work of the Missourians, the vessels still had a hard time, especially the tall-stacked transports; Grant noted that the ironclads "ploughed their way through without other damage than to their appearance. The transports did not fare so well."[31]

Despite this, Grant canceled orders for troops continuing into Yazoo Pass and sent them south into Steele's Bayou, warning his commanders to keep silent on the plan: "Keep this move an entire secret as it is not suspected by the enemy and there is no telling, sometimes, how they are enabled to get information." Even so, Grant was obviously excited: "The necessity of a large force descending the Yazoo, I think, has ended by the discovery of a route into the Yazoo from here by the way of Steele's Bayou and other cross bayous," he wrote one of his generals. In order to bypass the most congested portion of Steele's Bayou, Grant ordered Sherman's infantry up the Mississippi River to Gwin's Plantation at Eagle Bend, where the river and Steele's Bayou were no more than a mile apart. Landing there, the troops marched overland to the bayou where they boarded the transports, sparing them the torturous bayou trip. As the troops went forward and drove deeper into enemy territory, Grant was out of contact with the command for several days and began to worry that they may have run into trouble, writing that "they got in as far as Deer Creek without any great difficulty, but I fear a failure of getting farther."[32]

Failure was a mild word compared to what almost happened. Porter was so enthused with the route that he did not wait for infantry support, and Sherman trailed behind as the ironclads snaked their way through the treacherous bayous. Porter was able to make it easily up Steele's Bayou and even through the tangled Black Bayou, after which the wider Deer Creek allowed for easier travel. Then the Federal navy hit the Rolling Fork, which led to the Sunflower and Yazoo. They also hit Confederate resistance, mostly in the form of trees cut into the waterway to block travel. A crisis became evident when the Confederates also felled trees behind the gunboats. Porter knew he was in trouble without Sherman's infantry support and ordered his crews to prepare for a seeming pirate attack as in days of old; he even began to consider scuttling the vessels if the Confederates took advantage of the mess he was in. Even the sides of the ironclads were greased to keep the enemy from getting aboard. With the gunboats stuck, Porter wrote an urgent message to Sherman on tissue paper, as nothing else could be had, and sent a "negro, who had it concealed in a piece of tobacco," to deliver it. When he heard of the crisis, Sherman sent troops quickly, and they marched all night to reach the helpless gunboats, barely saving them from the swarming Confederates. They cleared the trees to their rear, and Porter backed his boats out until he reached a wide enough stream to turn around. It was a close call, but Porter made it. Steele's Bayou was clearly not the place to be unless a large portion of the army could provide support, and that was not possible in the wilderness of Mississippi.[33]

Four major attempts to get past Vicksburg on the west side of the river or to land on the dry ground east of it had been attempted, but by April each seemed increasingly unreliable. And that did not include the smaller efforts, such as Grant sending troops to "explore the system of Bayous from that point [Milliken's Bend] to Carthage, with a view of determining the practicability of turning sufficient water from, the Mississippi through that way to navigate with our fleet." This effort hinged primarily on Willow Bayou and Bayou Macon, and Grant never had much faith in the project: "I do not much think of using by Bayou Macon even if it can be used at this time. It would too much separate my forces." He added, "But [I] want to know if it can be used in case of necessity." Grant also sent an expedition inland from Greenville to stop the Confederate artillery from harassing boats on the river. He was obviously not about to leave any stone unturned to provide him an advantage, but chances of success were looking increasingly bad. Grant wrote of the high water and tough circumstances, "This is a terrible place at this stage of water. The river is higher than the land and it takes all the efforts of the troops to keep the water out." He even canceled plans for troops at Helena, Arkansas, to be shuttled down because of a lack of room to camp, and he likewise began to toy with the idea of evacuating others if the river rose too much: "It may become necessary also to move our forces from here to higher ground." Grant, however, had no such concerns living on the steamboat *Magnolia*, and remained as confident as ever amid the mounting failures. "Vicksburg will be a hard job," he wrote Julia, but added," I expect to get through it successfully."[34]

V

While Grant was exploring routes, conducting movements, observing progress, and planning future military actions, more methodical administrative and personal affairs also consumed his time. Indeed, the administrative work continued to mount as Grant's army grew larger, the lines of supply became longer, and the efforts to reach Vicksburg multiplied. Grant could not avoid the resulting minutiae, perhaps because he lacked staff officers. He often became involved in individual prisoner's cases, for example. He also had to order general officers out of private dwellings of loyal people, writing that "I am opposed to working any hardships upon such people when it can be avoided and especially where there are so many undeserving people occupying houses suitable for Officers Quarters. . . . Where there is great Military necessity for taking private houses from any class of people it will be done but even then the disloyal will be visited first." Concerning minutiae, Grant even stipulated how many trains to run in certain areas: "Can you not run three trains a day," he wrote Joseph Webster in January, "there is such complaint for want of forage." Moreover, larger numbers of men only increased the need for food. He continually pulled reinforcements down the river from stations farther north. To Hurlbut he wrote, "Seeing your last returns, I am satisfied that another division can be spared from your command." The arrival of these troops did not mean they were battle or campaign ready, however, and Grant worried over their conditions; he once wrote of "old and tired troops, whilst the others are raw, and with rather indifferent brigade commanders, I fear." In order to create the kind of environment he wanted, Grant issued orders that "the bars on all boats in Government service in this Department will be closed, and no spirituous, vinous, or malt liquors will be allowed to be sold on boats or in the camps. Card-playing and gaming is also strictly prohibited." To care for physical sickness, he authorized the United States Sanitary Commission to occupy a boat and provide "for the relief of the sick and wounded."[35]

Beyond these items of minutia, feeding and supplying such a force deep in enemy territory was a huge operation that took much of Grant's time. The army needed almost all items, from ammunition to horseshoes, except mules, and he recommended sending the surplus animals northward "and save the purchase above." He also needed boats to ship supplies and men, a requirement that actually forced McPherson to delay pushing his entire corps south. "Our wants for transportation here I have stated without exaggeration," wrote Lewis B. Parsons, Grant's superintendent of transportation, "and earnestly request, for the good of the whole service, that you will instruct the quartermaster of transportation to send back such boats as you can best spare as soon as can be safely done." Grant himself agreed, writing that he was going after Vicksburg but noting that he could not "say now how soon that may be, but I am making all the dispatch possible. The great drawback to contend against is to obtain sufficient transportation. Genl. Rosecranz is retaining about all on the Ohio river to supply his army, and a great share of that on the Mississippi is with the troops on the lower river." Grant even wrote, "I have been twice telegraphed by Gen. Halleck to send back boats." Eventually, Washington saw the great need in the Mississippi Valley and dispatched to Grant some of the vessels working to feed William S. Rosecrans's army in middle Tennessee, although Halleck stipulated that "boats will not be taken by force, unless it be found impossible to procure them by other means." Even then, Parsons mistakenly sent stern wheelers when Grant preferred side wheelers that could operate more easily in the narrow bayous.[36]

On top of supplying his own army, Grant also found himself forced to provide supplies for the naval assets that had penetrated the river between Vicksburg and Port Hudson. David G. Farragut especially needed coal, and Grant had no other choice but to send it to him by cutting loose unmanned coal-filled barges to float south; he also called for tugs to position the barges correctly. The barges had to run the gauntlet of Confederate batteries at Vicksburg but provided Farragut with the much-needed fuel. In return, Grant asked that the navy interdict trade along the Red River, which emptied into the Mississippi between Vicksburg and Port Hudson. If all this were not difficult enough, Grant was tasked with getting cotton north for the government to sell.[37]

As a large portion of Grant's department was occupied, he also had to oversee the civil affairs in the region, although he candidly advised a staff officer, "Now that I am out of the Dist. Of West Ten. I want to relieve myself as far as possible from the responsibility of administration of affairs there." He let Hurlbut govern trade in Memphis but worried that the general would resign because of a holdup in his promotion to major general. Grant assured Hurlbut that in governing Memphis he would "sustain you in forcing outside of our lines every disloyal person of whatever age or sex. I will also approve of closing all business with persons living outside of the city. In other words, if you deem it proper to prohibit intercourse between the country and city, do so." He also warned of "a disease that might be called *Cotton on the brain.*" Other government officials did not always agree with Grant's efforts. Although Grant had restricted trade below Memphis, the Treasury Department opened trade to Helena in mid-March and he could not argue with Washington; nevertheless, he still wanted to prohibit trade below Helena. Grant wrote Treasury Secretary Salmon P. Chase himself, describing "the difficulties a commander of troops in the field has to contend against while trade is allowed to follow the flag." He also gave power to his subordinates to "expel all citizens, both from the North and the South, who are troublesome or exercise an unhealthful influence upon the troops. I regard a mercenary, pretended Union trader within the lines of an army as more dangerous than the shrewdest spy."[38]

To compound matters for Grant, the number of contrabands continued to increase. Grant put many to work on the canal, but he found that it did not stem the tide: "In regard to the contrabands, the question is a troublesome one. I am not permitted to send them out of the department, and such numbers as we have it is hard to keep them in." Grant ordered, "The enticing of Negroes to leave their homes to come within the lines of the army is positively forbidden. . . . Those at present within the lines will not be turned out, but in future in the field no persons, white or black, who are not duly authorized to pass the lines of sentinels will be permitted to enter or leave camp." Much like when Grant expelled the Jews back in December, his order brought a swift rebuke: "It has been reported to the Secretary of War that many of the officers of your command not only discourage the Negroes from coming under our protection," Halleck wrote, "but by ill-treatment force them to return to their masters. This is not only bad policy in itself, but is directly opposed to the policy adopted by the government."[39]

Some of Grant's vast and wide-ranging correspondence and work during this period took on more unique forms. A major disagreement was developing amid higher level officers over Lew Wallace's famous march to Shiloh over a year earlier. Wallace was demanding answers to exonerate his actions and so Grant had his staff officers at the time, including McPherson who was now a corps commander, write their reports about the march. The results were remarkably in tune with each other, perhaps indicating that they got together to get their story straight, with the obvious scapegoat being Wallace. Conversely, Grant even corresponded with Confederates. General Carter L. Stevenson began the correspondence with Grant about Admiral Porter's order that "persons taken in the act of firing on unarmed vessels from the banks will be treated as highwaymen and assassins, and no quarter will be shown them." Grant later corresponded with Pemberton as well, but used the affair for his own good, writing Porter that he wanted the use of a tug so that he could "send my letter this afternoon the day being a very clear one to observe all that can be seen." Grant was using every possible advantage he could, including the pretense of correspondence for reconnaissance, in reducing Vicksburg.[40]

Grant's personal concerns also weighed on him at this time. When he left Memphis back in January, he had left Julia and son Jesse there. Julia, of course, had always been a calming force for him, and without her, Grant's staff officer

John Rawlins took over the guardianship role as Grant's confidant. Now, Grant saw no chance of seeing her and the children again any time soon, "until the reduction of Vicksburg is attempted." He told her to make a visit to the other children and "as soon as I am stationary I will write to you to join me again." That was not to be; he later wrote, "My whole time, if not occupied, at least my whole presence with my duties are required." He later added, "It is not atal probable that I will be up the river again until the decisive action takes place, and whilst here you cannot come down." Grant did take time to see to family business, however, including sending money home, buying property in Chicago, and writing Julia that "I will sign the deed you send me and forward with this if it can be done without going before a Notary. If this is required I will go before a Judge Advocate and sign and forward as soon as possible." Concerning the children, he advised Julia to go to his mother's or "take them to some town in Ohio Indiana or Illinois where they have good schools and take boarding for yourself and them"; he ultimately recommended Ottawa, Illinois, as a good place: "That is where Mrs. [W. H. L.] Wallace lives, and Col. Dickey who will resign and go home soon." He also told Julia, "Tell Jess he must be a good boy and learn his lessons. If he learns all his letters before I see him again I will give him something pretty."[41]

Perhaps because of oldest son Fred's health issues, Grant also hit upon a novel idea: "You will see from my letter that I want Fred to come and stay with me." Although in school in Kentucky at the time, Fred arrived with returning staff officers on March 29 following an eye-opening trip. At one point after being told to hide when the vessel on which he traveled passed near Greenville, from which boats normally took fire, young Grant ensconced himself "into the center of a coil of rope, deeming it a sure refuge." When all was safe, an officer told the boy, "See here, sonny, if them rebs had fired at us and hit our boilers, you would have gone straight up through the hurricane deck, and there would not have been a piece of you left to send home to your mamma." When Fred arrived, Grant was pleased at the boy's appearance: "Fred is looking well and seems as happy as can be at the idea of being here." Grant promised that the boy would write his mother twice a week and that he would "require Fred to read and study his arithmetic," though he added, "I will not be able to hear his lessons much however." For his part, Fred was more interested in the promised "beautiful Indian pony which Colonel [Theodore] Bowers, of father's staff, had provided for me." Fred soon settled into life on Grant's headquarters boat *Magnolia*. Perhaps to avoid intersibling rivalry, Grant also told Julia to "get Jess a suit of soldier clothes for his pa with stripes on his pants and eagle shoulder straps on his jacket. I think Jess would make a good Colonel." Evidently either Jess or Julia thought a colonel's rank far too low and had a major general's uniform made, just like his father's.[42]

At times Grant's personal and professional concerns melded together. One such case occurred soon after Fred arrived and Grant took him on a steamboat up the Yazoo. The general transferred to an ironclad for the dangerous portion of the journey, leaving a disappointed Fred behind, although the boy and a captain managed to sneak ashore while Grant was up the river. Fred remembered that "we drew marked attentions from the enemy and had to retreat to the steamer." More ominously, Fred also described some sort of "machine gun" contraption onboard one vessel, "a new invention, which it was determined to test when General Grant returned to the boat." Fred continued that "one of the cartridges exploded, and a fragment of the shell struck my father on the thumb, making a painful wound which caused him much suffering for some weeks, and greatly distressed me."[43]

Grant's personal and professional affairs also melded when politics came into question, such as when Halleck informed Grant, "There is a vacant major-generalcy in the Regular Army, and I am authorized to say that it will be given to the general in the field who first wins an important and decisive victory." The message had also gone to Joseph Hooker in Virginia and Rosecrans in Tennessee. Grant no doubt wished for the position as validation of his efforts but also because of financial security, about which he had always been bothered, although obviously the utmost reason he desired it was that only victory would win him the commission. Grant also cultivated his political connections, especially to his guardian congressman Elihu Washburne. He wrote the Galena representative in mid-March, "Now that Congress has adjourned I have thought possible you might want to make a visit to this part of the country. I need not assure you that I would be most glad to see you here and have you stay during the contest which will take place in the next thirty days from this writing." Grant was also careful to relate that some of the success (at that time) for the Yazoo Pass operation was due to Cadwallader Washburn, the congressman's brother. The general also defended the perceived lack of health in the army to the congressman, which had been making headlines, and gave a very positive assessment, writing, "We are going through a campaign here such as has not been heard of on this continant before." Washburne would soon visit, but unknown to Grant he came to shore up his own doubts that had emerged about his pet general, primarily from the mouth of his free-talking brother.[44]

Perhaps the most problematic personal event for Grant occurred in February. "I met with a great loss this morning," he wrote Julia. "Last night, contrary to my usual habit, I took out my teeth and put them in the wash bason and covered them with water. This morning the servant who attends to my stateroom, blacks my boots &c, come in about daylight and finding water in the bason threw it out into the river teeth and all." Grant immediately wrote the dentists who had made his teeth in Cincinnati to bring "material to take an impression and make me a new sett." He also asked Julia to find out if there was a dentist in Memphis who could do it and if so "hunt him up and tell him of my misfortune."[45]

VI

While the army's increasing size was a good thing, the growth also brought other problems, especially among growing command relationships. In addition to mundane and normal paperwork, such as reports, leaves, and returns (at one point Grant even personally ordered a new leather "letters received" book for headquarters), Grant continually begged for choice staff officers and their promotion. He endured a major shakeup with the loss of his medical director, surgeon J. G. F. Holston, to ill health. Grant soon found that he lacked staff officers; he informed Julia that "all were away at one point and another on duty and still others have been required, that is of a class that can do something." Grant also worked on getting competent officers for his army and keeping them there. When complaints about division commander Frederick Steele surfaced, he quickly defended him to Congressman Washburne, stating that "Gen. Steele is one of our very best soldiers as well as one of the most able" and that "a truer man is not in the Army. He will support the Government and maintain the laws, in good faith without questioning their policy." Grant was not afraid to be harsh to others who were not as able, even ordering the arrest of General Willis A. Gorman for diverting a gunboat bound for the Yazoo Pass operation so that it could escort a vessel carrying his son's cotton. In one amazing letter to Lincoln himself, Grant gave his opinion of officers who should be promoted, including John Logan, Marcellus Crocker, Mortimer Leggett, Thomas Ransom, John Stevenson, and Benjamin Grierson, and strongly suggested that there were other officers on the promotion list who should not be. He mentioned "some who have been named for promotion who really can render their country no service," including N. Brayman, Silas D. Baldwin, and Isaac Pugh. He held his harshest words for Napoleon B. Buford, telling Lincoln that he "would scarcely make a respectable Hospital nurse if put in petticoats, and certain is unfit for any other Military position. He has always been a dead weight to carry more burthensome with his increased rank."[46]

Grant had to endure and deal with backbiting and sniping among his command as well. "I am led to believe, and think there is no doubt of the fact, that Maj. Gen. C. S. Hamilton is making indirect efforts to get General McPherson removed from the command of his army corps, and to get the command himself," Grant informed Halleck. He added that "there is no comparison between the two as to their fitness for such a command." Grant admitted he found no military fault with Hamilton except "his natural jealous disposition, which influences his military conduct and acts prejudicially upon the service." Little did Grant know that Hamilton was even then writing derogatory letters to Washington politicians, one stating that "Grant is a drunkard." Hamilton believed that he outranked McPherson and was entitled to the command. Hurlbut, Hamilton's superior, would not back him and noted that Hamilton "seems disposed to provoke my good nature, to which there are limits." Hamilton even wrote Grant asking for a larger command with Hamilton reporting directly to Grant, not to Hurlbut. For his part, Hurlbut noted that "I can get along with almost anybody who has not confidential correspondents in high places," which was an odd statement since Hurlbut himself was carrying on a lengthy correspondence with Lincoln. The president at one point asked Hurlbut, "What news have you? What from Vicksburg? What from Yazoo Pass? What from Lake Providence? What generally?" Seeing that Hamilton and Hurlbut could not get along, Grant ordered Hamilton relieved and told him to report to the Vicksburg vicinity, where there were of course no corps commands available. Grant gave him the choice of a division, a smaller district, or to be relieved. Hamilton resigned.[47]

The Hamilton saga, however, paled in comparison to the continual criticism from a dishonored McClernand, who responded slowly to orders, if at all. Amazingly, McClernand wrote Grant on January 30,

> I understand that orders are being issued directly from your headquarters directly to army corps commanders, and not through me. As I am invested, by order of the Secretary of War, indorsed by the President, and by order of the President communicated to you by the General-in-Chief, with command of all the forces operating on the Mississippi River, I claim that all orders affecting the conditions or operations of those forces should pass through these headquarters; otherwise I must lose a knowledge of current business and dangerous confusion ensue. If different views are entertained by you, then the question should be immediately referred to Washington, and one or the other, or both of us, relieved. One thing is certain, two generals

> cannot command this army, issuing independent and direct orders to subordinate officers, and the public service be promoted.[48]

An amazed Grant responded firmly by issuing orders the same day: "Maj. Gen. U. S. Grant, commanding Department of the Tennessee, hereby assumes the immediate command of the expedition against Vicksburg, and [his] department headquarters will hereafter be with the expedition. . . . Army corps commanders will resume the immediate command of their respective corps, and will report to and receive orders direct from these headquarters." McClernand fired back, "I hasten to inquire whether its purpose is to relieve me from the command of all or any portion of the forces composing the Mississippi River expedition, or, in other words, whether its purposes is to limit my command to the Thirteenth Army Corps." He also offered a formal protest, but Grant informed him, "I regard the President as the Commander-in-Chief of the Army and will obey every order of his, but as yet I have seen no order to prevent my taking immediate command in the field."[49]

McClernand was not hindered. He continued his push for independent operations, desiring to attack other points on the western side of the river. Grant again responded firmly: "After reflection, I see but one objection to it. The objection is that all the forces now here to operate with are assigned to looking to the one great object, that of opening the Mississippi, and to take off the number of men suggested would retard progress." Grant also gave McClernand, who loved to toss around the president's name, a little taste of his own medicine. He reminded McClernand that "I know the President is looking forward with great anxiety to the completion of the canal . . . , so as to admit steamers through it. This work requires all the forces here."[50]

Amazingly, McClernand continued his peevishness. He wrote again on the last day of February, "Still keeping in view the proposed expedition to clear Arkansas and the west bank of the Mississippi River of an organized hostile force, I have continued to avail myself of all means of obtaining useful information in that respect." Later he continued to be unhelpful in an episode in which Grant had called for a detail, writing to Grant: "Of course, the detail will be furnished, but I think it probable that you would not have ordered it with a fuller knowledge of my operations."[51]

Ironically, Hamilton was also a problem for McClernand. Grant gave Hamilton the option of a division command in McClernand's corps, but McClernand childishly and jealously responded that Grant actually had command of all of his divisions except two small ones physically with McClernand. Grant realized he had perhaps overstepped his authority and humbly responded to

McClernand that "I readily perceive your embarrassment however and will relieve you from it either by assigning [Hamilton] direct to some specific duties within your army corps or by placing him elsewhere on duty." Even so, Grant did not let the comment about him commanding most of McClernand's corps himself go by: "I think you are mistaken."[52]

The bureaucratic and logistical obstacles extended over and above McClernand. Grant knew taking Vicksburg would require more troops than he had in his department, and he also knew that getting those from other departments would require going through Washington. "I would respectfully ask if it would not be [good] policy to combine the four departments in the West under one commander," he recommended. It was the very thing Halleck had so desired back in the spring of 1862, but unlike Halleck then (who wanted the larger command himself), the meek Grant added, "As I am the senior department commander in the West, I will state that I have no desire whatever for such combined command, but would prefer the command I now have to any other that can be given." While nothing came of the idea then, Halleck at least gladly agreed to Grant's suggestion that "both banks of the Mississippi should be under one commander, at least during present operations."[53]

VII

The most aggravating issue Grant struggled with between January and March 1863 was simply how to get to Vicksburg. He had tried several approaches, all at the same time, but none seemed to be working. The Steele's Bayou effort had almost ended in disaster. The Yazoo Pass operation was also failing; it was not quite the crisis that Steele's Bayou might have been, but Grant ordered it stopped on March 28.[54]

All the while, Grant was searching for some way to get to the high ground east of Vicksburg. Frederick Law Olmsted, who was then in the area, wrote a friend that Grant and Porter "looked to me like disappointed and anxious men." Exasperated, Grant finally decided that nothing would work except the grand attack he so feared. Accordingly, he began to concentrate his army even as the other efforts were still going on. "I will let them try Greenwood a short time longer," he wrote before canceling the Yazoo Pass operation, but added, "in the meantime I want concentrated as near here as possible all the troops now scattered from Young's Point to Helena."[55]

Grant's frustration can be clearly seen in a note he wrote to Sherman: "I regret the chances look so gloomy for getting through to the Yazoo by that route," he wrote. "I had made so much calculation upon the expedition down Yazoo Pass, and now again by the route proposed by Admiral Porter, that I have made really but little calculation upon reaching Vicksburg by any other than Haynes' Bluff." He added, however, "As soon as the admiral can get his gunboats back for service, I will concentrate all my forces and make a strike." He similarly wrote in late March in reference to Steele's Bayou, "This experiment failing, there is nothing left for me [to do] but to collect all my strength and attack Haynes' Bluff. This will necessarily be attended with much loss, but I think it can be done."[56]

Consequently, Grant began concentrating all his troops for the all-out assault up the bluffs Sherman had found so daunting in December. Most went to Milliken's Bend, including those from the Yazoo Pass operation, which worried Grant: "I do not much like taking troops that have been so long on board steamers, as General Ross' command has, immediately into the field, but it is a necessity." Despite many reports of sickness in the press and his own concerns, Grant's men were actually in good health and spirits: "The health of this command is not what is represented in the public journals. It is as good as any previous calculation could have prognosticated. I believe, too, that there is the best of feeling and greatest confidence of success among them." The only matter hurting morale was "the great delay in paying them"; Grant added that "many of them have families at home who are, no doubt, in a suffering condition for want of the amount due them, and they are bound for their support." Grant wrote the paymaster that "it is a matter of vast importance to the troops here that they receive their pay promptly . . . to the exclusion of all others if necessary." The reason: "A delay may find the troops actively engaged so that it will become impractacble."[57]

Nonmilitary problems also irritated Grant. The weather was still awful, and Grant told an absent staff officer that "the everlasting rains set us back here wonderfully in our work. It is impossible for us to get done more than one days work in three." In another letter he noted that "we are having a greatdeel of rain and mud so deep that it is almost impossible to get along on horseback." Grant was clearly impatient, and such impatience expressed itself in Grant's private correspondence. He wrote on February 14, "Hope in the course of ten days more to be making a move. My confidance in taking Vicksburg is not unshaken unless if our own people at home will give their moral support. At present however they are behaving scandalously. A soldier now geting home to Illinois, Indiana or Ohio there is no way of geting him back. Northern secessionest defend and protect them in their desertion. I want to see the Administration commence a war upon these people. They should suppress the disloyal press and confine during the war the noisy and most influential of the advocates." Nonetheless, Grant kept a generally optimistic attitude, writing, "A few weeks more I hope will settle the business here favorably." He also bragged about his own health: "I am well," he wrote Julia in March, "better than I have been for years. Every body remarks how well I look. I never set down to my meals without an appetite nor go to bed without being able to sleep."[58]

Still, Grant was running out of time, patience, and options. One friend described him plotting in his cabin on the *Magnolia*, mumbling that "the problem is a difficult one, but I shall certainly solve it. Vicksburg can be taken. I shall give my days and nights to it, and shall surely take it." Another visitor described his one-track mind:

> On board the head-quarters boat at Milliken's Bend, a lively gathering of officers and ladies had assembled. Cards and music were the order of the evening. Grant sat in the ladies' cabin, leaning upon a table covered with innumerable maps and routes to Vicksburg, wholly absorbed in contemplation of the great work before him. He paid no attention to what was going on around, neither did any one dare to interrupt him. For hours he sat thus, until the loved and lamented McPherson stepped up to him with a glass of liquor in his hand, and said, "General, this won't do; you are injuring yourself; join with us in a few toasts, and throw this burden off your mind." Looking up and smiling, he replied: "Mac, you know your whisky won't help me to think; give me a dozen of the best cigars you can find, and, if the ladies will excuse me for smoking, I think by the time I have finished them I shall have this job pretty nearly planned." Thus he sat; and when the company retired we left him there, still smoking and thinking.[59]

Messages from Halleck in Washington did not help Grant's mood. Perhaps thinking back to the lack of communication with Halleck back in February 1862, Grant gave explicit orders to send messages "promptly from Memphis if the lines are working, if not send them to Cairo to be telegraphed from there." Now, Halleck's messages arrived with perhaps too much regularity. One such letter of March 20 cautioned him not to divide his forces but to concentrate on "the great object on your line now . . .[:] the opening of the Mississippi River." Halleck also added that "the eyes and hopes of the whole country are now directed to your army. In my opinion, the opening of the Mississippi River will be to us of more advantage than the capture of forty Richmonds."[60]

Halleck's prodding must have added to Grant's impatience. His decision to begin operations against Vicksburg had netted little in the last three months, although he did take heart that "our labors, however, have had the effect of making the enemy divide his forces and spread their big guns over a great deal of territory." That was small consolation, especially since the public was beginning to wonder what was happening, and he certainly could not move the army back up the river to better camping ground; that would have been seen as a major defeat. At the same time, the army could not remain on transports and narrow levees much longer, especially with Halleck calling for the steamboats' return: "We cannot otherwise supply our armies in Tennessee and Kentucky." On top of all that, prime campaigning weather was just around the corner. With such prodding from Washington, Charles Dana reported that "Grant said confidentially that he had now tried unsuccessfully every conceivable indirect means of attacking Vicksburg, and that nothing but a direct assault upon the enemy's works remained."[61]

Perhaps most significant of all in stirring Grant to act rashly by assaulting Haynes' Bluff, Lincoln was also growing impatient. Grant corresponded with Lincoln on several matters, including about the president's desire for a commission for a friend's son, but Lincoln was far too savvy to directly advise his general. His advice arrived nevertheless. "I know that you can judge of these matters there much better than I can here," Halleck wrote Grant in early April. "But as the President, who seems to be rather impatient about matters on the Mississippi, has several times asked me these questions, I repeat them to you." Grant responded with uncharacteristic defense when he wrote, "The embarrassments I have had to contend against on account of extreme high water cannot be appreciated by any one not present to witness it." All the same, Grant realized that his time was about up. It was time to move; the Vicksburg Campaign was nearing a critical point.[62]

For all his impatience, Lincoln was not ready to replace his commander. He supposedly retorted to one Grant complainer, "He has given us about all our successes, and if his whiskey does it, I should like to send a barrel of the same brand to every general in the field." To another clamoring for Grant's removal, Lincoln supposedly said, "No, I rather like the man, and I think I will try him a little longer."[63]

It was a wise decision.

CHAPTER FOUR

"I THOUGHT THAT WAR ANYHOW WAS A RISK"

"I am very well but much perplexed," Ulysses S. Grant wrote to Julia on March 27, 1863, and he was indeed in a quandary. "Heretofore I have had nothing to do but fight the enemy. This time I have to overcome obstacles to reach him." Grant knew that he had failed in six different attempts to reach the high, dry ground east of Vicksburg, "the ground I so much desire," as he described it. "Foot once upon dry land on the other side of the river I think the balance would be of but short duration," he added. But time was not on his side. Halleck reiterated Washington's impatience on April 9: "You are too well advised of the anxiety of the Government for your success, and its disappointment at the delay, to render it necessary to urge upon you the importance of early action." If Grant was going to undertake a major land campaign, he had to do it during the prime campaigning weather of the spring. As a result, he turned to the only feasible option he had left: an assault up the steep bluffs north and east of Vicksburg to force his way onto the high ground. He knew it would be terribly bloody, but he had no other choice.[1]

Accordingly, Grant concentrated his army around Milliken's Bend and began to explore the best area to launch an attack at Haynes' Bluff. He personally inspected the sites in early April but did not like what he saw. The bluffs were steep, the deployment area narrow, and the Confederates were heavily entrenched at the top. "With present high water," he wrote, "the extent of ground upon which troops could land at Haynes' Bluff is so limited that the place is impregnable." The factors were stacked so much against him that Grant decided the assault was just not possible. "After the reconnaissance of yesterday," he wrote Porter, "I am satisfied that an attack upon Haynes' Bluff would be attended with immense sacrifice of life, if not with defeat." He added, "This, then, closes out the last hope of turning the enemy by the right." To his father, Grant described only "two points of land, Hains Bluff & Vicksburg itself, out of water any place from which troops could march. These are thoroughly fortified and it would be folly to attack them as long as there is a prospect of turning their position. I never expect to have an army under my command whipped unless it is very badly whipped and cant help it but I have no idea of being driven to do a desperate or foolish act by the howlings of the press." Then he added, "There is no one less disturbed by them than myself." There had to be another way.[2]

I

The pressure was beginning to get to Grant even before he was faced with the fiery rhetoric of his superiors. "It would be a great holiday for me to have one month to myself," he admitted to Julia in late March. He had to press on nonetheless. In fact, there might possibly be another way, although it had its share of problems. If Vicksburg's defenses could not be reached from the north, east, or west, and returning north to restart an overland campaign from Memphis would be seen as a major political reversal, Vicksburg could only potentially be gained from the south. Unfortunately, that possibility meant that Grant had to move the army south of Vicksburg on the Louisiana side, ferry it across the river, and then perhaps fight the rest of the way to Vicksburg with no solid supply line along the river. It was a gamble to be sure, but Grant had no other choice. In perhaps the most significant decision of the Vicksburg Campaign, and in what Bruce Catton has described as "one of the two or three important decisions of the Civil War," Grant decided to move his army south, cross the river, and approach Vicksburg from the south and east. If it worked, he would be a hero. If it did not, his career, and perhaps his life, might end. Grant later noted as much: "I thought that war anyhow was a risk; that it made little difference to the country what was done with me. I might be killed or die from fever."[3]

Because all the sounder plans had been tried and did not produce success, Catton argued that "it was time, therefore, to go beyond military logic." Although the path toward Grant's eventual arrival at this decision is not clear, the first solid mention of this possibility was on April 2. Grant by then had evidently come to the realization, over the course of several months, that it could be done. Actually, he later claimed that he had kept the idea in the back of his mind "the whole winter," adding that because it "could not be undertaken until the waters receded[,] . . . I did not therefore communicate this plan, even to an officer of my staff, until it was necessary to make preparations for the start." Over that winter, if he was thinking in those terms, several ongoing operations illustrated to him that certain parts of the plan could be achieved, and if all were put together the effort might actually succeed. For instance, Grant would need numerous vessels south of Vicksburg not only to silence the Confederate defenses at either Warrenton or Grand

Gulf, where he intended to land, but also to ferry his army across the river. One boat could ferry a few men at a time, but Grant did not want to chance putting men across piecemeal and allowing the Confederates to parry such weak thrusts. When he crossed the river, he wanted to do so in force, and that necessitated large numbers of boats to get the job done quickly. Grant first realized that he could send vessels past the Vicksburg river batteries when he shipped coal to Farragut. With that in mind, on March 25 Grant ordered his chief quartermaster, Charles A. Reynolds, to have transportation for fifty thousand men obtained as quickly as possible.[4]

Grant had already stationed troops to the area south of Vicksburg on the west side of the river, at the other end of the Confederate defenses, to watch for barges or restart them "should the barge run into the eddy." Grant had also put together an infantry expedition to destroy the batteries at Warrenton. He sent two regiments with Porter's aid, but bad weather and a lack of boats curtailed the effort. Grant wrote, "This is a bad day for troops to be out, but may be the more propitious for the plan." Despite setbacks like these, small numbers of vessels and troops were able to move to the river south of Vicksburg, making Grant think he could accomplish this in larger fashion. It was certainly a step in that direction, but Grant took a religious tone in explaining the less than stellar results heretofore: "It may all be providential however and I shall expect a change of apparent luck soon."[5]

Grant had also been working on, as directed by Halleck, sending major numbers of troops, perhaps even a corps, south of Vicksburg to operate with Nathaniel P. Banks around Port Hudson. The idea was that once Grand Gulf had been taken and a post established east of the river, McClernand's corps would head south to aid in reducing Port Hudson. They could then "come on up the river and maintain a position on high land near enough Vicksburg until they could be re-enforced from here sufficiently to operate against the city." Significantly, as Grant mulled over sending troops to Banks, the idea dawned on him that he could do the very same thing with his entire army, perhaps leaving one corps at Grand Gulf and taking the rest himself. Word from Halleck that arrived on April 10 further convinced him of the need to support Banks.[6]

If this scheme was to work, Grant would need the navy's complete aid, and he fully realized that this was a different situation than what he had enjoyed earlier in the war when the navy had been under army orders at Forts Henry and Donelson and Shiloh. Now, the navy was independent; Grant wrote one of his generals that "we cannot order them but only ask their co-operation." Indeed, all Grant could do was ask Porter to run the batteries and get below Vicksburg, and he broached the subject as early as March 29: "Will you be good enough, admiral, to give this your early consideration, and let me know your determination." Thereafter, he went onboard Porter's flagship *Benton* to discuss it in person, with Fred in tow. Just as Grant and Porter were beginning to get to serious work, Porter "called a man to show me all over the ship—everywhere but in the cabin," Fred later remembered. "Not then appreciating the reasons for this special courtesy," Fred related, "I enjoyed my explorations very much." Grant in the meantime talked with Porter about the plan, including how to communicate via rockets and whistles. Porter was agreeable to everything but was completely honest with the general when he described the ramifications over and above the potential loss of some or all of the gunboats: "I am ready to co-operate with you in the matter of landing troops on the other side, but you must recollect that, when these gunboats once go below, we give up all hopes of ever getting them up again." He continued, "If it is your intention to occupy Grand Gulf in force, it will be necessary to have vessels there to protect the troops or quiet the fortifications now there. If I do send vessels below, it will be the best vessels I have, and there will be nothing left to attack Haynes' Bluff, in case it should be deemed necessary to try it." With that said, Porter asked for time to accumulate coal and supplies. Grant also wanted the vessels back from the Yazoo Pass operation if possible and even asked for smaller yawls and skiffs, from as far away as Chicago, to be sent south.[7]

With Porter's agreement, Grant began planning in earnest. With the Lake Providence route being far too difficult to traverse with the river level falling, Grant opened a newly dried-out route on the western side of the Mississippi River to get the army south of Vicksburg. There was a wagon road from Milliken's Bend to New Carthage and on to the river, although high water in the adjacent bayous created the need for some water travel along the route until the level fell even lower in mid-April; at some points the wagon road was a mere twenty inches above the water. Even then, the roads, as Grant described them, "though level, were intolerably bad, and the movement was therefore necessarily slow." Adding to the frustration, breaches in the levee around New Carthage left that area "an island" for a time. Grant decided to change the route slightly, the end point now being at Perkins's Plantation, twelve more miles south, making a total distance of thirty-five miles from Milliken's Bend. Either way, Grant quickly occupied the route with troops. A new canal was also cut from the river to Willow Bayou, which promised to allow at least some communication for barges and small tugs, which Grant requested posthaste. With this route, Grant opined, he could "be able to move 20,000 men at one time." With these routes in order, Grant wrote of "having then fully determined upon operating from New Carthage either by the way of Grand Gulf or Warrenton." He was going to Mississippi or be defeated doing so; to McClernand he wrote, "It is no part of my present intentions to bring back the troops you have sent to Carthage ever by the route they went over."[8]

Grant had made his decision, but not everyone at his headquarters agreed. A free-for-all discussion took place in early April during which Grant, Sherman, McPherson, and a host of others openly discussed everything, including, as Sherman wrote, "that General McClernand was still intriguing against General Grant, in hopes to regain the command of the whole expedition, and that others were raising a clamor against General Grant in the newspapers at the North." Sherman noted that "even Mr. Lincoln and General Halleck seemed to be shaken." Later, Sherman privately argued with Grant against the move south of Vicksburg, stating, as Grant remembered, that he "was putting myself in a position voluntarily which an enemy would be glad to maneuver a year—or a long time—to get me in." Grant was not convinced, so Sherman wrote a letter to him on April 8 with his ideas of what should be done, writing that "the line of the Yalabusha [should] be the base from which to operate against the points where the Mississippi Central crosses the Big Black, above Canton, and, lastly, where the Vicksburg and Jackson Railroad crosses the same river. The capture of Vicksburg would result." He reminded Grant that the Tallahatchie and Yalobusha rivers had been high in the winter, but now in the spring "these streams will be no serious obstacle." Perhaps looking to Grant's political well-being, Sherman also called on Grant to query his other corps commanders as well, evidently thinking McClernand would agree with him. Sherman's friend Grant chose to ignore the advice and push on, hiding the letter from posterity. Grant's determined gamble was decided, and Sherman had no choice but to follow. Yet his loyalty was evident in a message he wrote to one of his division commanders: "I confess I don't like this roundabout project, but we must support Grant in whatever he undertakes."[9]

Sherman gave Grant his total obedience. He wrote later, however, that "I have never criticized General Grant's strategy on this or any other occasion, but I thought then that he had lost an opportunity, which cost him and us six month's extra-hard work, for we might have captured Vicksburg from the direction of Oxford in January, quite as easily as was afterward done." Sherman incisively noted that "the distance from Oxford to the rear of Vicksburg is little greater than by the circuitous route we afterward followed . . . during which we had neither depot nor train of supplies."[10]

There was also the chance of Confederate spies discovering Grant's preparations and countering them. Grant frequently saw Confederates spying on his army and transports. In one episode, he took a small boat with "a small white flag, not much larger than a handkerchief, set up in the stern, no doubt intended as a flag of truce in case of discovery." All the spies were brought to Grant, who found that one of them was none other than Jacob Thompson, who had been a cabinet secretary under James Buchanan. "After a pleasant conversation of half an hour or more I allowed the boat and crew, passengers and all, to return to Vicksburg, without creating a suspicion that there was a doubt in my mind as to the good faith of Mr. Thompson and his flag."[11]

All the while, Grant seemed to be renewed with vigor as a result of the forward movement. Charles Dana reported to Washington: "As for General Grant, his purpose is set in that direction." Another observer noted that all winter Grant had done everything methodically, rarely getting in a hurry or even riding faster than a slow trot; now, his "energies seemed to burst forth with new life" and he rode full speed everywhere he went. "He seemed wrought up to the last pitch of determination and energy." That there was a plan of action inspired much of the army as well, Sherman notwithstanding. "General Grant has ordered down the regimental and headquarters transportation," Hurlbut wrote from Memphis on April 9, "which looks as if he expected to be on hard land again." Hurlbut added that "the expedition against Vicksburg is not a failure, though it is well to let the enemy think so. In fact, it is my opinion that the right mode of attack has been at last attempted."[12]

II

As Grant neared his do-or-die crossing of the Mississippi River, he began to send a flurry of messages, some official and some personal, to shore up all aspects of his command and life before he went into communication blackout. "Ten days will probably take me away from here," he wrote Julia, "and I hope then soon to have the river open." Knowing he would be out of touch once he crossed the river and began actively campaigning, Grant certainly wanted his house in order in case it took longer than expected. "It is hard to tell when the final strike will be made at Vicksburg," he wrote, but added, "I am doing all I can and expect to be successful." Nevertheless, the correspondence piled up. In speaking of Colonel T. Lyle Dickey, Grant wrote, "I ought to write to him but I have so much of this to do, officially that I never write anything not absolutely necessary." On another occasion he admitted, "I have been intending to write to Emma for some time but somehow I am either too lazy or have too much to do."[13]

Grant's health also took a turn that made his workload more burdensome. Although he had been blessed with good health for months, Grant suffered a slight setback in early April when he informed Julia, "I am sorely afflicted at this time scarcely being able to sit, lay, or stand. Biles [boils] are the matter." Perhaps for that reason, Grant wanted Julia and the rest of the children to come down and see him. Grant's former headquarters boat *Tigress* was due to make a circuitous trip from Memphis down to the army during the time, staying two days, and Grant recommended that Julia and the children come down for a quick visit. "It is very pleasant now and the trip down here and back will do you good." Julia and the children soon arrived, despite the fact that Grant had decreed that no civilians could visit the army; he obviously made an exception for Julia. He also had a heart for others as well. In one sad case, a father came as close as Memphis to see his sons but was turned away. Grant wrote the mother, "I would always make an exception in favor of those who have children in the service." He also told her, "I cannot see your sons immediately as you request but I will take the very first opportunity of doing so and do all in my power to cheer them up."[14]

The father in Grant was especially glad to have Fred with him for longer periods. He wrote that Fred "enjoys himself hugely. His pony gets but little rest." In one letter to Julia he began that "Fred and I have just returned from a trip fifteen miles up the river where we had quite a horse back ride. He enjoys himself finely and I doubt not will receive as much perminant advantage by being with me for a few months as if at school." At the same time, Grant did not forget the other children. He wrote Julia that he had sent Buck "a lot of views [photographs] taken at Holly Springs for him to look at through his sterioscope. I hope he has not left it behind." Grant also recommended hiring a "Governess to teach the children, one who speaks German if possible."[15]

Grant was especially concerned about his personal financial situation, perhaps in case he did not survive the invasion. In late April he sent Julia explicit instructions about obtaining deeds for land near St. Louis and also what to propose for additional lands. Grant offered to buy one of Julia's family member's farms so that the relative could go to California, but Grant wanted it made plain that he was doing so simply to allow the trip rather than for selfish reasons: "If it was not that I am poor and have not a dollar except my savings in the last two years I would not hesitate to furnish him all the necessary money without any other guarantee than the conciousnous that I had done him a favor." Once signed over, Julia was to rent out this land to "some good and prompt tenant." To take care of all this business, Grant told her, she would have to go to Galena to obtain the money through credit. He noted that "some of them are seting so much higher merit upon money than any earthly consideration that I feel it a duty to protect myself." Fortunately, Julia and the children arrived only a few days later, so he was personally able to explain everything he wanted done.[16]

The more official communications hinged on many of the same issues Grant had been dealing with for months while in command of the Department of the Tennessee. In actuality, the administrative workload was every bit as daunting and time-consuming as the military operations themselves. Grant also had larger directives to enforce, such as Treasury department rules regarding shipping of goods and trade. With illegal trade becoming a major issue, Grant knew he could not oversee enforcement himself and detailed an officer to stop all boats at Memphis that were incoming from south of Helena, where trade was restricted.[17]

Interactions with civilians could be just as worrisome, as Grant never knew for sure what anyone's true colors were. In one instance, McClernand arrested a family Grant had allowed to travel north. Grant simply wrote McClernand that "if I have been deceived this is right but if not they are entitled to take their property and go on the permit previously given." Perhaps the most unwelcome correspondence was from his money-hungry father, who was interested in trade and getting rich. Grant responded to his "interogitories" and left no doubt that he hated these types of men who had "deceived" him: "I fee[l] all Army followers who are engaged in speculating off the misfortunes of their country, and really aiding the enemy more than they possibly could do by open treason, should be drafted at once and put in the first forlorn hope."[18]

Among the myriad of Grant's official matters vying for his attention, he had to rule on the status of paroled prisoners, decide whether to allow reporter Thomas W. Knox of the *New York Herald* to accompany the army, and choose which medical associations would provide for the sick and wounded in the campaign. He also reviewed a portion of McClernand's corps, Eugene A. Carr's and Andrew Jackson Smith's divisions, on April 8, although he informed McClernand, "I do not wish the troops to pass in review but merely to be drawn up in line so that I can ride by them and see the men." He also relieved officers and dealt with the fallout when congressmen became involved, as in the case of 2nd Illinois Cavalry commander Silas Noble. And, although he knew that his army's success would in large part depend on getting enough supplies, Grant still decided to replace his chief quartermaster. Amid other staff changes, Grant requested that quartermaster Lieutenant Colonel Charles A. Reynolds be transferred to a corps position "and some one better qualified for the very heavy business of the Department be given me. Col Reynolds is a very faithful officer, and I think can conduct the business of an Army Corps to the interests of the Public Service, but he is not quite up to his present duties[.]"[19]

Changes in higher-level general officers were especially onerous. In early April, David Stuart, who commanded one of Sherman's divisions, left the army because the senate did not approve his promotion to major general. Stuart had been a favorite of Grant and Sherman since well before Shiloh, and losing him was hard enough, but his replacement was concerning: Frank Blair, brother of Washington politico Montgomery Blair, a member of Lincoln's cabinet. Grant and Sherman could see that Blair could potentially be as difficult as McClernand. Sherman wrote that "Frank Blair is a 'disturbing element.' I wish he was in Congress or a Bar Room, anywhere but our Army." Grant was more diplomatic, but he let his disapproval of Stuart's handling be made known. For his part, and much to the relief of the officers, Blair soon became one of Sherman's and Grant's favorites, with Grant even admitting years later that "I dreaded his coming; I knew from experience that it was more difficult to command two generals desiring to be leaders than it was to command one army officered intelligently and with subordination. It affords me the greatest pleasure to record now my agreeable disappointment in respect to his character. There was no man braver than he, nor was there any who obeyed all orders of his superior in rank with more unquestioning alacrity. He was one man as a soldier, another as a politician."[20]

Grant was especially worried about the less active areas of his department, but he had Hurlbut there and gave him explicit instructions to "suppress the entire press of Memphis for giving aid and comfort to the enemy by publishing in their columns every move made here by troops and every work commenced." He was especially outraged that one particular editor had published the plan to move via New Carthage to Grand Gulf. Grant laid much of the blame on leaks from his own officers, especially "that incoragibly gassy man Col. [Josiah] Bissell of the Eng Regt. I sent him to you thinking he could not do so much harm there as here. His tonge will have to be tied if there is anything going on where he is which you don't want made public." He added, "I feel a strong inclination to arrest him and trust to find evidence against him afterwards."[21]

At the same time Grant was busily preparing for the campaign, he had to keep a steady eye on the main goal and not be sidetracked by the whims of other officers. For instance, when Major General Cadwallader Washburn, an officer with some clout, advised a foray into Arkansas, Grant told him that "the move would be a most excellent one if it could be made without interfering with operations here. My instructions nor the expectations of the public would admit of a diversion from the main object now. I think everything promises favorably here at this time." Still, he could not keep his eye from wandering to the preparations of the medical staff, ordering hospitals set up along the southward route of march. He wanted plenty of medical assets ready to cross with the army into Mississippi.[22]

All the while, Grant probed for the best routes possible for the invasion. "I am having a complete map of the East bank of the Mississippi made for you," Grant informed McClernand on April 13, "showing all the Streams and roads from Port Hudson to Vicksburg. I sent you a guide yesterday." On April 24, he similarly notified McClernand,

> I would like to have Gen. [Peter J.] Ousterhaus make a reconnoisance, in person, to a point on the Mississippi opposite the mouth of Bayou Pierre, and a short distance below, to where there is a road leading from the river to Grand Gulf. The map shows such a road. It is desirable to learn if there is a landing at that point, and if it can be done by inquiry to learn also the condition of the road on the opposite side. If a landing cannot be made in front of Grand Gulf it may be necessary to reach there by this route. The maps show this road, and also a road from the same point below Grand Gulf.

Grant even sent out staff officer James Harrison Wilson on a similar errand, "for the purpose of ascertaining if it is possible to reach the high lands of Mississippi from any point above Black River."[23]

No one could say that Grant was not prepared.

III

A confident Grant quickly put into motion the final plan for his move around the Confederate left. He assured Halleck that he would keep his army concentrated and "see to it that I am not cut off from my supplies, or beaten in any other way than in fair fight." He added that "the discipline and health of the army is now good, and I am satisfied the greatest confidence of success prevails."[24]

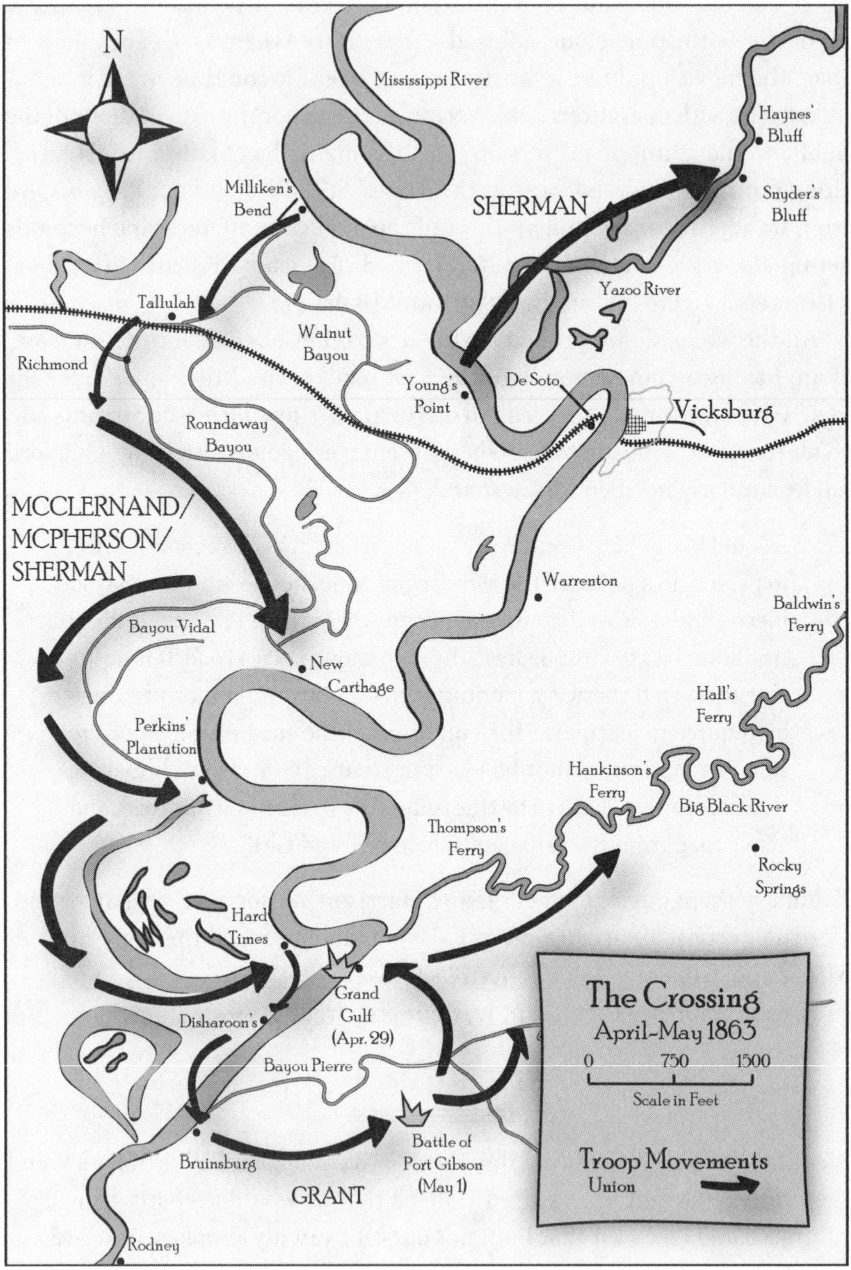
N
Mississippi River
Haynes' Bluff
Snyder's Bluff
Milliken's Bend
SHERMAN
Yazoo River
Tallulah
Walnut Bayou
Richmond
Young's Point
De Soto
Vicksburg
Roundaway Bayou
MCCLERNAND/ MCPHERSON/ SHERMAN
Warrenton
Baldwin's Ferry
Bayou Vidal
New Carthage
Hall's Ferry
Perkins' Plantation
Hankinson's Ferry
Big Black River
Thompson's Ferry
Rocky Springs
Hard Times
Grand Gulf (Apr. 29)
Disharoon's
Bayou Pierre
The Crossing
April–May 1863
0 750 1500
Scale in Feet
Troop Movements
Union
Bruinsburg
Battle of Port Gibson (May 1)
GRANT
Rodney

The plan was to move south and land at either Grand Gulf or Warrenton, with the former gaining precedence as the event drew closer. Yet there were positives and negatives to both. Warrenton was much closer to Vicksburg, but it was more heavily defended. Grand Gulf was almost a detached garrison. Warrenton was situated north of the Big Black River; if the army landed there, they would not have to fight their way across that barrier. On the other hand, the river might act as a shield if landing at Grand Gulf, allowing Grant's army to cross the Mississippi River more easily and gain a foothold on the east bank. For better or worse, Grant concentrated his focus on Grand Gulf, planning to land a large portion of his army there in one major movement. He hoped he could get the rest of the army up before the enemy realized what was happening.[25]

If this plan was to work, Grant needed significant cooperation and help. He needed the navy below Vicksburg to silence Grand Gulf's defenses and ferry the army across the river. He needed feints elsewhere to take the enemy's eyes off his true intentions. He also needed his corps commanders to work in tandem to make the landing as smooth as possible. Uniting all these components together into a rigidly timed operation would not be easy, but then Grant had never backed away from anything just because it was difficult.

One obvious issue was McClernand. Because his corps occupied the southernmost area of the army's encampment, his was the logical unit to lead the march south. Despite the geographical reasoning, numerous officers did not want their fortunes in the hands of the politician. Sherman argued long and hard for a change in the plan; Porter did likewise. Charles Dana reported to Washington, "I have remonstrated, so far as I could properly do so, against intrusting so momentous an operation to McClernand, and I know that Admiral Porter and prominent members of his staff have done the same, but General Grant will not be changed." That brought a quick reply from Stanton: "Allow me to suggest that you carefully avoid giving any advice in respect to commands that may be assigned, as it may lead to misunderstanding and troublesome complications." Grant argued that McClernand should lead based on geography, and Dana surmised that Grant was also thinking in political terms, remembering that Lincoln had wanted McClernand to play a major role in the effort. Moreover, McClernand was the senior corps commander and all for the plan while Sherman was very much against it. The only other corps commander, McPherson—whom Dana reported Grant "would really much prefer" to lead the effort—was farther to the north with his own corps. In the end, "Grant would not be changed," Dana wrote.[26]

With his mind made up about McClernand, Grant worked with other officers to accomplish the goal. He and Admiral Porter carefully planned the effort to send much of the flotilla south of Vicksburg. It was one thing to send ironclad gunboats, but Grant also needed transports and supplies. Porter worked with the quartermasters and supply officers to gather the material, but not enough transports were available for Grant's need below the city: "There has been great delay and neglect in the quartermaster's department in getting ready the barges," an aggravated Grant wrote on April 15, "and the reports of progress I have received I find on a personal inspection have not been realized." Grant was especially concerned for what transports he had, writing Porter that a Vicksburg newspaper advertisement had called for local planters to sell all small vessels to the Confederate army: "May this not be intended to make a raid upon our transports and burn at least a part of them?" Lastly, Porter also had to watch the moon's phases, as he needed to go on as dark a night as possible.[27]

That night came on April 16. As Porter ran the Vicksburg batteries with his gunboats, the entire Grant family watched from the tug *Henry von Phul* in the river north of Vicksburg. Grant described the Confederate response as "magnificent, but terrible." Fred later remembered the "river was lighted as if by sunlight" by Confederate fires on the bank, but recalled even more that his father stood by him on the hurricane deck watching and "quietly smoking, but an intense light shone in his eyes." James Harrison Wilson of Grant's staff remembered that Julia had numerous recommendations on what strategy Grant should take (which amused the general to no end). Meanwhile, one of the smaller Grant children sat in Wilson's lap, clutching tighter with each salvo. Although not nearly enough transports and barges were available then, Porter went anyway with what vessels he had, all of them lashed to the right sides of the armored gunboats to provide a shield. That proved successful despite the fires lit across the river and heavy Confederate artillery fire. The only steamer to be sunk was the *Henry Clay*. McClernand reported the next morning that the wreckage "was seen floating past New Carthage, on fire." It was loaded with important hay, cotton, and oats, but the crew swam safely to shore while the pilot was picked up "floating on a plank." Sherman was not worried, adding that "her load was small, and the boat itself a poor old concern." Seven gunboats and two transports made it safely, with only minor casualties.[28]

Grant himself went south to inspect the vessels on April 17 by the new land and water route to New Carthage. He returned the next day to Young's Point. Despite just getting over the severe case of boils that had left him hard pressed to even sit, he rode nearly thirty miles in one day. It was on this trip that Fred remembered his father displaying some of his admired horsemanship. At a slough where troops were crossing the single narrow bridge, Grant spurred his mount to a jump, "putting his horse at the opposite bank, which he just managed to reach." Fred recalled, "The rest of us preferred to wait our turn at crossing by the bridge, over which a wagon train was slowly passing." The delay, Fred remembered, allowed John Rawlins of Grant's staff "an admirable opportunity to display a talent which he exhibited on occasions,—that of ornamental profanity."[29]

With Grant's army moving below Vicksburg and on a tenuous supply line, Porter recommended haste. "My opinion is that they will move heaven and earth to stop us if we don't go ahead." But Grant needed more transports for the entire operation to succeed, and he ordered another group to run the batteries several nights later on April 22. The run was originally set to be made on April 20, but Grant complained that "the boats we expected to run the blockade . . . failed to get ready in time." Grant was so disturbed that he relieved the officers who were supposed to have prepared the boats, one of whom returned with Julia as she traveled back north and loudly predicting "with great confidence the failure of the expedition." The supply boats were ready two nights later, but this time the gunboats were not able to shield them. Under orders to merely float along until they reached the upper Vicksburg batteries, the crews were told "from that point all steam will be put on until the last battery is run." This time, five steamers made the run, with one turning back and one sunk. The stricken vessel was the *Tigress*, Grant's old headquarters boat at Shiloh. Porter thereafter cooperated in almost every request Grant made, although he would not risk his boats if he thought it was too much of a gamble. At one point, Grant asked Porter to send a gunboat up the Big Black River to keep the enemy from building small boats at a ferry, but Porter would not, deeming it "too risky." To make up for a diminished fleet, Grant ordered that field artillery be put on a steamboat to "improvise a gunboat."[30]

Even as Grant moved the navy south of Vicksburg and his headquarters to New Carthage on April 23 and thence to Smith's Plantation, he also formulated a series of feints to take the enemy's attention away from Grand Gulf. In addition to several smaller efforts in north Mississippi and along the Mississippi River, a few large feints took place: Hurlbut had issued an order that "the strongest and best mounted command will proceed with all possible speed, making direct for the Jackson and Meridian road, and break it up." He informed Grant that "this cavalry dash I desire to time so as to co-operate with what I suppose to be your plan, to land below Vicksburg, on south side of Black river." This effort turned into Colonel Benjamin Grierson's celebrated raid. Leaving on April 17, Grierson attracted most of the Confederate attention as he cut through north Mississippi and hit the Southern Railroad of Mississippi at Newton Station. From there, he moved south to Union-occupied Baton Rouge. The raid did relatively little damage, but it held Confederate attention for five critical days at the exact moment Grant was moving south in Louisiana and crossing the river. Grant described the feat as "the most successful thing of the kind since the breaking out of the rebellion."[31]

Grant had another feint in mind as well. In order to put more men ashore in Mississippi, McPherson was to "keep closed up" on McClernand, but Sherman was held back. As late as April 24, Grant told Sherman that if the water continued to fall in the river, "it may possibly happen that the enemy may so weaken his forces about Vicksburg and Haynes' Bluff as to make the latter vulnerable, particularly with a fall of water to give an extended landing." McClernand said the same thing, "That at least a feint should be made upon Warrenton and Haynes' Bluff—a feint to be pushed to a bold attack, if circumstances favor." It is unknown if Grant was already thinking in those terms, but Grant gave Sherman the go-ahead, "if you think it advisable" (showing sensitivity to Sherman's earlier defeat there), to make a reconnaissance at Haynes' Bluff. Sherman agreed despite concerns that an eventual withdrawal would again look bad for him in the Northern press. "The troops will all understand the purpose," Sherman wrote, "and will not be hurt by the repulse. The people of the country must find out the truth as they best can; it is none of their business. You are engaged in a hazardous enterprise, and, for good reasons, wish to divert attention; that is sufficient to me, and it shall be done." Sherman played his hand perfectly, although he saw evidence that an actual attack might work. He resisted the temptation, though, and he wrote a division commander, "It won't do to make a foothold at Haynes' Bluff and Grand Gulf too."[32]

Other smaller raids and marches also took place, one by Frederick Steele's division inland from Greenville, Mississippi, and more by Federal cavalry from Hurlbut's command around Memphis and Corinth, even including Abel Streight's famous "Mule March." In mid-April Grant even had an artillery battery fire into Vicksburg to distract the Confederates. The officer in charge of the battery reported that he "commenced firing upon the court-house and the railroad depot in Vicksburg with two 30-pounder Parrott rifles, placed in casemate battery opposite the town." The battery fired from April 17 to the night of the twentieth. At first, the firing was inaccurate but then it became better, "the shells apparently bursting at the height and distance of the dome of the court-house, and at the very center of the ridge pole of the depot."[33]

With the navy positioned and the feints in place, Grant was ready to make the real move below Vicksburg. Consequently, he needed the complete support of his corps commanders. McClernand led the way, as his corps was the closest to New Carthage. As if emboldened by his first chance at real movement, McClernand became almost cooperative for a time. Grant nevertheless scolded that "in leaving here, you left 1,000 men, sick and straggling, without any provision either of tents or medical attendance. Great difficulty has been experienced in providing for them." Undaunted, McClernand worked hard to move his corps and its many supplies by the water and road route from Milliken's Bend to New Carthage, writing excitedly that "my present movement, if properly sustained, ought, and I believe will, eventuate in the extinguishment of the rebellion in the Gulf States, and limit it to the East." Indeed, it had to be sustained, and Grant needed no lecture from McClernand to realize that. Knowing full well that the army could gain many provisions and foodstuffs from civilians along the way, Grant and McClernand were most concerned about ammunition, which could not be harvested from the Mississippi planters' fields. "I have been more troubled to know how to supply you with ammunition, until water communication is established," Grant wrote McClernand, "than on any other subject. If roads hold good, there will be no difficulty, but, without them, there will be." He added by way of reminder, "It is not safe to send [ammunition] by the river, as we do coal."[34]

The decision to live off the land as much as he could was an outgrowth of what Grant had learned earlier, particularly in the Mississippi Central Campaign when his army had used much of the local infrastructure to its advantage. Now, Grant would do the same in an area that had seen no conflict and was not heavily garrisoned by Confederate troops. The use of local commodities was also part of a slow but sure change related to how to fight the war. The term "total" or "hard" war has normally been reserved for the 1864 campaigns led by Sherman and Philip Sheridan, and perhaps could be applied to Sherman's earlier Meridian Campaign. Interestingly, Grant wrote as early as April 1863 that the "rebellion has assumed that shape now that it can only terminate by the complete subjugation of the South or the overthrow of the Government. It is our duty, therefore, to use every means to weaken the enemy, by destroying their means of subsistence, withdrawing their means of cultivating their fields, and in every other way possible."[35]

An obvious part of this changing philosophy of war was taking the Southerners' chief means of food production: their slaves. Having been advised strongly by Washington, Grant ordered his commanders to encourage all contraband to join them. Indeed, the adjutant general of the army, Lorenzo Thomas, was on site, organizing black regiments and making speeches touting the colored troops. Grant did his part to facilitate the formation of black regiments, placing Brigadier General John P. Hawkins in command of all African American organization and troops in the department. For his part, Thomas reported back to Washington that Grant's "army is in fine condition, unusually healthy, and in good heart."[36]

IV

The actual crossing could not come soon enough for Grant. McClernand continually moved his corps south in mid-April, discovering more and more of what lay on the other shore; the troops also found mills on the western side of the river that could be used to feed the army. McClernand and Grant constantly fine-tuned the plan, even discussing whether to land on the Mississippi River bank itself or move up the Big Black River and land near one of two major roads that led to Vicksburg. Despite the options, however, Grant insisted that he wanted Grand Gulf seized first. Only after Grand Gulf was seized could other moves be made, including potentially providing aid to Banks at Port Hudson; Grant even wrote Banks as much. Perhaps Grant saw this movement as a chance not only to allow McClernand to hold the position in Mississippi until he could get McPherson and Sherman across the river but also then, potentially, to get rid of McClernand by sending him to Banks.[37]

Obviously, the navy was going to have to play a critical role, and Grant frequently conferred with Porter. On one occasion he took a small boat to Porter's flagship but decided to leave late in the night. Porter sent Grant back in his own cutter with navy men, but several staff, led by staff officer James Wilson, returned in the boat on which they had originally arrived. Grant's boat became lost and could not find the way back to headquarters, so they returned to the fleet to stay the night. Wilson later reappeared, having come to look for the general. With his guide, Grant chose to return to headquarters in the wee hours of the morning. It did not occur to anyone just how hazardous all this had been. Wilson later wrote, "I thought but little of the adventure at the time, but it is easy to see now that had the general's cutter been capsized, rowed as it was by a crew of landsmen unused to such navigation, nothing could have saved him from drowning."[38]

Despite the danger everywhere, Grant sent out orders to govern the "present movement to obtain a foothold on the east bank of the Mississippi River, from which Vicksburg can be approached by practicable roads." He fashioned the three corps into wings for the invasion, with McClernand holding the right and Sherman eventually the left, closest to Vicksburg and perhaps the most dangerous position. McPherson, who was the least experienced, was given the center. Grant's orders covered everything, from hospitals and tents to supplies, and "authorized and enjoined [the troops] to collect all the beef-cattle, corn, and other supplies necessary for the army on the line of march, but wanton destruction of property, taking of articles, unless for military purposes, insulting citizens, going into and searching houses without proper orders from division commanders, are positively prohibited."[39]

As the time for the crossing approached, McClernand and Grant continually discussed how best to approach Grand Gulf. The corps commander had been sending out reconnaissances all the way down to the mouth of Bayou Pierre to find the best place to land, and Grant himself reconnoitered Grand Gulf on April 24 with Porter. Grant began to have doubts: "I forsee great difficulties," he wrote Sherman, "in our present position, but it will not do to let these retard any movements." Grant mostly dwelled on how the force was "very destitute of all preparations for taking care of wounded men." Most of the medical supplies had unfortunately been on the *Tigress*, the one boat that was sunk in the second passage of Vicksburg. Evacuating wounded was another concern, and Grant cautioned Sherman to keep up the roads back from New Carthage. Sherman was perhaps in an "I told you so" mood and warned his division commanders that they had to keep the road open even if they had to plank it or "General Grant's army and Admiral Porter's fleet will be caught unprovided unless every possible means be adopted to relieve their wants."[40]

Despite the close proximity and planning, Grant's problems with McClernand were increasing. Although the politician had moved south with little issue in Louisiana, Grant was losing patience as it took the corps commander two or three days before he was ready to cross. "I have been fretting here for several days to get ready to attack Grand Gulf," Grant wrote Julia on April 28, "with weather roads and water all against me." He could have added McClernand to the mix. One issue was that McClernand insisted that his brand new wife accompany him on the operations. Dana derisively wrote, "Though it is ordered that officers' horses and tents must be left behind, McClernand carries his bride along with him." Dana reported the problems to Washington, writing that when Grant arrived at Porter's flagship on April

27, he "at once sent for General McClernand, discussed with him the point of attack, and ordered him to embark his men without losing a moment." Grant was incredulous that some of McClernand's troops were still stuck across some of the waterways while one of the transports was being used to carry "General McClernand's wife, with her servants and baggage." McClernand even held a formal review of his troops and ordered an artillery salute fired, "notwithstanding that positive orders had repeatedly been given to use no ammunition for any purpose except against the enemy." Grant wrote McClernand "a very severe letter" in the midst of the delay, but he did not send it once he learned that McClernand had finally gotten his transports together and loaded with two divisions of troops on April 28.[41]

By then Grant concluded that the "enemy cannot fail to discover my plans," which indeed they had, but he went on with the operation anyway. McClernand decided the actual landing would be made by the division under Peter J. Osterhaus, a German who had confessed a lack of confidence in himself to Grant upon entering his duties with him; Grant stood by him anyway and Osterhaus soon made a fine general. Yet landing at Grand Gulf was easier said than done. Porter was unable to silence the batteries there on April 29. Grant, Fred, and staff watched from a tug in the river; "We have had terrific cannonading all day, without silencing the enemy's guns," a dejected Grant wrote Sherman. After the fighting, Grant and Fred went aboard Porter's flagship *Benton* to confer about what to do next, and Grant's view was intensely chaotic: "The sight of the mangled and dying men which met my eye as I boarded the ship was sickening." Fred similarly saw the sights, later writing that he "was sickened with the scenes of carnage." Included among the wounded was Porter himself who, Fred related, "had been struck on the back of the head with a fragment of shell, and his face showed the agony he was suffering." Still, the admiral took time to acknowledge the boy, asking him if he wanted to stay on the boat with him and work as one of the fallen gunner's replacements. Looking around at the blood, Fred simply mumbled, "I do not believe that papa will allow me to serve in the navy."[42]

Realizing Grand Gulf was much stronger than anticipated, Grant and Porter put in place "an alternative plan," Dana reported, "which he had in mind from the first." Grant determined to drop down below Grand Gulf and seek another landing spot, "either at the lower end of Grand Gulf or below Bayou Pierre." Obviously, it had to be done quickly, as all of McClernand's divisions and one of McPherson's were on the transports and barges, and another of McPherson's was waiting to be loaded. Grant sent out more reconnaissance to find the best place to land around Rodney or Bruinsburg. "I had sometime previously ordered a recconiscence to a point opposite Bruinsburg," Grant reported, "to ascertain, if possible, from a person in the neighborhood the character of the road leading to the highlands back of Bruinsburg." He added, "During the night I learned from a negro man that there was a good road from Bruinsburg to Port Gibson, which determined me to land there." Grant noted that this was "the first point of land below Grand Gulf from which the interior can be reached." With the location set, Grant then had to get the troops south of Grand Gulf, which he did by ordering them off the transports after dark at Hard Times and marching them south across the neck of land where the river made one of its notorious circular bends. Marching on top of the levee, the troops soon reached Disharoon's Plantation, where Fred recalled the slaves "turned out to welcome us with great rejoicing, deeming us the messengers of the Lord, bringing them freedom." Meanwhile, the gunboats and transports once again ran the Confederate batteries, this time at Grand Gulf on the night of April 29.[43]

Grant was under extreme pressure at this point. He confided to Julia that, personally, "I feel very well but a goodeal disgusted." Simple things got to him amid all the pressure he felt: "The want of a servant to take care of my things and pack up when we leave any place has left me now about bare of some necessary articles. I am always so much engaged on starting from anyplace that I cannot look after things myself." The change in landing spots added to the pressure. Acting on the sole advice of a slave was worrisome, and he had it verified and "the information was found correct," Grant later wrote. Nonetheless, landing below Bayou Pierre added another degree of difficulty in that not only would the army have to cross the Big Black River but it would also have to first negotiate the wide and formidable bayou, which actually split into two large waterways nearer to the inland town of Port Gibson. The Confederates could contest the crossing of these perpendicular waterways much as they had in the earlier Mississippi Central Campaign. On the other hand, landing south of the bayou would force any Confederates that would contest the landing to make the long, circuitous route via Port Gibson, taking much more time and hopefully giving Grant an easier landing. No matter the pros and cons, Grant had no choice. He ordered McClernand to land at Bruinsburg.[44]

With the decision made, Grant rode through the dark night to Disharoon's Plantation as well, almost being thrown from his horse in the process. Dana described the incident when Grant's horse stumbled in the pitch-black night: "I expected to see the general go over the animal's head." Grant held on, and never uttered a negative word. An amazed Dana recalled, "I had been with

Grant daily now for three weeks, and I had never seen him ruffled or heard him swear." Expecting as much, Dana admitted, "I never heard him use an oath."[45]

With the first streaks of dawn on April 30, the navy began the tedious ferrying process that would mark one of the largest amphibious landings in American history prior to World War II. Soon Grant was across, as were the first elements of the army. The transfer utilized transports as well as gunboats; a grateful Grant later wrote that Porter "volunteered to use his entire fleet as transports. I had intended to make this request, but he anticipated me." By 11:00 A.M., McClernand had landed three divisions ashore, with two more ready to cross, at the burned-out village of Bruinsburg ("now not a house was to be seen,—fire had destroyed the whole town," Fred remembered) and each had drawn three days' rations from the transports; McClernand had, to Grant's great dismay, neglected to issue them beforehand, causing several hours' delay. A frustrated Grant repeatedly ordered haste; Dana reported that although "all seems now to be going on well, . . . had any other general than McClernand held the advance, the landing would certainly have been effected at daylight." It nevertheless succeeded, perhaps because Lincoln had declared a month earlier that that very day, April 30, was to be a day of "national humiliation, fasting, and prayer."[46]

Yet crossing was not enough on its own. "I deemed it a matter of vast importance that the highlands should be reached without resistance," Grant later wrote, so McClernand quickly moved his corps forward during the afternoon and night. If the Confederates wanted to dislodge the Union foothold, the best ground to do so was where the lowland in the valley of the Mississippi rose into the surrounding hills. For the Union, moving quickly was essential. And it paid off. As McClernand marched uncontested into the hills overlooking the Mississippi River Valley, he could breathe a sigh of relief. So could Grant, who informed Halleck, "The move by Bruinsburg undoubtedly took the enemy much by surprise."[47]

Back at Bruinsburg, Grant oversaw the crossing as McClernand moved inland. He eventually crossed over all four of McClernand's divisions and one of McPherson's despite the collision of two boats that resulted in the loss of an Illinois battery, horses and all. Another of McPherson's divisions was not far behind and crossed on May 1. By daylight that day, Grant had upward of twenty thousand men on the Mississippi shore. To Halleck he wrote on April 29, "I feel that the battle is now more than half won." Later, while writing his memoirs, Grant could still feel the sense of accomplishment, eloquently writing,

> When this was effected I felt a degree of relief scarcely ever equaled since. Vicksburg was not yet taken it is true, nor were its defenders demoralized by any of our previous moves. I was now in the enemy's country, with a vast river and the stronghold of Vicksburg between me and my base of supplies. But I was on dry ground on the same side of the river with the enemy. All the campaigns, labors, hardships and exposures from the month of December previous to this time that had been made and endured, were for the accomplishment of this one object.[48]

V

"I am pushing forward the Thirteenth Army Corps, with the hope of seizing the bridge across Bayou Pierre," McClernand informed Grant during the night of April 30. The concern for the bridge was evident: taking it intact and crossing the troops before the Confederates could respond and defend it was vitally important. But McClernand was perhaps lulled into a false sense of security when the vanguard marched miles through the Mississippi countryside without seeing so much as a single Confederate. The feints must have worked. McClernand made it past the famous Windsor mansion and on toward Port Gibson, where he could seize the first crossing of the branch of Bayou Pierre. From there it was not far to the main branch of the bayou. Hopefully by nightfall, McClernand could be across it.[49]

At the same time, back at Bruinsburg, Grant began to organize what he could in terms of transportation for the army. The wagon train was left west of the river in the hopes that it would be brought across at a more suitable place such as Grand Gulf, once it fell, but Grant needed instant transportation to carry ammunition.

> I directed, therefore, immediately on landing that all the vehicles and draft animals, whether horses, mules, or oxen, in the vicinity should be collected and loaded to their capacity with ammunition. Quite a train was collected during the 30th, and a motley train it was. In it could be found fine carriages, loaded nearly to the top with boxes of cartridges that had been pitched in promiscuously, drawn by mules with plough-harness, straw collars, rope-lines, etc.; long-coupled wagons, with racks for carrying cotton bales, drawn by oxen, and everything that could be found in the way of transportation on a plantation, either for use or pleasure.

It was certainly no time to worry about appearances, or paperwork for that matter. Grant added, "The making out of provision returns was stopped for the time. No formalities were to retard our progress until a position was secured when the time could be spared to observe them."[50]

Unfortunately for Grant, what seemed to be an easy invasion of Mississippi soon became more difficult. The terrain was awful, and Grant wrote Halleck that it was "the most broken country I ever saw. The whole country is a series of irregular ridges, divided by deep and impassable ravines, grown up with heavy timber, undergrowth, and cane." Then, as McClernand neared Port Gibson early on May 1, he met Confederates. A portion of the Confederate command at Grand Gulf had frantically moved south of Bayou Pierre when they realized that the Federals had crossed farther to the south. A motley collection of brigades, augmented by some reinforcements throughout the day, provided a determined defense in the wilderness and ridges southwest of Port Gibson, beginning before daylight around the A. K. Shaifer House and continually moving east toward Magnolia Church and finally near Willow Creek. McClernand sent forward divisions under Eugene Carr, Andrew Jackson Smith, and Alvin Hovey against the Confederates on the Rodney Road and detached Osterhaus's division along a side road to flank the enemy. There, they met more Confederates on the Bruinsburg Road. McClernand was able to push forward on both fronts, aided by the just-arrived lead division of McPherson's corps under John A. Logan.[51]

Once artillery was heard to the east on May 1, around 7:00 A.M., Grant quickly readied to go to the front. He left staff officer William S. Hillyer at Bruinsburg to superintend the crossing, ordering him to come to his headquarters later. When Hillyer asked where that would be, Grant humorously replied, "Well, I don't exactly know till I've consulted Pemberton!" Grant rode to the front carrying nothing; he even had to borrow a horse from Andrew Jackson Smith. War correspondent Sylvanus Cadwallader later recalled that the stories of Grant having nothing but the clothes on his back "are so literally true that no exaggeration is possible." Grant noted that the entire wagon train was left west of the river, and "my own horses, headquarters' transportation, servants, mess chest, and everything except what I had on, was with the train." He also left Fred behind on the steamboat, where the boy had fallen asleep on the deck during the monotonous crossing. Grant left explicit orders with Lorenzo Thomas to keep Fred there when he awoke, but Fred managed to talk his way into going ashore "to join a party in chasing a rabbit." Fred then followed the wagon train and secured a ride on a mule until he found better company with an artillery battery and then an infantry regiment. He moved so far forward that he soon reached his father, but Fred's "guilty conscience so troubled me that I hid from his sight behind a tree." He later wandered around the fought-over ground where the sights nearly made him sick; he sat down at a tree, "the most woe-begone twelve-year-old lad in America."[52]

Grant had seen the same thing, riding along both fronts of the battle. Governor Richard Yates of Illinois was with him, and at one point they came under fire. Grant was by this time tired of governors getting in his way; Frederick Law Olmsted remarked to a friend after a visit to Grant's headquarters in April that "Grant is, in his good nature, nearly driven crazy by them." Now, Grant puffed on his cigar and calmly noted, "Governor, it's too late to dodge after the ball has passed." Grant even had to nudge McClernand and Yates forward when the politicians stopped to give speeches. More troubling, McClernand continually called for reinforcements, and Grant personally moved one brigade of McPherson's corps to Osterhaus's support, but he later reported how he could not see the need: "I had been on that as well as all other parts of the field," Grant wrote in his report, "and could not see how they could be used there to advantage." Still, it was a tough fight; Grant informed Porter that "[John S.] Bowen himself is here." Despite the hard fighting, the results were glorious. Grant informed Sherman that he had met the enemy "in a very strong position near Port Gibson, 4 miles south, and engaged them hotly all day, driving them constantly. Our victory was complete. We captured 500 prisoners, four guns, killed General Tracy and a large number of the enemy. Our own loss will not exceed 150 killed and 500 wounded." Even with that, Grant was not satisfied. "Push the enemy," he wrote McClernand late in the day, "with skirmishers well thrown out, until it gets too dark to see him; then place your command on eligible ground, wherever night finds you. Park your artillery so as to command the surrounding country, and renew the attack at early dawn. If possible, push the enemy from the field or capture him."[53]

During the chaotic advance, Grant finally caught up with his wandering son. Grant later admitted that he "hoped to get away without him until after Grand Gulf should fall into our hands." Fred of course wandered much of the day but was soon overtaken by Charles Dana, who had likewise been left; the two moved on together. Grant was drinking coffee at a campfire when the two harried interlopers arrived, and he was amused that they had procured "two enormous horses, grown white from age, each equipped with dilapidated saddles and bridles"; Fred later wrote how "the sight of a small boy on the big white horse made some sport on the road for the soldiers I passed or those who passed me." In the midst of tedious operations, Grant showed remarkable composure at the appearance of his son: "He supposed I was still onboard the boat." Fred later recalled, "In later years he often told the story of my following him to the battle of Port Gibson, with more interest and satisfaction than he manifested to me at the time." Grant had nothing to give them, noting that Fred "forged around the best he could." Dana actually remained horseless until a captured Confederate officer begged Grant to let him keep his horse, which he said was his personal possession and not owned by the Confederacy. Grant responded, "I have got four or five first-rate horses wandering somewhere about the Southern Confederacy. They have been captured from me in battle or by spies. I will authorize you, whenever you find one of them, to take possession of him. I cheerfully give him to you; but as for this horse, I think he is just about the horse Mr. Dana needs." Dana later recalled, "Whenever I went out with General Grant anywhere he always had some question to ask about that horse."[54]

Grant was intent on moving on, but he had to do so cautiously. It helped that good news was coming frequently now, including information that Benjamin Grierson had traversed the entire state of Mississippi and "had the whole state on edge." Additionally, the Confederates did not contest the battlefield the next morning, much to Grant's delight, and the Federals moved on at daylight. Grant set up headquarters quickly in a house in Port Gibson, and Fred found a local dog to keep his attention; it was there that one of McClernand's staff officers, sent to Grant hours before and taking a widely circuitous route all the way back to the battlefield, reported to Grant, "I am sent by Genl. McClernand to inform you that we have Port Gibson." Neither Grant nor his staff could refrain from laughing. Nevertheless, Grant soon got to work and took care of what had to be done. Not wanting to take any men from his mobile force, he asked Porter to see to the prisoners captured at Port Gibson. While he did not know any of the ground ahead of him, he was aware that he had to attain the crossing points of Big Bayou Pierre, Little Bayou Pierre being the branch that shot off to the southeast and ran through Port Gibson itself. The main channel was some three miles north of the town, and there were only two crossing points in the Port Gibson area that Grant could use. One was at the bridge over which the railroad from Port Gibson to Grand Gulf ran and was the farthest down the watershed. The crossing to the east was a bridge at Grindstone Ford. Making the bridges vitally important was the fact that, in Grant's words, Bayou Pierre was "high and the current rapid."[55]

Grant ordered McClernand to take these crossing points. Fortunately for Grant, renewing the battle the next day, May 2, was not possible, because "in the morning it was found that the enemy had retreated across Bayou Pierre" to await reinforcements, Grant wrote. Confederate local commander John S. Bowen, Grant's friend in Missouri before the war, even sent him a message asking for "a suspension of hostilities" for an entire day for the purpose of "burying my dead and looking after my wounded." Grant was in no position to provide such an interval, informing Bowen that he knew the Confederate was awaiting "reinforcements and additional munitions of war." Grant pushed on.[56]

Grant found that the bayou was "not fordable for many miles up." He therefore set to work to rebuild the suspension bridge over the lower fork at the town itself, with engineer James H. Wilson of his staff superintending "what might be called a raft-bridge" out of any and all materials found nearby, including buildings and fences. In addition to this, he ordered McPherson to send one of John A. Logan's brigades to "proceed to the ford, 3 miles above the town, under the guidance of the black boy sent herewith." Grant also wanted a brigade to take the bridge on the Grand Gulf road and even to spur the enemy onward: "Let the brigade push across the bayou and attack in flank the enemy, now in full retreat through Willow Springs, demoralized and out of ammunition." Fred actually accompanied Logan, with the politician general telling Fred while in Port Gibson, "Come, my boy, and I will show you the prettiest fight you will ever see." Grant also sent components of McPherson's corps northwest toward Grindstone Ford, where that destroyed suspension bridge had to be rebuilt as well. That was done overnight from May 2 to May 3, with Grant himself onsite and pushing troops across as soon as daylight dawned. The Confederates fired into the head of the column with artillery and small arms, but Grant was able to get across despite noting that McPherson "had a skirmish nearly approaching a battle." The affair mainly prompted Grant to secure the roadways to his rear, and he left ample reserves to meet any threat.[57]

As important as Bayou Pierre was, the capture of Grand Gulf was even more important. Grant admitted to Julia, "I feel every confidance of success but may be disappointed. Possession of Grand Gulf too I look upon as virtual possession of Vicksburg and Port Hudson and the entire Mississippi River." He also sent Porter a message asking him to be at Grand Gulf around 10:00 A.M. on May 3. Accordingly, Grant sent portions of McPherson's corps northwest along the isolated railroad line, and Eugene Carr's division took the crossing, although the enemy had burned the railroad and suspension bridges. Grant was especially interested in the Grand Gulf approach, because as long as Grant's forces stayed south of Bayou Pierre, the Confederates could hold Grand Gulf. In actuality, it would have been perfectly logical for Grant to pause south of Bayou Pierre and hold the crossings, giving himself the much-needed time to bring up the remainder of McPherson's corps as well as Sherman's, but Grant was not about to let a golden opportunity slip through his grasp. Continuing on past Bayou Pierre would outflank Grand Gulf. If supplies of ammunition and other items that could not be taken on the march toward Vicksburg had to come by way of the Bruinsburg–Port Gibson route, Grant would be in bad shape. Significantly, taking Grand Gulf would allow for supplies and troops to be unloaded north of Bayou Pierre.[58]

And it worked. The Confederates left Grand Gulf before dawn on May 3, blowing up the magazines and dismounting and spiking the heavy guns. Without any infantry components nearby as yet, Grant had to rely on the navy to take possession. Porter landed and quickly took official charge of the Confederate bastion that had held out so long under his direct fire. Because Grant had outmaneuvered the enemy and turned the position, Porter was able to occupy it without firing a single shot. Grant himself rode to Grand Gulf with a small cavalry escort later on while pushing most of his troops forward to Hankinson's Ferry on the Big Black River. There they skirmished with the enemy and made Pemberton think that Grant was about to cross and invest Vicksburg from the south or, as Grant put it, that these fords "were objects of much solicitude to me." At times, small reconnaissance groups even crossed the river at Hankinson's as well as Hall's Ferry farther to the north, pressing toward Warrenton.[59]

All the while, Grant was having trouble keeping track of Fred. The boy had gone with Logan on his march but wandered for a while on his return, his horse actually falling at one point and injuring the boy's leg. Fred eventually found a house with a porch full of sleeping officers; he "crawled in for a nap between two of them." The officers were not amused and "said things" until Grant told them who he was, whereupon their opinions changed drastically. Colonel John B. Sanborn even offered Fred his overcoat for a pillow. Fred grew cold toward morning and went inside and crawled between two others in a bed, finding out the next morning they were "two large negroes." Eventually, Fred made his way back to Grant and accompanied him on the ride to Grand Gulf.[60]

Grant was ecstatic when he found that Grand Gulf was in Porter's hands; "Grand Gulf is now the base of supplies," he informed McClernand on May 4. He later noted, "I went to the Gulf myself, and made the necessary arrangements for changing my base of supplies from Bruinsburg." His staff rode along; Grant, showing his humorous side, told the energetic young staff officer Wilson: "Wilson, there's a fallen tree you haven't jumped yet." Grant informed Julia in a quick note from Grand Gulf that "I have been on horseback since early this morning, rode in here leaving my army fifteen miles in the country, have written dispatches and a report for Washington and have to go back tonight." He also took advantage of his first bath in over a week: "When I reached Grand Gulf May 3d I had not been with my baggage since the 27th of April and consequently had had no change of underclothing, no meal except such as I could pick up sometimes at other headquarters, and no tent to cover me. The first thing I did was to get a bath, borrow some fresh underclothing from one of the naval officers and get a good meal on the flagship." Grant also told Julia, "Fred is very well, enjoying himself hugely. He has heard balls whistle and is not moved in the slightest by it. He was very anxious to run the blockade of Grand Gulf."[61]

Congressman Washburne and Governor Yates of Illinois, along with Lorenzo Thomas, were also at Grand Gulf by this time. They were all there to observe Grant, and they witnessed one of the most significant victories of the campaign. Porter later said that Thomas actually had orders to relieve Grant if he thought it necessary; according to Julia, she had alerted Grant to Thomas's mission, so the general may have indeed known about Thomas's potential action. For his part, Thomas showed little heart for the undercover work, especially now that Grant had captured Grand Gulf. Cadwallader noted that Thomas had "became so interested in negro regiments" that he delayed his arrival; "he stopped at nearly every landing on the river and spent what seemed to be an unnecessary time at each, until he was suspected of purposefully evading the disagreeable subject." Grant ended up reassuring all three, plus Charles Dana; he also now had a major victory under his belt. But Grant had a campaign to conduct, and there was little time to lose dealing with politicians; he departed a little after midnight and arrived at Hankinson's Ferry just before dawn.[62]

Dana accompanied Grant on the trip to Grand Gulf and left a vivid account of what Grant was thinking during this time. He reported that the general's mind was firmly on supplies. While much could now be brought across the river to Grand Gulf and sent to the army, Grant was becoming even more convinced that he could also glean much from the land itself. He had learned what abundance lay across the fields in north Mississippi, and if this portion of the territory was anything like what he had already seen, he could supply his army with many essentials right off the land. "During this ride to Grand Gulf," Dana recalled, "Grant made enquiries on every side about the food supplies of the country we were entering. He told me he had been gathering information on this point ever since the army crossed the Mississippi, and had made up his mind that both beef and cattle and corn were abundant in the country."[63]

Grant was admittedly proud of what he had accomplished thus far: "My victory at this place, over Bowen, is a most important one. Management I think has saved us an immense loss of life and gained all the results of a hard fight. I feel proud of the Army at my command. They have marched day and night, without tents and with irregular rations without a murmer of complaints." Grant was, of course, enduring the hard times as well. The general often slept at the foot of a tree before his headquarters equipment and horses came up after he had reached Hankinson's Ferry. His fare changed only slightly even once his possessions arrived. Dana described it: "I get my meals in General Grant's mess, and pay my share of the expenses. The table is a chest with a double cover, which unfolds on the right and the left; the dishes, knives and forks, and caster are inside. Sometimes we get good things, but generally we don't. The cook is an old negro, black and grimy. The cooking is not as clean as it might be, but in war you can't be particular about such things." As such, Fred decided he could do better elsewhere. He noted that Grant was so busy riding from corps to corps that "this made his headquarters so uncomfortable, and his mess so irregular, that I, for one, did not propose to put up with such living, and I took my meals with the soldiers, who used to do a little foraging, and thereby set an infinitely better table than their commanding general. My father's table at this time was, I must frankly say, the worst I ever saw or partook of."[64]

With the major prize of Grand Gulf in his possession, Grant now paused to regroup and bring up the rest of the army for the trials that lay ahead. He had left Grand Gulf the same night he rode in, leaving Fred with staff officer Clark B. Lagow. Meanwhile, Grant made his headquarters at Hankinson's Ferry and directed the movements of the army from there. McClernand took a position on the right, covering the various Bayou Pierre crossings and concentrating mostly near Willow Springs, just north of Bayou Pierre. McPherson wound up on the left. Grant was confident despite his displaced plans. He described his troops as "composed of well-disciplined and hardy men, who know no defeat, and are not willing to learn what it is." He added, "This army is in the finest health and spirits. Since leaving Milliken's Bend they have marched as much by night as by day, through mud and rain, without tents or much other baggage, and on irregular rations, without a complaint, and with less straggling than I have ever before witnessed." Grant repeated that sentiment to Sherman: "The enemy is badly beaten, greatly demoralized, and exhausted of ammunition," he wrote. "The road to Vicksburg is open. All we want now are men, ammunition, and hard bread."[65]

VI

Grant used the small delay to get his forces in order, and he soon sent out a number of instructions. While keeping his troops basically in camp, mainly reconnoitering for food, he stipulated that they would not move each day "before the cool of the evening." He also made sure that various naval components were stationed at important places around Grand Gulf as well as at the Big Black River. He also called up additional troops, such as Jacob Lauman's division of Hurlbut's Sixteenth Corps from the north. Additional officers similarly arrived, such as Michael K. Lawler, who was immediately put into a command. To replace some of Hurlbut's losses with troops that could be used more effectively, Grant sent most of the department's cavalry to him in north Mississippi. Grant told Hurlbut to use these horse soldiers "as much as possible for attracting attention from this direction." He also ordered that the cavalry be firm but delicate. "In other words," Grant wrote, "cripple the rebellion in every way, without insulting women and children or taking their clothing, jewelry, &c."[66]

Grant most wanted Sherman and his troops in Mississippi. The red-headed general had feinted near Haynes' Bluff north of Vicksburg until he received Grant's order to rejoin the army. Sherman was convinced his efforts had worked: "Great activity being seen in Vicksburg, and troops pushing up this way." He wanted the ruse to remain in effect until night before leaving, telling a subordinate: "By prolonging the effort, we give Grant more time. Therefore, move quietly after dark (8 P.M.), slowly, till we are about Johnston's, and then let out for home." For his part, Grant ordered Sherman to "make all possible dispatch to Grand Gulf."[67]

Once Sherman got the order, he moved quickly. He remembered Grant telling him "to hurry up, cross at Grand Gulf, and hurry forward." Sherman alerted his commanders, "There are now six divisions of our men across and operating east of Grand Gulf. Let us catch up as quickly as possible consistent with bringing our men there in good fighting condition." Once across, Sherman was to move to Hankinson's Ferry and relieve McPherson so McPherson could push on. Grant ordered Sherman to follow, destroying the bridge at the ferry. Sherman did so despite what he described as "a good deal of scrambling to get across."[68]

One of the main reasons Grant wanted Sherman was, of course, to beef up the army's numbers in hostile territory. Another reason was that Sherman was bringing with him the wagon train and as many supplies as he could. By May 6 the army had been in Mississippi six full days, and rations were beginning to run low. Grant told officers west of the river, "You will give special attention to the matter of shortening the line of land transportation from above Vicksburg to the steamers below." He reminded them that "everything depends upon the promptitude with which our supplies are forwarded." Of course, the supply line became much shorter once Grant moved to Grand Gulf on May 3 and made his base there. He ordered staff officer William S. Hillyer, who had been left there, to "see that the Com.y [Commissary] at Grand Gulf loads all wagons presenting themselves for stores with great promptness. Issue any order in my name that may be necessary to secure the greatest promptness in this respect. . . . If necessary for promptness relieve the present Com.y and call on Sherman for an officer to take his place." Grant also told Sherman to send 120 wagons to Grand Gulf with a hundred thousand pounds of bacon, with "coffee, sugar, salt, and hard bread." He added, "It is unnecessary for me to remind you of the overwhelming importance of celerity in your movements."[69]

A baffled Sherman did not see how he was to do it all. "Some other way must be found to feed this army," he told a subordinate, but Grant would not take no for an answer. The commander wanted supplies and Sherman would do his best to get them to him. Fortunately, the river was falling, which meant the surrounding lakes and bayous were also falling, so there was more land to work with. By May 5 the river and surrounding waterways had fallen so much that a route only eight miles long was established between Young's Point "to below Warrenton batteries." With such a short supply line, Grant ordered, "We will risk no more rations to run the Vicksburg batteries."[70]

Just because moving the supplies to Grand Gulf was now easier did not mean that all the logistical problems were solved. In order to keep the river free of Confederates north of Vicksburg, Grant ordered another expedition toward Greenville to clear out an additional rumored battery. Getting the provisions to the various commands in the field east of the river was also problematic and McClernand pestered Grant about it. On May 3 McClernand informed Grant that "my corps will be out of rations to-morrow. I am, as you are aware, without means of transportation. I ask that you will cause rations to be sent out immediately." McClernand then took his complaint to another level by charging favoritism: while McPherson's corps soon had an almost full complement of wagon trains, McClernand had only three wagons east of the river. When McClernand's corps became stuck behind McPherson's wagon train at one point, McClernand erupted. "The officer in charge of transports has given preference to the Seventeenth Army Corps in everything," he wrote. "The baggage of that corps is being sent forward, to the exclusion of ammunition and provisions for the Thirteenth Army Corps; priority is given to forage over necessary supplies for the Thirteenth Army Corps."[71]

That exchange was mild compared to Grant's growing wrath toward McClernand. Grant had had enormous problems with McClernand getting ready to cross the river, and he also had issues during the fighting on May 1. At one point, McClernand was sent a message only to respond that "he had fought the battle so far and fought it well, and would not be interfered with by anybody." Of course, the courier reported this to Grant, who fumed at the response. According to staff officer Wilson, he and others actually tried to make amends, counseling Grant to congratulate McClernand on a well-fought battle. By this time Grant had evidently had enough and refused. McClernand was finally starting to get under the calm-mannered Grant's skin.[72]

Despite the continual concern over supplies and McClernand's nonsense, Grant was comfortable enough to probe ahead even while waiting for Sherman and the army's transportation system to arrive fully. As early as May 4, McClernand explored forward to the Big Black River at Hall's Ferry and even toward Edwards Station. And with that exploration came renewed confidence. "Everything here looks highly favorable at present," Grant wrote Hurlbut, "the only thing now delaying us is the ferriage of wagons and supplies across the river to Grand Gulf. . . . Rations now are the only delay."[73]

CHAPTER FIVE

"YOU CAN DO A GREAT DEAL IN EIGHT DAYS"

"Since General Grant commenced to move his columns," wrote brigade commander George B. Boomer to his sister on May 6, "he has displayed great tact and skill, together with immense energy and nerve." Boomer had earlier voiced his opinions of the impending failure of the various expeditions, but now he was brimming with confidence as he sat poised to move forward with the rest of the Union forces. "The passage of this army over the Mississippi River and up to this point is one of the most masterly movements known in the history of any warfare, and it is a success." But it was obviously not over: "We shall soon commence the second movement, when you will probably hear of a tremendous battle, and I trust a victory."[1]

Ulysses S. Grant was confident as well. He had written on the last day of March that "once landed on the other side of the river I expect but little trouble." He was wrong, of course, but he still remained confident after he crossed the Mississippi River and especially after he secured Grand Gulf. This confidence continued on through the early stages of the inland operation. "All looks well," Grant wrote Halleck on May 8, and he was correct. He had obtained much more than just a foothold in Confederate Mississippi, although he had fought a major battle to do so, which he had hoped to avoid certainly until moving farther inland, perhaps even to Vicksburg itself. That the Confederates were able to muster even somewhat of a resistance as close to the Mississippi River crossing as Port Gibson was surprising and was evidence that even with all the feints Grant had employed, he had not totally caught the Confederates off guard. Yet he had surprised them enough to get much of his army ashore and inland to the high ground before that battle was fought, and he had won it in convincing fashion. Had he not been able to get inland before meeting the Confederates and, certainly, won the first battle, things would look completely different now.[2]

Fortunately for Grant, things were looking good. The army was situated north of Bayou Pierre, where Grant had originally wanted to start the campaign, and he had possession of Grand Gulf too. He was currently in the midst of a pause that would allow him to bring up more troops, particularly

Sherman's Fifteenth Corps, but more importantly additional wagons and supplies. Once they arrived, Grant planned to restart his advance, although he would not aid Banks. Now that the situation had changed, Grant planned to move on. "I shall not bring my troops into this place [Grand Gulf]," he informed Halleck on May 3, "but [will] immediately follow the enemy, and, if all promises as favorable hereafter as it does now, not stop until Vicksburg is in our possession."[3]

The decision to advance was indeed contradictory to Grant's original plan. He had talked of sending McClernand's corps south to aid Banks after gaining a foothold in Mississippi. Whether that plan was ever firm is questionable; perhaps Grant kept talking about it to keep off pressure from above. Banks, after all, outranked him. Whether it was a firm plan or not mattered less than whether it was a realistic plan. No commander would want to reduce his force once he confronted the enemy in hostile territory. The idea of splitting his force was ludicrous; if that was going to happen it would have been much better to have done it while the Army of the Tennessee was still shielded on the western side of the river. Fortunately, Banks made it easy for Grant. At Grand Gulf, Grant received word that Banks would not be able to cooperate on the Mississippi River for some time.[4]

With the Confederates scattered and on the run, Grant simply could not wait for Banks. He quickly informed the politician general that he would not be receiving any help, although Banks was still counting on Grant's troops, even writing on May 3, "Can you not forward these troops now?" The fact that Banks was even then moving away from Grant and the Mississippi River, even being at Alexandria on May 8, certainly negated for Grant any requirement to cooperate, especially if he could reduce Vicksburg in the time that Banks would need to complete his efforts up the Red River. In fact, Banks wrote that he would not be ready and able to cooperate until perhaps June. Grant had always regarded anything other than operations on the Mississippi River as "a waste of time and material," so sending a corps to Banks in early May, which he could not use for some time, would consequently leave a reduced Grant sitting for nearly a month on the same side of the river as the enemy, waiting for Banks to return. The Confederates would no doubt concentrate on Grant during the interim.[5]

Accordingly, Grant made the decision not to support Banks at all, writing him that although he had intended to send a corps after "gaining a foothold at Grand Gulf," he was changing his plan. "Meeting the enemy, however, as I did south of Port Gibson, I followed him to the Big Black, and could not afford to retrace my steps." He added, "Many days cannot elapse before the battle will begin which is to decide the fate of Vicksburg." Grant also mentioned a rumor that he had heard about Port Hudson being all but abandoned, which would of course negate any need for a detachment. Grant then went so far as to actually call on Banks to support him at Vicksburg. "It is impossible to predict how long it [the fighting at Vicksburg] may last. I would urgently request, therefore, that you join me or send all the force you can spare to co-operate in the great struggle for opening the Mississippi River." He particularly asked that Colonel Benjamin Grierson's cavalry brigade be sent back to him, as it "would be of immense service to me now."[6]

Grant had made a major decision, to be sure, one that effectively catapulted the campaign into a new realm. He had a foothold east of the river, but he no longer saw it as a base for later operations; instead, he would move out from that foothold. Grant knew this decision would not be popular in Washington, but being mired in the depths of the Mississippi countryside had its advantages. He later wrote how he "knew well that Halleck's caution would lead him to disapprove of this course; but it was the only one that gave any chance of success." Then he added, significantly, "The time it would take to communicate with Washington and get a reply would be so great that I could not be interfered with until it was demonstrated whether my plan was practicable." He later described how he knew it would take days for his message to get to Washington and receive a reply. Hopefully he would have Vicksburg by then, if he moved with haste. "I remember how anxiously I counted the time I had to spare before that response could come," Grant said years later.[7]

He guessed he had a little over a week. "You can do a great deal in eight days," Grant quipped. But he had to hurry.[8]

I

Having made the decision to concentrate on Vicksburg alone, with more supplies pouring in and being turned out in local plantations' mills, and with Sherman's troops crossing the river, Grant restarted the campaign. In an uncharacteristic move, the mild-mannered Grant issued congratulatory orders to his troops for the victory at Port Gibson but then called them to more duty: "A few days continuance of the same zeal and constancy will secure to this army the crowning victory over the rebellion. More difficulties and privations are before us. Let us endure them manfully. Other battles are to be fought. Let us fight them bravely. A grateful country will rejoice at our success, and history will record it with immortal honor."[9]

But restarting the campaign necessitated yet another major decision: how best to get to Vicksburg. Grant could certainly cross the Big Black River at any of the southern ferries near Grand Gulf and approach from the south. He believed the Confederates would expect that, however, and knew the enemy would concentrate their forces in the triangle of land between the Mississippi River, the Big Black River, and the Southern Railroad of Mississippi. Entering this heavily defended triangle would probably precipitate a battle in a rather restricted area that would deprive him of much chance to maneuver. "The broken nature of the ground would have enabled him [Pemberton] to hold a strong defensible line from the river south of the city to the Big Black," Grant later wrote, "retaining possession of the railroad back to that point." Choosing not to put his army in such a binding position, Grant selected to simply move his forces in such a way, particularly at Hankinson's Ferry, that would lead Pemberton to believe that he intended to cross there and move to Vicksburg from the south.[10]

Instead, Grant opted to march northeast, parallel with the Big Black River, to the east-west railroad and cut the line of supply to Vicksburg. As early as May 4, Charles Dana described Grant planning to push "his army toward the Big Black Bridge and Jackson, threatening both and striking at either, as is most convenient." The newly arrived Sherman similarly wrote as early as May 5 that "the enemy has escaped across Big Black River, and Grant will now probably strike in the direction of the Jackson Railroad." Such a maneuver would allow Grant to move northward to the much more easily traversed ground east of Vicksburg instead of being tied up crossing the substantial Big Black River in a restricted area. Marching parallel with the river on the east side of the Big Black would also shield Grant's most vulnerable left flank as he moved north; at the same time, the right flank, which Grant worried much less about, would still have some cover in the form of a tributary of Bayou Pierre, Tallahalla Creek, which paralleled the Big Black River's northeast-to-southwest trajectory for at least a portion of the way, nearly to Raymond. McPherson later described this geography as "the divide between Big Black and north fork of Bayou Pierre."[11]

Moving in such a manner did have its problems, though. Two major creeks slashed across the front of this corridor between the Big Black River and Tallahalla Creek. Moving northeast up this ridge toward the railroad, Grant's forces would first come to Fivemile Creek just past Cayuga and Utica. Pressing on, the army would then face Fourteenmile Creek nearer to Edwards and Raymond. If the Confederates remained behind (west of) the Big Black River, these creeks would likely present little problem. If the enemy contested their crossing, however, Grant might have another fight on his hands. Fortunately for him, Grant was well informed the whole way, having scouts out front and taking in every piece of information he and his staff could glean from captured letters, local newspapers, and civilians both black and white.[12]

Adding to the potential danger from the terrain was probable Confederate resistance, which came in the form of two major concentrations of troops at Vicksburg on the river and Jackson to the east. It was not acceptable military theory to cross a major river in the face of a large enemy who could concentrate on him, which Grant did as a last resort because the Confederate forces in the Vicksburg area, although not concentrated, together vastly outnumbered the troops Grant initially put across the river. Now, he was going to willingly march between the two forces defending Mississippi, putting his army between the two and in danger of being assaulted by both. Grant knew that Halleck would not approve this plan either. He was "too learned a soldier to consent to a campaign in violation of all the principles of the art of war," Grant noted, but Grant knew Pemberton, although he did not know his strength. After the war, Grant dangerously admitted that he had "entirely under-estimated Pemberton's strength."[13]

In the end, the chances of success moving northeast to the railroad and cutting Vicksburg off from the outside world were far greater than diving off into the convoluted and restricted ground west of the Big Black River. Grant had the advantage of maneuver, and he would use it.

II

The forward movement from the Willow Springs area began on May 7, with a confident Grant looking toward the decisive encounter of the campaign. "Two days more, or Tuesday next," Grant wrote Julia by courier to Grand Gulf on May 9, "must bring on the fight which will settle the fate of Vicksburg." He added, "No Army ever felt better than this one does nor more confidant of sucsess. Before they are beaten they will be very badly beaten." McPherson thus began his move northeast, keeping his left near the Big Black River and soon reaching Rocky Springs. He watched the various ferries across the river such as Hall's and Hankinson's; the enemy actually placed a battery across Hall's Ferry to contest that crossing. At the same time, McClernand moved northeast on the center of the ridge, with Sherman following both. Despite the reorganization, it was a fluid situation; rumors from "fugitive Negroes,"

McClernand reported, stated that the enemy was concentrating at Edward's Station, east of the Big Black River.[14]

Grant was not to be denied, however. He moved his own headquarters forward to Rocky Springs on May 7. Over the course of the next few days, he positioned the army in a north-facing line, changing the pattern by moving McClernand's Thirteenth Corps to the left nearer the Big Black River while McPherson marched across his rear and took station on the right. Sherman eventually moved into the center between them. "The change of route for the march of your Corps was on the strengt[h] of reports made by one of the Engr officers from Head Quarters who went beyond Cayuga to-day," Grant wrote McClernand on May 8. Grant also warned McClernand to be wary on this most exposed flank, writing that "it was my intention here to hug the Big Black River as closely as possible." McClernand accordingly watched all the fords "till our troops were well advanced." Next to the right were Sherman's two divisions (Frank Blair's was still on the move to join the army) in the center, and then two divisions of McPherson's Seventeenth Corps (John McArthur's was still on the move also) on the right moving parallel with Tallahalla Creek to the east. McClernand moved through Auburn, where Grant advanced his headquarters on May 10, McPherson through Utica, and Sherman in the middle near Cayuga, all reaching the Fivemile Creek watershed by May 10. Fearing a Confederate defense of Fivemile Creek, Grant made sure all the corps commanders moved "on the same general front." In telling them to halt and reconnoiter to the front toward Fourteenmile Creek, he also ordered them to "have all the lateral roads leading from your line of march carefully examined, to facilitate communication with the other corps in case of necessity." Fortunately for the Union advance, the Confederates did little to hold the Fivemile Creek line.[15]

Not everyone was as bold and confident as Grant. As they progressed north, Grant's corps commanders began to show extreme nervousness. McClernand lectured Grant that "the political consequences of the impending campaign will be momentous," and he did not always fully understand Grant's orders in the unknown terrain. "Is there not some mistake about this," he wrote of Grant's orders on May 8, adding, "I have with me an intelligent negro, who has been driving a team at intervals for fourteen years from Port Gibson to Edwards Station."[16]

Supplying the army was the biggest worry. Officers in the rear had been working diligently to shift supplies to the Grand Gulf area, having moved "over 300,000 rations of hard bread, coffee, sugar, and salt, 225,000 rations of salt meat, and 130,000 of soap" by May 8. That said, the real trick was getting the supplies to the front from Grand Gulf, and that distance was now growing daily as the army marched farther northeast. Grant continually cautioned his corps commanders to keep teams traveling back and forth to Grand Gulf to bring up supplies, and he put a capable officer, J. Condit Smith, in charge of the trains. "Send all the teams you can spare, after putting three days' rations in the men's haversacks, back to Grand Gulf for rations and ammunition," Grant wrote McClernand on May 7. Still, there was bound to be trouble in supplying the army on one road from Grand Gulf. Sherman lodged his concerns with Grant on May 9: "There are 500 wagons across [west of] the river, and with each is an officer pressing to have it cross over, as if the absolute safety of the army depends on that wagon. Make some uniform and just rule, and send somebody back to regulate this matter, or your road will be crowded and jammed unless it is done." Sherman went so far as to demand, "Stop all troops till your army is partially supplied with wagons, and then act as quickly as possible, for this road will be jammed as sure as life if you attempt to supply 50,000 men by one single road."[17]

Grant would have none of it. He planned to "disregard his base and depend on the country for meat and even for bread. Beef-cattle and corn are both abundant everywhere." Grant had learned in north Mississippi just how much food could be procured and later admitted that back in December, "had I known the demoralized condition of the enemy, or the fact that central Mississippi abounded so in all army supplies, I would have been in pursuit of Pemberton while his cavalry was destroying the roads in my rear." Now Grant was putting that lesson, as well as what he had learned since crossing the river, to good use. He responded to Sherman, "I do not calculate upon the possibility of supplying the army with full rations from Grand Gulf. I know it will be impossible without constructing additional roads. What I do expect, however, is to get up what rations of hard bread, coffee, and salt we can, and make the country furnish the balance." He reminded Sherman (who was not present to observe it) that after McClernand and McPherson crossed the river, they "started from Bruinsburg with an average of about two days' rations, and received no more from our own supplies for some days. Abundance was found in the mean time. Some corn meal, bacon, and vegetables were found, and an abundance of beef and mutton." As to stopping the advance again, Grant would not hear of it. "A delay would give the enemy time to re-enforce and fortify," he wrote, adding to the worried Sherman, "you are in a country where the troops have already lived off the people for some days, and may find provisions more scarce, but as we get upon new soil they are more abundant, particularly in corn and cattle." It was much better, Grant argued, to move forward quickly. Historian J. F. C. Fuller likened Grant to Napoleon, whom he quoted as saying, "It may be that I shall lose a battle, but I shall never lose a minute."[18]

Nevertheless, unguarded wagon trains were ripe for raids by roving Confederates, so Grant stipulated that large bodies of Union troops, brigades at the least, be detailed to guard the trains as they proceeded north. At first this was easily done as Sherman shuttled his corps across the river brigade by brigade and then north to join the army. Later, divisions left behind to guard the Louisiana route, such as McArthur's division of McPherson's corps and Blair's of Sherman's corps, moved with the supplies. Yet even then, the supplies were still not totally safe; at one point, Grant ordered Sherman to put a brigade at a critical crossroads until the wagon train moved through, but Sherman had already passed that point and did not learn of Grant's order until after the fact. "I feel somewhat uneasy for our trains that are out now but hope they will get through all right," Grant wrote on May 9. Fortunately for him, the wagon train that Sherman missed passed unscathed. Grant also ordered staff officer William S. Hillyer at Grand Gulf—which he ordered fortified on the land side—to hold all wagons loaded and ready to march until more troops crossed and could escort them. Grant wanted mostly "bread salt and coffee," and stipulated that Hillyer "send all the supplies of Ammunition and provisions you can with every body of troops coming this way."[19]

And it was a lot of supplies; Grant ordered "100 rounds of ammunition for 50,000 men and 100 rounds for all Artillery in the field." While ammunition could not be spared, Grant could, and did, change what food supplies came as he moved on: "Reduce the meat ration to one quarter to the whole ration of bread coffee and salt and . . . drop the sugar altogether." He also cautioned Hillyer not to let politics or bullishness get in the way of what was shipped to whom: "There has evidently been a great deal of pulling and hauling among Divisions to get the advantage in transportation."[20]

Water also became scarce as the army moved north in the dry days of May. "Roads are very dusty; middle of day hot, but mornings and evenings cool," Sherman reported. By May 10 McPherson, who was moving on the high ground between the river and creek, reported that "there are no streams on the road, and the troops have suffered some for want of water." He even admitted, "I had to be guided to-day in selecting camps somewhat by the chances of getting water." Sherman agreed, similarly reporting that he had "ridden forward a mile or so, and water is very scarce to Fourteen-Mile Creek."[21]

As had become custom by now, McClernand continued to allow his disposition to get the best of him. When one of Grant's staff officers carried a message to the corps commander to watch one of the Big Black River ferries they had passed, McClernand exploded, "I'll be —— if I'll do it—I am tired of being dictated to—I won't stand it any longer, and you can go back and tell General Grant!" The staff officer did, of course, but McClernand was not the only one having such outbursts: even McPherson could be susceptible in the growing nervousness brought on by the isolated campaign, and once told staff officer James Harrison Wilson that "he would be damned if he'd do any such thing." While Wilson was less dramatic with his friend McPherson, who was evidently having a bad day, he once challenged McClernand to a fistfight for cursing him, or so he claimed: "Although you are a major general, while I am only a lieutenant colonel, I will pull you off that horse and beat the boots off of you!" A much older McClernand wisely backed down and stated that he was not cursing him but simply "expressing my intense vehemence on the subject matter, sir, and I beg your pardon." Grant took the story in stride but did relate that he was going to get rid of McClernand the first chance he had; other than that, the episode merely gave the headquarters staff a chuckle. Thereafter, when anyone cursed around Grant's headquarters, they were said to be simply expressing their "intense vehemence on the subject matter."[22]

McClernand also continually griped about transportation, but Grant, either tiring of such foolishness or having no time to bother with McClernand's pettiness, wrote back firmly:

> I have passed one and a part of another of your divisions, and am satisfied that the transportation with them, to say nothing of the large number of mules mounted by soldiers, would carry the essential parts of five days' rations for the soldier, and Negroes now riding. You should take steps to make the means at hand available for bringing up the articles necessary for your corps. Equal facilities have been given each of the army corps in all respects, no special order having been given to favor any one, except to give the first 30 wagons to the Thirteenth Corps.

In another episode, McClernand was told to send a certain battery to Sherman's corps because it had six brigades across the river "and but four batteries, and all of them smooth-bore guns." Grant told McClernand to send the 1st Iowa Battery, which had been transferred to him from Sherman back at Milliken's Bend, but McClernand sent a different one. Grant calmly but quickly ordered McClernand to send the correct artillery unit as requested.[23]

It did not help the frayed nerves that everyone also wondered where the Confederate army was; Dana reported on May 4 that "General Grant is of the opinion that Pemberton will endeavor to bring on the decisive battle within the next ten days." Rumors abounded, with McClernand advising on May 8 that three Confederate deserters "report[ed] the enemy to be concentrating between the bluffs on the east side of Big Black and Bolton. Edwards Station is about the center of this line on the east side of the Big Black." McClernand most worried over "reports and what should be the policy of the enemy," and that once the army swept northeast toward the railroad, the enemy would "cross the Big Black in our rear, and isolate us by cutting our communications." He recommended covering the ferries by moving the army to the left, perhaps even transitioning to a western alignment instead of northern. Grant took the advice, but not to the extent of repositioning the army. He simply detailed individual regiments supported by cavalry to hold each river crossing in the rear. Other rumors indicated different Confederate intentions, such as letters found in the Auburn post office indicating that the enemy was stockpiling "many millions rations in Vicksburg for the siege." One rumor even noted that "some of the citizens in the vicinity of Utica say Beauregard is at or near Jackson."[24]

In the midst of all this, Fred managed to wander off on numerous occasions, but Grant seemed to be mostly unconcerned, knowing that he had tens of thousands of soldiers who would help look after him. Fred befriended a young orderly on Grant's staff, and the two boys seemed to get into more trouble than they should have. At one point they rode too far forward and stumbled on a house with several horses tied in front. They devised a plan to capture the riders who were inside but "not until we had gone too far to retreat did the idea occur to us that the would-be captors might possibly become the captured." The group turned out to be Federals, thankfully part of Sherman's signal corps scouting to the front. On returning, Fred noted, "We had some difficulty in convincing the pickets that we were entitled to pass."[25]

The unease of moving ever closer to the enemy was understandable. All expected a battle soon, and McPherson and Sherman were unhappy about the absence of their respective divisions (led by McArthur and Blair): "We want every available man in the field when the battle comes off, which cannot now be long delayed." Grant, on the other hand, displayed no anxiety, and Sherman realized it: "He is satisfied that he will succeed in his plan, and, of course, we must do our full share."[26]

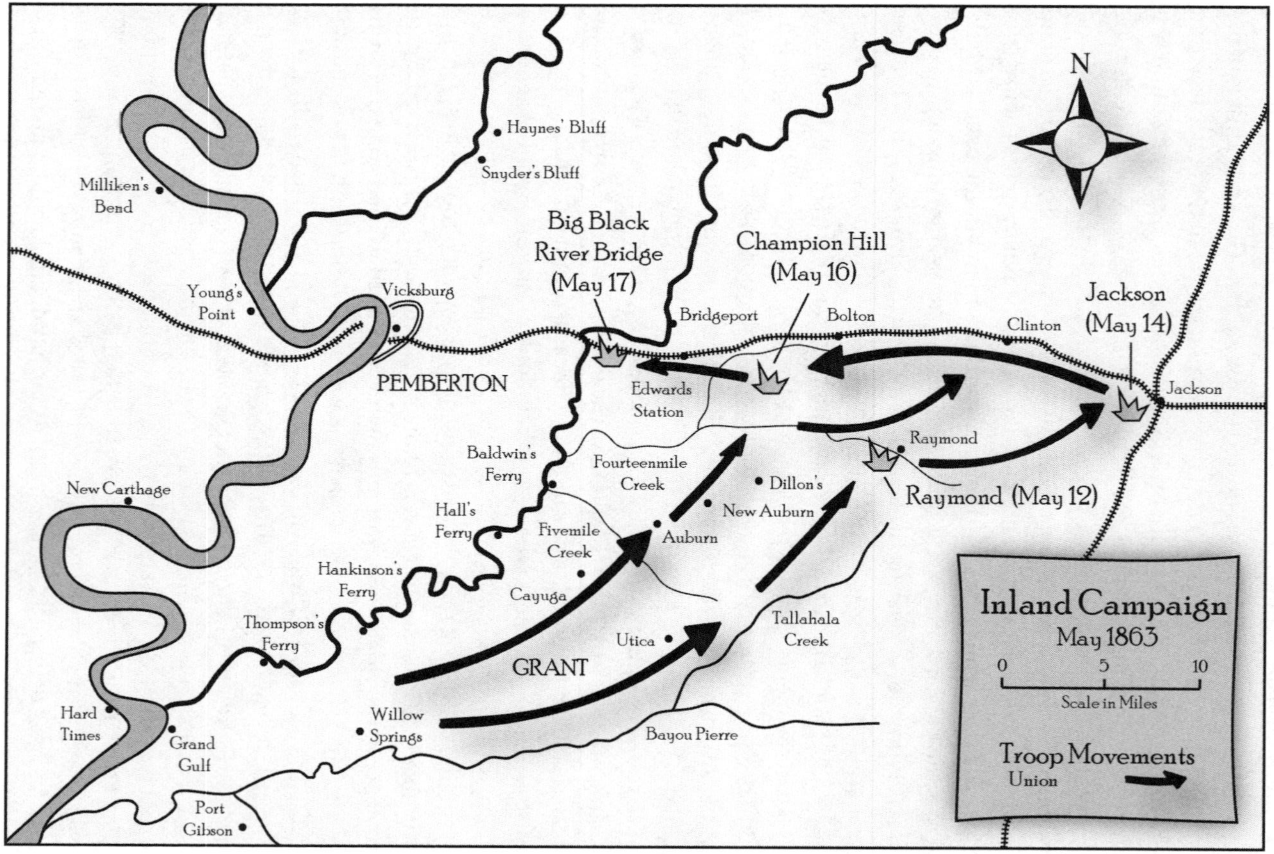
Inland Campaign
May 1863
0
5
10
Scale in Miles
Troop Movements
Union
N
Haynes' Bluff
Snyder's Bluff
Milliken's Bend
Young's Point
Vicksburg
PEMBERTON
Big Black River Bridge (May 17)
Champion Hill (May 16)
Jackson (May 14)
Raymond (May 12)
Bridgeport
Bolton
Clinton
Jackson
Edwards Station
Raymond
Baldwin's Ferry
Fourteenmile Creek
Dillon's
New Auburn
Auburn
Hall's Ferry
Fivemile Creek
Cayuga
Hankinson's Ferry
Thompson's Ferry
Utica
Tallahala Creek
GRANT
New Carthage
Hard Times
Grand Gulf
Willow Springs
Bayou Pierre
Port Gibson

III

Grant had been extremely fortunate since crossing the Mississippi River. He had been met at Port Gibson by a substantial enemy contingent, forcing him to fight a battle, but since then his forces had seen few Confederates as they quickly moved northeast toward the railroad in what historian Terry Winschel has labeled "Blitzkrieg, U. S. Grant Style." Anticipated resistance at Fivemile Creek did not materialize, but Grant could not expect that to remain the case. Grant's three corps were nearing the Fourteenmile Creek watershed, which provided ample places for the Confederates to resist. They were also nearing the Southern Railroad of Mississippi, which was Vicksburg's lifeline. While Grant, mostly accompanying Sherman's corps, had only rumors and spotty intelligence to go on, it seemed clear that the enemy would fight for the railroad at some point, and that point was drawing nearer.[27]

As expected, McClernand's advance cavalry met the enemy on May 11. They were in the Fourteenmile Creek valley, "in too strong force to allow the party to proceed farther," McClernand reported to Grant. Furthermore, "negroes informed the officer in command that the enemy intended to offer obstinate resistance at that creek." McClernand continued: "There is little or no water between here and Fourteen-Mile Creek; so we will probably have to fight for the water of that stream." Significantly, Grant's already underpowered cavalry was becoming worn out due to the heavy workload and dry surroundings.[28]

With success at some points and the lack (or mere rumors) of firm Confederate resistance, Grant planned to move on and take multiple crossings of Fourteenmile Creek on May 12. He wanted the moves to be more than just isolated, however, so he ordered McClernand forward on the left "so that your entire corps will arrive on the Fourteen-Mile Creek simultaneously and in a compact line. It is also important that your corps reach the creek at or about the time that Sherman's does." McClernand gave detailed instructions pertaining to where each division should go, but then added, "If in approaching the creek an engagement ensues, of course the different divisions of the Thirteenth Army Corps will be applied as circumstances may dictate." Skirmishing did develop that next day, but nothing major erupted on McClernand's front, despite Grant thinking it was the most dangerous area. He informed McPherson on the morning of May 12, "I will ride over to see you this evening, but I cannot do so until I know McClernand is secure in his position." McClernand, meanwhile, pushed on, easily taking the Whittaker

Ford crossing of the creek with Alvin Hovey's division. He sent a force forward on the road to Edwards, "thus holding the creek and the road beyond it." About the same time, Andrew Jackson Smith took and held Montgomery Bridge over the creek farther to the west without much resistance.[29]

The other two corps were moving toward Fourteenmile Creek as well. Sherman reported that "our men here are all healthy, and now make their marches regularly and without straggling." He took his Fourteenmile Creek front at Dillon's Plantation, although the enemy destroyed the bridges before he could get there. Meanwhile, McPherson moved toward the little village of Raymond just north of the creek where Grant hoped to find ample supplies. Grant told McPherson to "use your utmost exertions to secure all the subsistence stores that may be there [Raymond], as well as in the vicinity." He betrayed some unease, writing, "We must fight the enemy before our rations fail, and we are equally bound to make our rations last as long as possible." He reminded McPherson that "upon one occasion you made two days' rations last seven. We may have to do the same thing again." It was not quite that grim as yet, as Grant noted: "One train of wagons is now arriving, and another will come with Blair, but withal there remains the necessity of economy in the use of the rations we have, and activity in getting others from the country." While the food shortage was not yet a crisis, Grant certainly wanted McPherson to take advantage of any supplies he found at Raymond.[30]

In a total surprise, McPherson did not find any supplies at Raymond as Grant had hoped. Instead, he found an enemy brigade under John Gregg. McPherson was shorthanded—he had sent Colonel Clark Wright's 6th Missouri Cavalry, which normally led the corps, to cut the railroad some twenty miles to the east. John Logan's division was thus the first to encounter the enemy as it approached Fourteenmile Creek south of Raymond. The stubborn Confederate force put up such a fight that McPherson had to deploy Marcellus Crocker's division as well, and for hours the battle raged amid the heat and dust of the creek valley. Finally, McPherson was able to push the enemy back, but the battle at Raymond had much larger ramifications on Grant's army than the mere numbers would indicate.[31]

Grant, who had been with Sherman in the center much of the day on May 12, had planned to make his final push to the railroad the next day, sending orders for Sherman to "strike the railroad between Bolton and Edwards Station." But the sounds looming from the east were ominous. "McPherson is undoubtedly in Raymond and has had, from the amount of firing heard, a hard fight," Grant informed McClernand. As of this point, the overall plan was still in place, Grant said, adding that McPherson "will also move on to the railroad toward Bolton," but he noted that this plan could change once he found out the details of the Raymond encounter. Meanwhile, in order to keep the enemy confused, Grant wanted McClernand to provide a bold front to the west, the direction the main Confederate body was apparently located. "Edwards Station is evidently the point on the railroad the enemy has most prepared for receiving us. I therefore want to keep up appearances of moving upon that place, but want to get possession of less guarded points first. You will, then, move to-morrow, to keep up this appearance, a short distance only from where you now are."[32]

Even with his basic plan in place, Grant continued to improvise. Because of McPherson's "severe fight of several hours, in which we lost from 400 to 500 killed and wounded," he informed McClernand, Grant was now more aware of the possible threat from the east. Ironically, McClernand had alerted Grant of threats from the east as early as May 3, and McPherson also reported rumors of a Confederate concentration: "It is rumored, but with how much truth I have not been able to ascertain, that heavy re-enforcements are coming to the enemy from Jackson to-night, and that we may expect a battle here in the morning." The rumors turned out to be true, and with an unknown Confederate force appearing from that direction, Grant now had to worry about more than just his left near Vicksburg and the Big Black River. He had to deal with at least some Confederate force in the east, evidently based out of Jackson, the state capital, and he did not know its strength. If Grant plunged headlong into the area between them, he could be caught between two enemy forces of unknown size. Grant obviously had to account for the new threat, so he changed his plans while at his headquarters at Dillon's Plantation.[33]

Without much recourse other than to neutralize any opposition in what would be his rear when he reached the railroad and turned west toward Vicksburg, Grant decided to go in full force in the opposite direction to capture Jackson, removing it as an area from which the Confederates could hamper him. "I have determined to follow," Grant continued as he described the Confederate retreat to Jackson, "and take first the capital of the State." He later reported, "I therefore determined to make sure of that place and leave no enemy in my rear." Then, Grant noted, he could "work from there westward." Despite the obvious need, the plan had drawbacks. Moving east would leave his rear uncovered against the Confederate force operating around Edwards Station. Likewise, moving east, as Grant put it, "uncovered my own communication." As a result, it was here, Grant later wrote, that he fully "cut loose altogether from my base," and one admirer later described how "it was like Cortez burning his ships." Although trains guarded by Blair's division were then on the way from Grand Gulf, as well as another guarded by a brigade of McArthur's division, no more trains would leave Grand Gulf thereafter. "I then had no fears for my communications," Grant wrote, "and if I moved quickly enough could turn upon Pemberton before he could attack me in the rear."[34]

Grant thus put into action his original plan, but included in it the quick move east toward Jackson. He had already issued orders for different movements, but they were, he wrote, "annulled by new ones." He informed Halleck of the change by a courier who rode "to Grand Gulf through an unprotected country." Grant's new orders called for McPherson to move north to the railroad at Clinton the next morning, May 13, but then instead of turning west and meeting the enemy near Edwards Station, he would turn east and take Jackson. At the same time, Sherman was to move to Raymond and follow the direct route to Jackson, coming in from the southwest while McPherson came in from the northwest. To cover the rear of the two corps while they were marching east, McClernand was to move three divisions of his corps north across Fourteenmile Creek toward the enemy, keeping his attention, while Smith's division was to stay at Old Auburn and await the arrival of the wagon train heading inland with Blair's division of Sherman's corps. Despite the explicit orders, McClernand still had questions; he wrote a subordinate that "the general is inexplicit as to the detachments guarding Baldwin's Ferry, but I cannot believe that he instructs that they should be left behind and exposed to the danger of capture or dispersion."[35]

Minor confusion aside, the corps commanders put the plan into action the next day, May 13. Grant himself moved his headquarters to Raymond and then farther north. According to plan, McClernand blustered in front of the enemy near Edwards Station on May 13 while Sherman and McPherson had their backs turned to the enemy. McClernand sent most of his corps north of Fourteenmile Creek and then three divisions west toward Edwards Station and across Bakers Creek, which flowed into Fourteenmile Creek. At one point, McClernand's troops approached within two and a half miles of Edwards, although some delay occurred due to a destroyed bridge over Bakers Creek. Having made his show, McClernand then withdrew the divisions back toward Raymond and Bolton, skirmishing lightly with the enemy but worrying over "trouble in effecting so delicate a movement with my flank and rear both exposed to attack." Grant was actually appreciative, later writing that McClernand performed his job "with much skill and without loss."[36]

With their rear covered, and with McClernand positioned to hold the rear as well as support either wing of the forces moving on Jackson, McPherson and Sherman, with Grant along, rushed east for the capital. McPherson reached Clinton at 3:00 P.M. on May 13 and was ordered to move to Jackson the next morning. Sherman was given the same orders, and he told his soldiers matter-of-factly, "The men and officers must keep their posts. Thirst and fatigue are to be expected, but the safety and success of all will make all good soldiers bear cheerfully the deprivation of rest and water. . . . Our corps must be first in the breach, but must be compact and strong." Mother Nature soon intervened in the operation, however: "the rain fell in torrents all the night before and continued until about noon of that day," Grant wrote, "making the roads at first slippery and then miry."[37]

All the while, new information continued to come in, allowing Grant the freshest possible intelligence. Early on May 14, for example, McPherson reported at 5:30 A.M. that "General Crocker's division is all on the march for Jackson. General Logan's division is just stretching out on the road. I have had a regiment of infantry and Logan's pioneer company, under charge of my engineer and General Logan's destroying the railroad." But the big shock was what came next. "General Joe Johnston is in Jackson," McPherson continued, "and it is reported they have 20,000 men. I do not think there is that many, though they have collected considerable of a force. They have fortified on the different roads on this side of town, and are forming abatis."[38]

For all the rumors of a strong force and major commander, the capture of Jackson was instead a minor military affair. Only a few Confederates contested the advance once it started after the rain ended on the afternoon of May 14, mostly on McPherson's front as he moved east along the railroad. Grant rode with Sherman's troops to the south, actually coming under fire at one point in a thick wood. Staff officers yelled that they were firing at Grant, but Grant bolted into the woods directly toward the firing. The staff, along with Fred, followed closely and the enemy fled. Grant took possession of a house nearby and Sherman joined him there when the corps arrived, the two generals directing the movements from the porch until a portion of Sherman's men broke under fire and the two mounted and reformed them. Later, Grant personally led a flanking movement to the southwest, which met no opposition, allowing Sherman to walk into town.[39]

Caught up in the glory, Fred again got loose and rode directly into Jackson. He moved so fast that he later recalled how "the Confederate troops passed me in their retreat." Fred was wearing blue but admitted that "I was so splashed with mud, and looked generally so unattractive, that the

Confederates paid no attention to me." It did make him think later, though: "I have since realized that even had I been captured it would not have ended the war." Nevertheless, Fred was rewarded for his haste; he saw the stars and stripes raised by Cornelius Cadle above the capitol dome and even went into the governor's office, where he confiscated a pipe from the desk.[40]

Grant had easily taken Jackson, and soon met his victorious corps commanders Sherman and McPherson in the hotel next to the state house. There, he informed the generals of his army's progress and ordered troops to get to work to destroy roads and rail lines, making the city unfit as a transportation center and neutralizing it to the point that no threat could emanate from it. Sherman's troops did most of the work: "The destruction of the roads will be extended out as far as possible, and must be complete. The rails and ties will be taken up and placed in stacks, and the ties set on fire, in order to warp the rails and so render them unfit for use. Dispatch is of the utmost importance." With Jackson in Sherman's sufficient hands, Grant consequently turned his attention back to the west, toward Vicksburg and more importantly toward the main enemy army defending it.[41]

Grant's main concern was evident from his orders. He sent McPherson west and left Sherman in Jackson only long enough to destroy the transportation there. His major concern was McClernand's front, and Grant soon informed him that "it is evidently the design of the enemy [Johnston] to get north of us, and cross the [Big] Black River and beat us into Vicksburg. We must not allow them to do this. Turn all your forces toward Bolton Station, and make all dispatch in getting there. Move troops by the most direct road from wherever they may be on receipt of this order." He also advised McClernand that Sherman and McPherson would follow him, leaving only enough troops to destroy Jackson's transportation arteries. Grant also sent word for Frank Blair, who was guarding the approaching wagon train from Grand Gulf, to move his division forward and join the army.[42]

If Grant had thought the Confederate defense would stiffen when he reached the railroad or even when he threatened the state capital, he was mistaken. But now that he was oriented westward and beginning to move toward Vicksburg itself, something was bound to happen. He kept cavalry to the front to scout, and the 6th Missouri Cavalry of McPherson's corps, which was in Bolton, reported increasing signs of Confederate activity. "Reports are fully ripe that the enemy are in strong force at Edwards Depot," McClernand informed Grant on May 14. Grant would soon find out that the rumors were true.[43]

IV

Even in the midst of such major campaigning when one would have thought that Grant would let administrative tasks slip, the general carried on a muted form of correspondence on matters only indirectly related to the military movements. On May 9, for instance, Grant had to correct brigade commander Michael K. Lawler for paroling prisoners and releasing them. He reminded him that such actions did not meet the terms of the Dix-Hill Cartel, which labeled any parole not at the designated points null and void. "Besides this prisoners running loose throug[h] our camp is giving the enemy an advantage which they pay men for risking their lives to obtain. I want no more liscenced spies within our lines."[44]

Prisoners were indeed a problem, and growing more so by the battle. Nonetheless, the wounded were an even greater difficulty. Grant frequently left hard-hit units on the battlefield to police the area and care for their wounded while he moved on with the main army. At times, Grant sent teams of wagons to retrieve the wounded and communicated with Confederate commanders about getting his wounded out. "My only desire," he wrote, "is to know that there is no unnecessary suffering among the unfortunate wounded."[45]

Fortunately, Grant's health remained strong. He wrote Julia on May 9, "I am very well camping in the forest of Mississippi"; he also notified her that Fred was fine too. Grant even took time at one point to rest. Spending the night in Jackson on May 14, Grant and Fred stayed in the Bowman Hotel, in the same room Joseph E. Johnston had used the night before. He briefly made his headquarters at the next-door state house.[46]

Grant did not have to deal much with the local population. "People all seem to stay at home and show less signs of fear than one would suppose," he wrote Julia amid the marching and fighting. "These people talk a greatdeel about the barbarities of the Yankees but I hear no complaints where the Army has been of even insults having been offered." Most people just wanted to escape. Correspondent Sylvanus Cadwallader told of meeting a group of schoolchildren who had been turned out "on account of the approach of our army." Upon the troops' arrival the children "took to the fence corner thickets, like a covey of quail." Their teacher was a Northern woman, who like many citizens of this area had migrated from upstate New York (hence the many town names such as Cayuga, Utica, etc.). She begged to be sent home, and Grant obliged her after warning that she was on her own and would probably not meet anything but men along the route north on the other side of the river. She took the offer anyway. Others could only ask for guards on their property. "By far the greater number were left to the tender mercies of Confederate friends," Cadwallader reported.[47]

Grant could at times also be firm, such as when he and Sherman visited a factory in Jackson, which was amazingly still producing cloth despite the quick abandonment of the city by the government and the fighting that had raged on the outskirts. "Our presence did not seem to attract the attention of either the manager or the operatives, most of whom were girls," Grant noted. The generals watched for a while as the workers produced cloth marked C.S.A. Eventually, Grant turned to Sherman and told him they "had done work enough." Sherman quickly sent the workers home with all they could carry, and the building and cotton soon went up in flames.[48]

V

"Move your command early to-morrow toward Edwards Depot," Grant wrote McClernand on May 15, "marching so as to feel the force of the enemy, should you encounter him, and without bringing on an engagement, unless you feel entirely able to contend with him." Because of Grant's wise positioning, McClernand was "already one day's march from there [Jackson] on their way to Vicksburg." If everything went right, Grant would hopefully have the river city in a few days.[49]

May 15 saw Grant's campaign nearing its climax. He probably had no grasp of what historians would see 150 years later, but he was cognizant that he and his army were nearing the critical phase. For one, the supply situation was tenuous; although trains were due to arrive out of Grand Gulf in rear of the army, no more were to be put on the road. Grant had now been in Mississippi for fifteen days, and it was paramount that he reach a place where a secure line of communication and supply could be established. Fortunately, he was nearing that point. The closer he came to Vicksburg the closer he would also come to the Yazoo River. Haynes' and Snyder's Bluffs had always been the problem points, but now he had them outflanked and once they were occupied, the Federal navy and transports could easily deposit more than ample supplies for the army operating against Vicksburg.

But the real issue was that, as Grant moved west, he was coming closer to the Confederate army defending Vicksburg. Reports indicated that the army was not inside Vicksburg itself but actually east of the Big Black River near Edwards. As Grant neared Edwards, he was also nearing the main enemy force. A large and important battle was bound to take place in the near future, one that would possibly determine the campaign. The fighting at Port Gibson, Raymond, and to an extent at Jackson had been tough, but these clashes were not campaign-swaying affairs. Had Grant been defeated in any of them, disaster could possibly still have been averted. But now the pitched battle between the majority of both forces was looming, and if defeated here, Grant might be hard pressed to recover. In fact, the Union army might find it difficult to survive, deep as it was in Confederate territory between two enemy forces and without a secure line of reinforcement and supply. Grant might even perish himself. On the other hand, if Grant could win a decisive victory over the Confederate army defending Vicksburg, he might be able to walk right in to the river city. Grant wrote Sherman early on May 16, "I have evidence that the entire force of the enemy was at Edwards Depot at 7 P.M. last night, and was still advancing. The fight may, therefore, be brought on at any moment. We should have every man in the field."[50]

Grant was well situated for the climactic battle. Positioning his corps in a line extending southward from the railroad near Bolton, he intended to approach Edwards and the Confederate army on a broad front with massive force. "McClernand faced about and moved promptly," he later wrote. Hovey's division moved the next day, May 16, on the Jackson Road from Bolton. McPherson's two divisions followed him. A middle road existed between the Jackson and Raymond Roads, and McClernand positioned Peter J. Osterhaus's and Eugene A. Carr's divisions there. On the Raymond Road to the south, Smith's division moved west, followed by Blair's newly arrived division of Sherman's corps. Sherman's men who stayed behind to finish up with the destruction of Jackson's railroads also moved west; Sherman was impatient to get the job done so he could rejoin the army for the climactic fight.[51]

Grant told McClernand, "You will therefore disencumber yourself of your trains, select an eligible position, and feel the enemy." Even then, significantly, Grant stipulated, "Don't bring on a general engagement till we are entirely prepared." McClernand informed his commanders that "the movement will be toward Edwards Station, with the purpose to feel the enemy and engage him if it be found expedient to do so. Let each division keep up communication with that or those next to it, and all move on parallel with each other as near as may be." Feeling the rush of battle and chance for glory, McClernand self-interpreted the orders to make sure his corps's division under Smith left its encampments on the Raymond Road before Blair's, so that McClernand's corps would lead the march on all three roads.[52]

What lay ahead of these divisions was unknown. McClernand informed Grant on May 15 that a captured letter placed the Confederate strength at forty thousand and the Federal army at seventy thousand. The next morning as McClernand neared the enemy and began to pick up prisoners, the captives estimated the Confederate strength at between fifty and sixty thousand. McClernand soon found the main body, not just rumors. He reported to Grant that morning that Hovey, on the Jackson Road, "finds the enemy strongly posted in his front, showing two pieces of artillery at the distance of some 400 yards." Hovey also picked up indications of a large force farther south, causing those Federals on the Jackson Road to wonder if they had not "passed a large force toward Raymond, and to our rear." That was exactly where Smith's and Blair's divisions were, so any move could conceivably be handled. McClernand thus inquired of Grant, "Shall I hold, or bring on an engagement?"[53]

Grant was on the Jackson Road early on the morning of May 16, having spent the night at Clinton, but he quickly surmised that something momentous was happening; indeed, Grant was getting firm intelligence that the campaign was reaching its climax. Earlier, a spy purposefully kicked out of Memphis by Hurlbut "with a good deal of parade" brought a note from Johnston he was supposed to carry to Pemberton, ordering him to attack Grant at Clinton. Then, two railroaders who had been through Pemberton's army during the night relayed the estimated size and position of the Confederate forces. "I naturally expected that Pemberton would endeavor to obey the orders of his superior," Grant wryly noted later, but that was not the case. Pemberton at the time was actually marching away from Grant's army trying to cut the Federal transportation line that no longer existed. Grant quickly sent orders hurrying McPherson and Sherman westward, telling McPherson, "You will, therefore, pass all trains, and move forward to join McClernand." Grant rode forward as well, spurred by a message from McPherson: "I think it advisable for you to come forward to the front as soon as you can." Evidently, McPherson was writing in response to a visit from McClernand, who seemed dead set on finally commanding the army while Grant was not on site. Finding out all he could as he traveled, Grant soon began to get a better picture, telling McClernand around 10:15 A.M., "From all information gathered from citizens and prisoners, the mass of the enemy are south of Hovey's position. McPherson is now up with Hovey, and can support him at any point." Yet Grant seemingly did not have enough information to fully commit to battle, reporting later that "I would not permit an attack to be commenced by our troops until I could hear McClernand, who was advancing." He told

McClernand to "close up all your forces as expeditiously as possible, but cautiously. The enemy must not be allowed to get to our rear." Meanwhile, the skirmishing soon "amounted almost to a battle," Grant later wrote.[54]

The battle soon expanded along the Jackson Road as Hovey advanced, supported by McPherson's two divisions, first Logan's and then Crocker's. The Federals swept up the high ground and drove the enemy from Champion Hill itself back to the crossroads where the Jackson and Middle Roads met. Evidently, Grant became caught up in the fighting on his front and forgot to send word to McClernand to press the attack; it was only 12:35 P.M. when Grant sent McClernand orders: "As soon as your command is all in hand, throw forward skirmishers and feel the enemy, and attack him in force if an opportunity occurs. I am with Hovey and McPherson and will see that they fully co-operate." Unfortunately, McClernand was on the Middle Road, and it took time for the message to get to him and then for him to react. In the meantime, the Confederates brought reinforcements from their right near the Raymond Road and drove Hovey's troops back from the crossroads and hill, almost splitting the force on the Jackson Road. Crocker, who was sick, barely arrived in time with his brigades to stem the tide and push the Confederates back toward Bakers Creek, retaking the hill and crossroads even as Grant himself waded into the fighting. Meanwhile, because of the delay in communication, little combat occurred on the Middle and Raymond Roads, for which Grant severely and perhaps incorrectly faulted McClernand when he wrote his memoirs.[55]

Grant himself was in the middle of the fighting, mostly keeping his headquarters at the Champion house on the flatland just north of the hill. There, the Confederate counterattack by Grant's former neighbor John Bowen came altogether too close for comfort before being driven back. Grant ranged out along the lines at other times, including to the right where he noted and praised the work of Logan's troops: "Go down to Logan and tell him he is making history to-day," Grant told a staff member. Logan was moving forward across a road that neither he nor Grant knew was the Jackson Road. "Neither Logan nor I knew that we had cut off the retreat of the enemy," Grant later wrote, but he unwittingly ordered Logan back to support the more pressed divisions around the hill itself and the Confederate counterattack. Grant later complained in his memoirs that "had McClernand come up with reasonable promptness, or had I known the ground as I did afterwards, I cannot see how Pemberton could have escaped with any organized force." Significantly, Grant never moved toward his left in the direction of McClernand.[56]

As it turned out, the fighting on the Jackson Road and at the crossroads was enough to cripple the enemy, which retreated haphazardly southwest toward the only available crossing point of Bakers Creek, on the Raymond Road. While a small force on that road thwarted Smith's and Blair's timid advance, the rest of the Confederate army escaped either across the creek or to the south. By dark, the Confederates were mostly in rapid flight west toward the Big Black River, and by Grant's personal order McClernand's divisions were in pursuit. It had not been a complete victory, but Champion Hill had been decisive. Grant had met the main enemy force and had thrashed it. "I am of the opinion that the battle of Vicksburg has been fought," Grant wrote Sherman that night.[57]

Grant was not about to let up, however, and he personally directed Carr to pursue with his division. In the same note to Sherman, he added, "We must be prepared . . . for whatever turns up." Grant had the enemy on the run, and he followed quickly. He sent much of McClernand's corps directly west with McPherson and left a staff officer near Bolton to route Sherman's just-arrived troops north to Bridgeport to cross the Big Black River there. Grant hoped to outflank any Confederate defense of the river with Sherman's movement, although Blair's division from the main army, detached to rejoin Sherman, actually beat him there by an hour or so. Grant pursued ahead of the army himself, riding that night until "finding ourselves alone we stopped and took possession of a vacant house." There Grant waited but no troops came up, so he decided to go back. After a mile or so, he met the head of the approaching column, and there, without tents, he occupied the "porch of a house which had been taken for a rebel hospital and which was filled with wounded and dying who had been brought from the battle-field we had just left." Grant was amazed at how "while a battle is raging one can see his enemy mowed down by the thousand, or ten thousand, with great composure; but after the battle these scenes are distressing, and one is naturally disposed to do as much to alleviate the suffering of an enemy as a friend."[58]

Fred was also out front, at one point reaching a hospital where Confederates were being attended. "They were not feeling very friendly toward the Yankees," he later wrote, ". . . and I passed on." Later, several Federals tried to capture him before they found out who he was. Suddenly, their hate turned to shouts of "three cheers for young Grant," and Fred admitted, "I began to feel more comfortable." Later, he stayed with his father that night. Fred years afterward marveled at how "even after the great battle and victory of that day, and with the expectation and cares of another battle on the morrow, [Grant] was, as ever, most considerate of the comfort and welfare of his young son."[59]

Grant had no such mercy for the enemy. He had McClernand's command on the march at daylight the next morning, May 17, but soon ran into Pemberton's army again. The enemy contested the Big Black River crossing, as Grant suspected they would, at a line about a mile east of the crossing of the Jackson Road and railroad. Grant wanted to hold the enemy in place and allow Sherman to get in their rear. He informed Sherman, "I will endeavor to hold the enemy where he is, to give you time to cross the river, if it can be effected." He also wanted to gain multiple crossing points for the main body of his army, adding that "the moment the enemy begins to give way, I will endeavor to follow him so closely that he will not be able to destroy the bridge."[60]

Grant laid out his plans well, and Sherman, to whom Grant ordered the only pontoon train in the army, assured him on May 17 at midday that "you may count on my being across in three hours." Even Sherman was gaining confidence with every hour, now writing, "Shall I push into the city, or secure a point on the ridge?" Grant was feeling an even greater wave of excitement, especially with the renewal of fighting on May 17. The enemy held a line east of the river and bridge, but an attack by Lawler's brigade of Carr's division, followed by the rest of the corps, quickly ousted them. The Federals captured sixteen hundred prisoners and nearly twenty guns as the fleeing Confederates burned the railroad bridge. Despite a wound to division commander Osterhaus, the May 17 battle of Big Black River Bridge was a great victory for Grant's troops. A clear path toward Vicksburg was now in view in the wake of the retreating and broken Confederate army. Grant showed his excitement by telling Sherman to "secure a commanding position on the west bank of Black River as soon as you can," adding that "if the information you gain after crossing warrants you in believing you can go immediately into the city, do so. If there is any doubt in this matter, throw out troops to the left, after advancing on a line with the railroad bridge, to open communications with the troops here. We will then move in three columns, if roads can be found to move on."[61]

Even during these most climactic and exciting moments of the campaign, Fred caused Grant consternation, though Grant later wrote that Fred "caused no anxiety either to me or to his mother." The freedom Fred enjoyed led to a close call for him at the Big Black River Bridge. Fred had ridden there, and a Confederate on the opposite bank shot at him and managed to slightly wound him in the leg. Fred went down, convinced he was dead; he shouted to Grant staff officer Clark Lagow, who quickly arrived: "I am killed." Lagow told the boy to wiggle his toes, and it was clear that nothing was broken. Lagow then "recommended our hasty retreat," which they accomplished.[62]

Grant also had to worry about his own, mostly political, well-being, because right in the middle of the fighting a courier (Grant later remembered it being a general officer named William Dwight) arrived with a note from Halleck via Banks ordering Grant to cooperate with the army in Louisiana. Grant told him that "the order came too late, and that Halleck would not give it now if he knew our position." The courier protested, rising up on his toes in exasperation. At that exact moment, however, Grant heard "great cheering to the right of our line and, looking in that direction, saw Lawler in his shirt sleeves leading a charge upon the enemy." Grant mounted and rode away. He later added, "And saw no more of the officer who delivered the dispatch; I think not even to this day." Still, Grant was smart enough to know how to mend fences, and quickly informed Halleck that he had heard Banks was off in Louisiana: "I could not lose the time," he said. Fortunately, Grant had some leeway; Halleck biographer John F. Marszalek has noted that Halleck often gave his generals the final say on all orders from so far away, lecturing that since they were there and he was not, they had the right of decision.[63]

Nevertheless, Grant was in a strong military and political position, although he came under fire, both literally and for his decisions, on occasion. When he rode the night of May 17 over to Sherman's position at Bridgeport, where the latter had laid the pontoon bridge made of "India-rubber boats," Grant let some of his early war overconfidence creep in again. Sherman described how "we sat on a log, looking at the passage of the troops by the light of those fires; the bridge swayed to and fro under the passing feet, and made a fine war picture." Grant was thinking. "The enemy have been so terribly beaten yesterday and to-day that I cannot believe that a stand will be made unless the troops are relying on Johnson's arriving with large re-enforcements, nor that Johnston would attempt to re-enforce with anything at his command if he was at all aware of the present condition of things." Grant was so confident that he boasted to Sherman that he would "either have Vicksburg or Haynes' Bluff to-morrow night."[64]

Haynes' Bluff was one thing, and it was indeed possible to have possession by the end of May 18. On the other hand, Vicksburg was not to come so easily. In fact, much more work would be necessary before he could take possession of the hill city itself.

Ulysses S. Grant. After a rocky start in the war, Grant became a national hero with his success at Vicksburg. He continued his success for the rest of the war, finally reaching the highest office in the land.

All images courtesy of the Library of Congress.

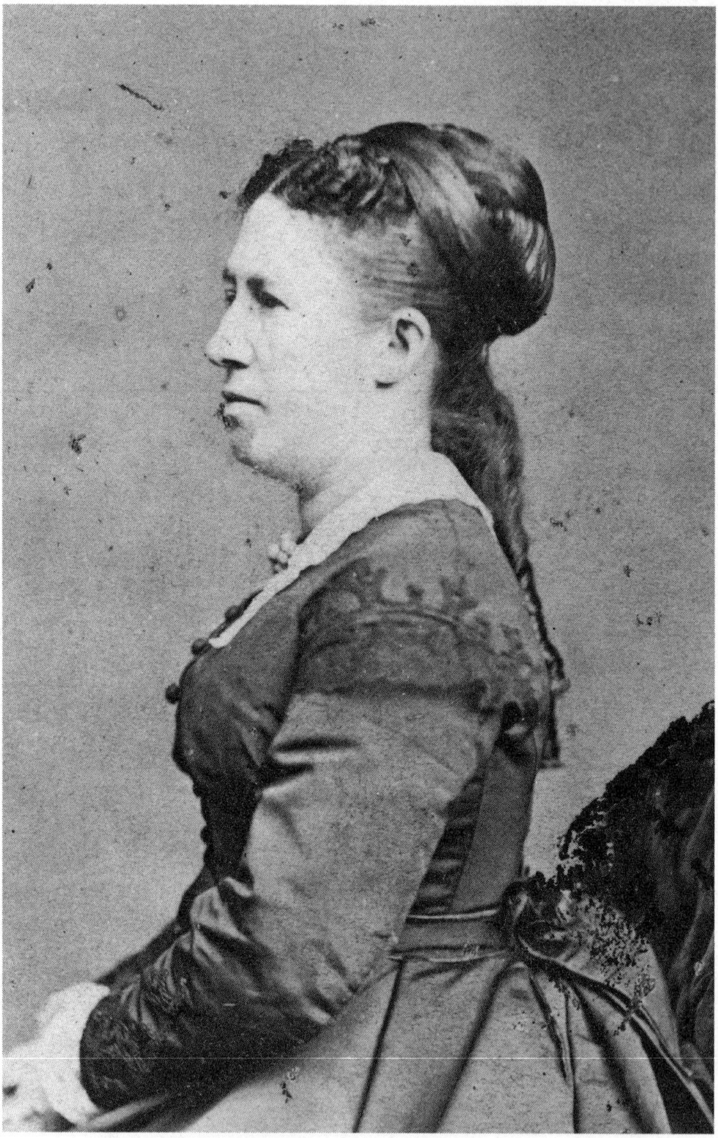

Julia Dent Grant. Grant's wife, Julia, was his cornerstone during the Vicksburg Campaign, taking care of all the family business and giving him a family outlet from his administrative and military duties.

Frederick Grant. Grant's twelve-year-old son Fred (seen here in later life) accompanied his father during much of the Vicksburg Campaign, giving the general a personal family connection amid all the fighting. Fred was wounded at Big Black River Bridge.

Jesse Grant. Out for any monetary gain, Grant's father, Jesse, became a problem for the general as he attempted to administer his department. That Jesse did not get along with Julia did not help.

Abraham Lincoln. One of President Lincoln's most important decisions during the war was keeping Grant in command in the Mississippi Valley. Many called for Grant's relief, but Lincoln stuck with him and won large dividends in the process.

Edwin M. Stanton. As secretary of war, Stanton oversaw much of Grant's administrative, political, and military efforts.

Henry W. Halleck. Formerly Grant's superior in the Mississippi Valley, Halleck served as general in chief during the Vicksburg Campaign. He was a frequent correspondent with Grant during the fighting.

Nathaniel P. Banks. Banks, Grant's co-commander in the Mississippi Valley, operated to the south near Port Hudson. He was not especially helpful or cooperative, viewing his own efforts as more important than Grant's.

David Dixon Porter. As Grant's naval co-commander, Porter was open to whatever Grant requested. His agreement to run the batteries at Vicksburg was a key in the successful campaign.

Lorenzo Thomas. As adjutant general, Thomas came to the Mississippi Valley with discretion to relieve Grant if he thought it necessary. Fortunately for Grant and the United States, he chose not to do so.

John A. McClernand. As Grant's most senior corps commander, McClernand was also his most problematic. Grant finally had to relieve the politician general during the siege.

Edward O. C. Ord. Although of solid ability, Ord had none of McClernand's political clout. He nevertheless replaced the politician during the siege.

William T. Sherman. Despite being against the final push to Vicksburg by way of Bruinsburg, Sherman was Grant's closest friend and most trusted corps commander. Grant placed him in charge of the rear during the siege, where Grant feared a Confederate relief attempt.

Frederick Steele. Steele was a solid division commander who took charge of Sherman's corps when the latter took command of the rear defense. Steele ably commanded the corps for the remainder of the siege.

James B. McPherson. Despite his youth and inexperience, McPherson was a Grant favorite and protégé. Even so, Grant took care to make sure he had the safest tasks during the campaign.

Stephen A. Hurlbut. Although not at the actual scene of major operations, Hurlbut commanded one of Grant's corps in north Mississippi and west Tennessee. His diversions were a major reason why Grant was so successful.

John A. Rawlins. Often referred to as Grant's conscience, Rawlins was a close friend and confidant to the general. They had known each other since their Galena, Illinois, days, and he served Grant well.

Benjamin H. Grierson. One of the most spectacular events of the campaign came when Grierson led a small cavalry brigade through Mississippi, disrupting communications and supply but more importantly turning Confederate attention from Grant's crossing of the Mississippi River.

John C. Pemberton. Grant largely outgeneraled Pemberton, the Confederate commanding officer at Vicksburg. It did not help that the Confederate commander was torn between conflicting orders from his president and theater commander.

Joseph E. Johnston. Although not even in the state, Johnston, Pemberton's theater commander, had plenty of advice for Pemberton. Once he arrived in Mississippi, he showed none of the decisiveness he had earlier recommended.

Shirley House. One of the great wartime photographs, this image shows the Shirley House on the Vicksburg siege lines.

CHAPTER SIX

"TO CARRY VICKSBURG BY ASSAULT"

"I am not in any way authorized to say so," Admiral David Dixon Porter wrote Hurlbut in Memphis on May 18, "but my opinion is that General Grant should be re-enforced with all dispatch, and with every man that can be sent him from all directions. He will have the hardest fight ever seen during this war. The attention of the nation should now be devoted to Vicksburg." Porter was worried, and he was not the only one, just perhaps the one closest to the scene. The farther out from Vicksburg that officials were, the more panicky they became. Hurlbut in Memphis, for example, wrote Halleck telling him that Southern papers were reporting that "heavy reinforcements are moving on General Grant from South Carolina, Georgia, and Tennessee." Two days later he wrote, "This city (Memphis) is full of rumors of disaster to General Grant."[1]

Other reports also indicated that a major disaster had befallen the Federal army, including one stating that as many as thirty thousand Confederates were reinforcing Johnston, who had fought Grant and "had taken large number of prisoners." The fear of Johnston's arrival shook officials as high as the War Department in Washington. Halleck informed William S. Rosecrans and Ambrose Burnside, "Dispatches just received say that General Joe Johnston, with a considerable force, has left Tennessee to re-enforce Vicksburg." He warned of Confederate raids to hide this transfer and recommended offensives to counter them. It seems that Grant's campaign was causing worry on both his own side and the enemy's. Even Abraham Lincoln pondered news gleaned from Confederate papers about Grant's progress in Mississippi.[2]

In the midst of all these negative rumors, a few optimistic ones appeared as well. Some spoke of positive events such as Vicksburg having been evacuated. Grenville Dodge at Corinth wrote, "It was said . . . that Pemberton was a traitor, and had sent a bouquet to Grant, so arranged as to give position of rebel troops." In the midst of the land campaign, Hurlbut also wrote, "We in the rear, and the country behind us, are watching with unspeakable pride the glorious track of the Army of the Tennessee. Every sort of congratulation for the glory already won, and the crowning victory to come."[3]

In reality, the only person who knew the real story was Grant himself, and he was doing just fine. By May 18 when he made his headquarters at Evans's Plantation three miles west of the bridge across the Big Black River, and when many of the rumors and worries were circulating hundreds and thousands of miles away, Grant had actually defeated the enemy five times in the previous seventeen days. Even better, the two victories over the past two days at Champion Hill and Big Black River were almost crushing in nature. Now, the enemy was hastily withdrawing back into Vicksburg's defenses, leaving all outlying areas to Grant's forces. Many of these places, such as Warrenton, were important and had been a thorn in Grant's side for months, but the chief prize was to the north. Grant planned to take possession of what he hoped was an evacuated Haynes' and Snyder's Bluffs. "My first anxiety was to secure a base of supplies on the Yazoo River above Vicksburg," he later wrote. Grant even rode on ahead of the army with Sherman ("Sherman was equally anxious," Grant noted) to see if Haynes' Bluff had indeed been evacuated; they even rode as far forward as the "advanced skirmishers." Taking these areas on the Yazoo River, which Grant had been trying to secure for months now, would provide the Federals with access to a waterborne outlet, which the navy and transports could easily use to ferry supplies to the army. Grant consequently sent Porter a request to "please send a boat up to Haynes' Bluff, which I think is evacuated. Our cavalry have gone up to see."[4]

Haynes' Bluff was indeed evacuated, and Grant must have known that this was the clincher; now he could supply his army indefinitely, outlasting any Confederate defense of Vicksburg. Grant could also see into Sherman's mind: "In a few minutes Sherman had the pleasure of looking down from the spot coveted so much by him the December before on the ground where his command had lain so helpless for offensive action." Sherman was all smiles, and profusely praised Grant. "He turned to me," Grant later remembered, "saying that up to this minute he had felt no positive assurance of success. This, however, he said was the end of one of the greatest campaigns in history and I ought to make a report of it at once. Vicksburg was not yet captured, and there was no telling what might happen before it was taken; but whether captured or not, this was a complete and successful campaign."[5]

It was indeed a significant moment. Provisions had always been Grant's major concern during the inland campaign, and while the soldiers had been forced to stretch rations, they were now holding a supply base that could quickly be filled to the brim with every conceivable necessity. Grant, in fact, considered it the key to victory. He had maneuvered to get to the high ground east of Vicksburg, fighting his way there, and now he had taken possession of the critical supply area. With full supplies and reinforcements, Grant could do just about anything he desired at Vicksburg. Despite all the rumors, Grant was making great progress. "I have sent for forage and supplies to be sent to Lake's Landing at the mouth of Chickasaw bayou," he wrote in mid-May. Now, it was just a matter of hours before supplies would arrive and roads would be opened to the landing.[6]

I

Although he had won major victories over the last two days and Haynes' Bluff was in his hands, Grant was not about to let the enemy regain any momentum. He wrote Porter about how shocked the enemy must be: "We beat them badly on the 16th, near Edwards Station, and on the 17th, at Black River Bridge, taking about 6,000 prisoners, besides a large number killed and wounded. Two [actually only one] divisions were also cut off from their retreat, and have gone eastward, many of their men throwing down their arms and leaving. The enemy only succeeded in getting back three pieces of artillery." To keep the enemy on the run, Grant pressed his three corps forward early on May 18. Sherman's troops, by that time, had moved to Bridgeport where Blair's wayward division rejoined him. He pressed forward across the river after the pontoon bridge was emplaced and, by direction of Grant himself at a crossroads, moved on the right of the army toward Vicksburg, taking firm possession of Haynes' and Snyder's Bluffs. Later while watching Steele's division deploy on the far right of the Vicksburg enclave, Grant and Sherman came under fire from the enemy, one ball hitting a man directly beside them.[7]

McPherson and McClernand moved as well, although the Confederates had destroyed the bridge at the Big Black River. Grant later wrote that "but for the successful and complete destruction of the bridge, I have but little doubt that we should have followed the enemy so closely as to prevent his occupying his defenses around Vicksburg." Despite the failure, the troops began to fashion "floating bridges" near the burned railroad bridge site, with McPherson creating a pontoon bridge of cotton bales and Thomas Ransom felling trees from both banks and planking them with whatever material could be found nearby. McPherson moved across the bridge above the railroad and marched in the center along the Jackson Road, while McClernand moved along the Jackson Road as far as Mount Albans, where he was to find an alternate route to the south. Grant cautioned his commanders to move quickly, ordering them to leave behind all wheeled vehicles "except ambulances and ammunition wagons." Grant made his headquarters that night at Cook Plantation, just a few miles from Vicksburg.[8]

Even in the midst of the climactic approach to the hill city, Grant kept a gentle heart for the enemy population in the area through which he was marching. During one incident, Grant and his staff passed a woman flagging them down in front of a tattered cabin. Grant sent an aide back to see what she wanted, and he returned with news that she and her husband were Northerners who had moved south just before the war, that her husband was sick, that they were very poor, and she just wanted to welcome the Federals. Grant rode back to meet the woman and then continued westward. After a few miles he suddenly turned to his staff and ordered that a guard be placed at the home. He rode on again, but after a few more miles he suddenly hesitated again and ordered a surgeon to go back to see to the sick man. Grant stopped yet again after a few more minutes and ordered supplies taken to the house. At the same time, Grant could also be firm. While stopping at a house to get water, Fred remembered how the "Confederate proprietress expressed her opinion scornfully, that we could never take Vicksburg." Her declaration was evidently based on the paltry number of troops she saw at the time, as the head of the column was just arriving. Grant simply noted that he "would capture Vicksburg if it took thirty years to do so." Just then the column burst over the crest of a ridge, and the woman "retired, much chagrined."[9]

Grant also began to bring in reinforcements. Jacob Lauman's division of Hurlbut's Sixteenth Corps had just arrived at Young's Point from Memphis, and Grant originally intended for it to go south and cross at Grand Gulf, with Grant stipulating that one of his least favorite brigade commanders, Isaac Pugh, garrison Grand Gulf itself. With the enemy having moved back into Vicksburg, Grant ordered the division instead to Haynes' Bluff: "General Grant is investing Vicksburg, and directs that all troops and gunboats come to his assistance immediately up the Yazoo." Those who had made it south of Vicksburg on the western side of the river were to use "forced marches" if necessary. Likewise, McPherson had nearly an entire division, McArthur's, garrisoning Grand Gulf. Now that it looked like Haynes' Bluff would be the army's supply depot and Pugh would soon garrison there, Grant called McArthur north. McArthur marched up the road through Warrenton toward Vicksburg's southern flank.[10]

Grant also wanted the navy ready to help, and he communicated with Porter. "My forces are now investing Vicksburg," he wrote on May 19. He told Porter where the forces would be located and asked, "If you can run down and throw shell in just back of the city, it will aid us, and demoralize an already badly beaten enemy." Sherman also communicated with Porter, at one point requesting fire and adding, "I would get General Grant to make this request, but he is far on the left flank and it would take hours to find him." Grant was indeed along the lines, mainly near the unguarded left, confident that Vicksburg would surrender in a day or two. He even wrote a brigade commander left at Champion Hill to bring all prisoners forward and send them to Young's Point "if we are not in possession of the city when they arrive."[11]

Despite Grant's confidence, there was one obstacle in the way of an easy capture: a strong line of forts connected by heavy rifle pits guarding every route into Vicksburg. What to do next was the main question. The normal procedure for this type of offensive was a siege operation, which all the graduates of West Point understood. Such action would take time, as a line would have to be established to hem in the enemy. Then, formal approaches would have to be started, with saps and tunnels moving toward the enemy lines. Only once the siege lines and approaches reached a sufficiently short distance from the enemy lines could an assault have a great chance of succeeding. Grant's army had by this time mostly accomplished the first goal, that of fanning out to encircle Vicksburg, although he was not able to fully do that because of a lack of troops. Grant reported that "the three army corps covered all the ground their strength would admit of, and by the morning of the 19th the investment of Vicksburg was made as complete as could be by the forces at my command." Still, simply fanning out did not necessitate the use of siege operations, which would be long and arduous, and possibly not even needed.[12]

Grant hated to use up all that time on siege operations if it was not totally necessary. Plus, spending weeks if not months on siege efforts brought back into play Johnston's forces to the east. Yes, Jackson had been removed as a threatening supply position for any attempt to relieve Vicksburg, but Grant had not garrisoned the capital, and thus the Confederates could reestablish the city as a support base for Johnston if Grant dallied too long in front of Vicksburg. Other factors influenced Grant's thinking as well. His belief that the enemy was so badly demoralized and that they "would not make much effort to hold Vicksburg" was at the forefront of his mind. Thus, he entertained the possibility of storming the works and taking Vicksburg sooner rather than later. It might be bloody, but it also might save lives in the end if he could avoid a formal siege and more huge battles, perhaps with Johnston. In addition, Grant's political and personal affairs would be greatly affected by the success or failure of this campaign, and the sooner he succeeded the better. With so much depending on the reduction of the citadel and opening the river, Grant made one of the most important decisions of the campaign: to assault the Confederate entrenchments. While the various corps continued to file into position around Vicksburg, even on the morning of May 19, Grant sent out orders: "Army corps commanders will push forward carefully, and gain as close position as possible to the enemy's works until 2 P.M. At that hour they will fire three volleys of artillery from all the pieces in position. This will be the signal for a general charge of all the corps along the whole line."[13]

Grant was confident of success. He added, "When the works are carried, guards will be placed by all division commanders, to prevent their men from straggling from their companies." Grant was intent on ending the campaign that had started some six months ago by nightfall of that day, May 19.[14]

II

Unfortunately for Grant, reality did not cooperate with the timetable. He had been in this situation before in February 1862, although then it was the weather that would not cooperate with him. He had wanted to march after his victory at Fort Henry to Fort Donelson, but he had to wait nearly a week before he could begin marching. He had learned patience since then, a trait that continued to grow as he toiled through the months of little success in getting to Vicksburg. But this patience failed him miserably on May 19.[15]

Grant hoped the three Union corps would be in position by early afternoon to launch their single major attack and finish the campaign. Yet few if any of McClernand's and McPherson's corps brigades were in front of Vicksburg and on line ready to attack at the appointed hour. Grant noted that "the Thirteenth and Seventeenth Army Corps succeeded no further than to gain advanced positions covered from the fire of the enemy." Those that did make it were so small in number that it would have been suicidal to attempt to assault the Vicksburg works with them. In addition, such a late arrival left little time to reconnoiter and find the best avenues of advance. As a result, McClernand and McPherson did not participate in the scheduled 2:00 P.M. assault in any major way.[16]

Only Sherman's corps northeast of Vicksburg had arrived with any strength by that time. He began to unfold his three divisions as they approached Vicksburg, with Steele moving toward the river to cut off any escape route in that direction. The brigades of this division fanned out north of Mint Spring Bayou and began to examine the ground and take firm positions. Blair's division took position next to, or on the left of, Steele, where the Confederate line curved from a northern orientation to facing east. At the apex of the

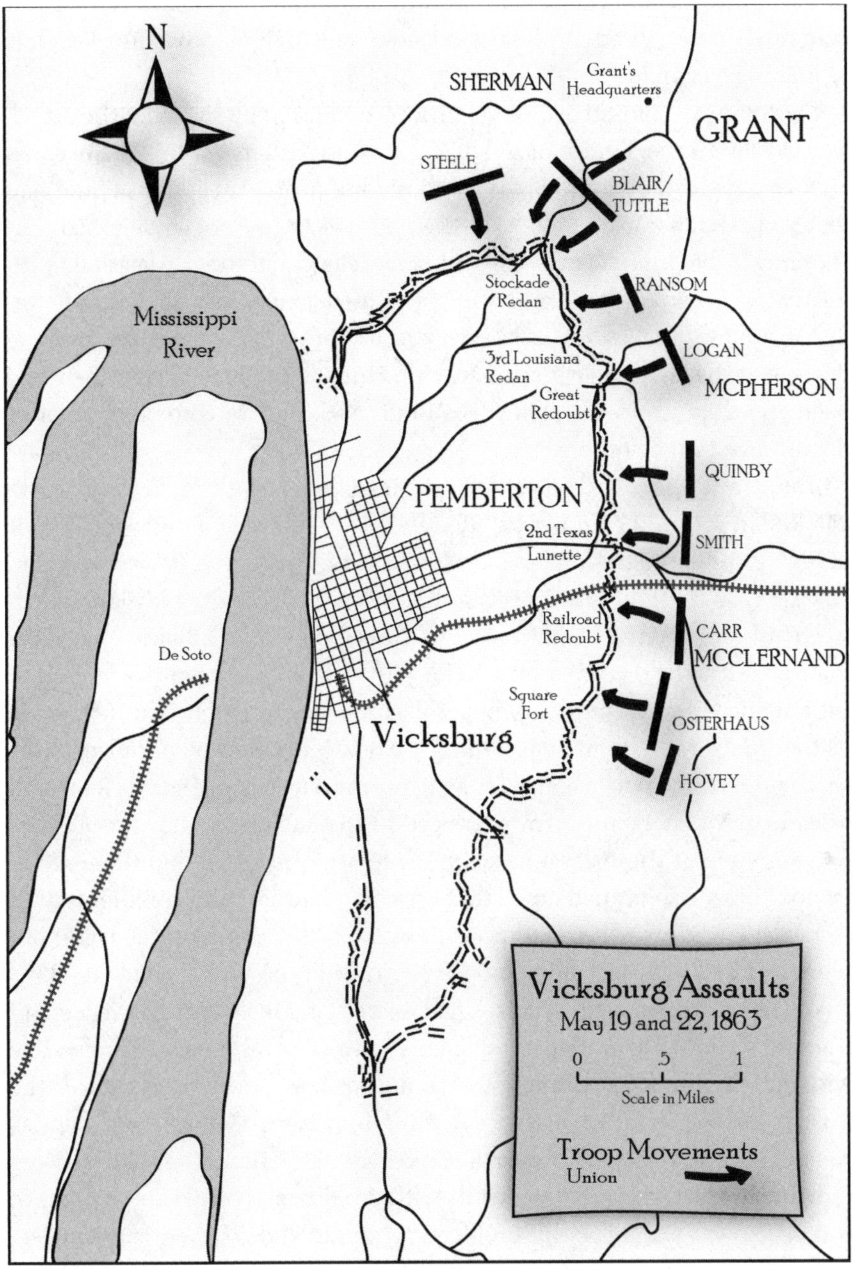
N
SHERMAN
Grant's Headquarters
GRANT
STEELE
BLAIR/ TUTTLE
RANSOM
Stockade Redan
Mississippi River
3rd Louisiana Redan
LOGAN
Great Redoubt
MCPHERSON
QUINBY
PEMBERTON
2nd Texas Lunette
SMITH
Railroad Redoubt
CARR
MCCLERNAND
De Soto
Square Fort
OSTERHAUS
Vicksburg
HOVEY
Vicksburg Assaults
May 19 and 22, 1863
0 .5 1
Scale in Miles
Troop Movements
Union

curve was a large fortified complex sitting on the Graveyard Road called the Stockade Redan, because a portion of the defenses included a stockade wall on the northern face. Most of the work was an earthen V-shaped redan that contained infantry and artillery. It looked strong to the approaching Federals of Blair's division.[17]

Sherman had only these two divisions emplaced by the time the attack was to commence; James Tuttle's brigades were still marching in. Sherman attacked anyway. In doing so, he shattered many preconceptions Grant had fostered. The major one was that the Confederates were so dejected that they might fold immediately. Instead, they defended their fortifications with gusto. Unknown to Grant and Sherman, the defenders of the Stockade Redan, primarily the 36th Mississippi, had not been part of the Confederate debacle of the last few days at Champion Hill and Big Black River. They had been guarding Haynes' and Snyder's Bluffs and thus were not as tired or as demoralized as the others.[18]

The attacking Federals also found the terrain to be formidable. The Stockade Redan sat on the Graveyard Road, which ran along a narrow corridor of high ground separating forks of Mint Spring Bayou that flowed west and Glass Bayou that initially flowed south. Deep and shielding lowlands with steep hillsides covered the entire face of the complex. Blair's division made the main attack along the Graveyard Road, with Thomas Kilby Smith's brigade to the left and Giles A. Smith's to the right, supported by Hugh Ewing's brigade farther to the right. John Thayer's brigade of Steele's division performed isolated supporting maneuvers across Mint Spring Bayou, and Thomas Ransom's brigade of McPherson's corps advanced to the left across the fork of Glass Bayou. None of these assaults were successful, however, and the Federal troops became so pinned down that Sherman had to wait until nightfall to retract his command. Grant himself observed the action on the right, but there was little else he could do once he saw that the assaults had failed.[19]

Grant probably wished that he had exercised a little more patience and waited for his full army. He had chosen not to do so, and now he had to live with the consequences. Grant tried to put a positive spin on the action. At the least, it had been a reconnaissance in force, indicating that the Confederates were not going to be easily overtaken. At the same time, the soldiers were growing impatient as well, especially with the slow arrival of supplies. Grant was of course working on this problem: "The 20th and 21st were spent in perfecting communications with our supplies," he wrote a few weeks later. "Most of the troops had been marching and fighting battles for twenty days, on an average of about five days' rations drawn from the commissary department," he wrote. "Though they had not suffered from short rations up to this time, the want of bread to accompany the other rations was beginning to be much felt." To illustrate, as Grant rode the lines in the days after the assault, he heard a soldier in a low voice call out "Hard Tack." He remembered that "in a moment the cry was taken up all along the line, 'Hard Tack! Hard tack!'" Grant knew the troops had suffered for lack of bread on the campaign, but told them that "we had been engaged ever since the arrival of the troops in building a road over which to supply them with everything they needed." Grant marveled that "the cry was instantly changed to cheers." He also noted that by the night of May 21, "all the troops had full rations issued to them. The bread and coffee were highly appreciated." Other items were also welcomed, such as tents and cooking utensils.[20]

Grant had to decide what to do next. The idea of siege always loomed in his mind, but he was not quite ready to bow to that necessity. He still thought an all-out assault might be successful, ending the campaign in days rather than the weeks or months a siege would require. Consequently, he opted to assault again, this time after a couple of days of major preparation and when the entire army was in position to participate. Such a delay would also give plenty of time to open the supply base at Haynes' Bluff and thoroughly feed the men and restock ammunition. Grant set the assault date as May 22.[21]

Much of the prodding for another assault came from McClernand. The politician general seemed to have quieted down during the land campaign, but now that Federal troops had enveloped Vicksburg, he began to interfere again. Not all of it was his fault. He and Grant often just could not understand each other. McClernand had earlier been confused when Grant did not indicate what to do about the Big Black River fords prior to Champion Hill; McClernand had decided to remove the garrisons himself. On the march from the Big Black River on May 18, McClernand had to write Grant, asking, "You say take a parallel road if I find one; I suppose you mean to divide my forces on two roads, if I can. If I am mistaken, please correct me." Later, McClernand ordered Alvin Hovey's division up from the Big Black River when Grant, not through McClernand, had ordered Hovey to stay. All McClernand had been told was that a brigade was to stay at the river bridge. Finally, Hovey himself had to write Grant for clarification.[22]

McClernand began inching forward after the initial assault on May 19, perhaps prodding Grant to try again on May 22. Having missed the earlier fighting, McClernand was eager to get involved and wrote McPherson on May 20, "I propose to make a charge upon the enemy's lines within an hour or two"; he requested McPherson's aid in guarding the corps's right flank. The assault never came, perhaps because McPherson alerted Grant and Grant stopped it, but McClernand actively felt out the enemy works nonetheless. He informed Grant, "I am close up to the enemy's works all along my line. Have lost in killed and wounded a number of men to-day, but have silenced most all the guns in my front." Then he added, "I propose to assault the enemy's works in the morning, and have made arrangements with that view." Even Charles Dana became caught up in the proposed assault, writing Washington on May 20, "Probably the town will be carried to-day."[23]

Grant would not allow the assault to take place on May 21, but he was thankful for the intelligence he received from McClernand, who reported "a formidable line of earthworks, chiefly square redoubts or lunettes, connected together by a line of rifle-pits, and the whole line in a very commanding position." He also mentioned rumors of a second and third line behind the first. With such a formidable enemy position, McClernand backed away from attacking on May 21, informing Grant, "I do not think the position can be carried with our present extended lines." He counseled massing for an attack on a small front and punching a hole in the enemy lines, or else "perhaps, a siege becomes the only alternative."[24]

Grant continued with plans to assault on May 22, cautioning his commanders to watch for a breakout attempt in the meantime, possibly at night. Grant also wanted the navy involved as much as possible, writing Porter on May 21, "I expect to assault the city at 10 A.M. to-morrow. I would request, and earnestly request it, that you send up the gunboats below the city and shell the rebel intrenchments until that hour and for thirty minutes after." He also requested the mortars to fire throughout the night: "I would like at least to have the enemy kept annoyed during the night."[25]

By May 22, Grant was ready to try again. "My arrangements for drawing supplies of every description being complete," Grant reported, "I determined to make another effort to carry Vicksburg by assault." He had weighed the pros and cons thoroughly and believed that another assault would work and that it was warranted. In his report in early July, he enumerated the reasons. One was that it might just succeed, which would alter the entire course of the campaign and relieve the need for a long siege with all its attendant dirty work. Another was that Grant knew that Johnston was gathering a force to his rear and would soon attack him if matters were not concluded soon. Moreover, taking care of Vicksburg immediately would allow Grant to turn and fight Johnston, "securing to ourselves," Grant wrote, "all territory west of the Tombigbee, and this before the season was too far advanced for campaigning in this latitude." Other important reasons included not requiring heavy reinforcements, which would have to be sent to him, allowing them to be used elsewhere that summer. There was a morale factor as well. The troops probably would not put the required effort into digging the necessary fortifications for a siege if they were not convinced that a siege was the only option.[26]

Orders went out to the three corps commanders, and Grant, to be sure, called them together as well for personal instructions. "A simultaneous attack will be made to morrow at 10 A.M. by all the army corps of this army." He even had them coordinate their watches with his: "All the corps commanders set their time by mine, that there should be no difference between them in movement of assault." Grant ordered them to use the rest of May 21 to reconnoiter the ground and move infantry and artillery to commanding positions near the enemy lines. An artillery bombardment was to begin early the next morning, with the infantry drawn up "in columns of platoons, or by a flank if the ground over which they may have to pass will not admit of a greater front." The lightly burdened troops, each carrying only a canteen, ammunition, and one day's rations, were to step off promptly at 10:00 A.M. with bayonets fixed and not fire "until the outer works are carried." Grant ended the orders with a reminder of the importance of the assault: "If prosecuted with vigor, it is confidently believed this course will carry Vicksburg in a very short time, and with much less loss than would be sustained by delay. Every day's delay enables the enemy to strengthen his defenses and increases his chance for receiving aid from outside."[27]

Others were confident as well, with Sherman issuing orders to his corps that "as soon as the enemy gives way, he must be pushed to the very heart of the city, where he must surrender." He also reminded the troops to follow the retreating enemy "at their heels, and not permit them to rally in an interior work." Sherman ended his message, "We must have Vicksburg, and most truly have we earned it by former sacrifices and labors."[28]

III

Federal artillery pounded the Confederate lines prior to the scheduled 10:00 A.M. assault, and the Southerners responded, at one point almost hitting Grant himself. A shell landed close by as he talked with Logan, and Fred later described how the general was "covered with yellow dirt thrown up by the explosion." With the decision made and the action set in motion, Grant moved to the center of the line so he could be within range of all his commanders and could see much of the assaults himself. "I had taken a commanding position near McPherson's front," he noted in his report, "and from which

I could see all the advancing columns from his corps, and a part of each of Sherman's and McClernand's."[29]

Grant picked certain units to make the assault, because, as he noted, "each corps had many more men than could possibly be used in the assault over such ground as intervened between them and the enemy." He ordered Blair's division, the same troops who assailed the Stockade Redan on Sherman's front, to make the assault this time on the Graveyard Road. Giles and Thomas Smith's brigades supported Ewing and even filed off to the side to launch their own assaults. As on May 19, Ransom's brigade of McPherson's corps advanced as it connected with Sherman's troops. But just as on May 19, none of the attacks on the Stockade Redan were successful.[30]

To the south, McPherson also launched assaults on both sides of the Jackson Road against the 3rd Louisiana Redan. Logan's division undertook the assault, with Isaac Quinby's (who had returned to the army and replaced the sick Crocker) to the left in case the lines were broken. John E. Smith led his brigade forward on the north side of the Jackson Road while John D. Stevenson attacked to the south, with Mortimer Leggett's brigade in support. The assaults also failed here, although they reached the parapets in front of the Confederate works.[31]

McClernand made three separate attacks, the first one against the 2nd Texas Lunette on the Baldwin's Ferry Road. William P. Benton's brigade of Carr's division and Stephen Burbridge's brigade of Andrew Jackson Smith's division hit the Confederate works south of the road but were unable to make any more progress than Sherman and McPherson's troops did. Farther to the south, Osterhaus's troops, supported by a brigade of Hovey's division, assaulted the Square Fort but could not take it. The only thing close to a breach came in the area between Carr's and Smith's attack to the north and Osterhaus's to the south where Michael Lawler's brigade of Carr's division and William J. Landram's brigade of Smith's division assaulted the Railroad Redoubt. A few Union troops managed to push through and enter the Confederate stronghold, but these were quickly stopped. It was the only success of Grant's May 22 assaults.[32]

Unfortunately, this paltry achievement was enough for McClernand to send Grant a message that he had broken through and desired support. Grant had by this time moved over toward Sherman's forces to get closer to the action. The commander responded that McClernand should employ some of his unused troops, but McClernand had not kept any troops in reserve, and a second message, arriving just as Grant was conferring with Sherman on the right, stated "positively and unequivocally that he was in possession of and still held two of the enemy's forts; that the American flag waved over them, and asking me to have Sherman and McPherson make a diversion in his favor." Grant was disinclined to believe McClernand after all the trouble he had caused him over the course of the campaign, and he blurted out, "I don't believe a word of it." Sherman, who was with Grant, argued, however, that they could not afford to quit now if McClernand had had any success. Still wary, Grant ordered Sherman to renew his attacks, which Sherman did about 2:00 P.M., and then rode back to McPherson to get him restarted as well. On the way a third message from McClernand arrived, and then a fourth. Back at his original position where he could see McClernand's troops, although not well enough to refute McClernand's claims, Grant still doubted any success, writing in his report that "the position occupied by me during most of the time of the assault gave me a better opportunity of seeing what was going on in front of the Thirteenth Army Corps than I believed it possible for the commander of it to have. I could not see his possession of forts nor necessity for re-enforcements." All the same, Grant could not "disregard his reinterated statements, for they might possibly be true; and that no possible opportunity of carrying the enemy's stronghold should be allowed to escape through fault of mine." New areas of assault were consequently added, with Steele's division of Sherman's corps on the far right attacking on John Thayer's front; Tuttle's division likewise renewed the offensive on the Stockade Redan. Quinby's division struck near the 2nd Texas Lunette, but without success. Most notably, McClernand was unable to build on his limited success either, and Dana lambasted him to Washington: "McClernand's report was false, as he held not a single fort, and the result was disastrous."[33]

Grant considered relieving McClernand on the spot because of the misinformation. Sylvanus Cadwallader had observed the assaults and later informed Grant of the lack of breaching the enemy lines; "I was questioned closely concerning it," he later wrote, "and shall never forget the fearful burst of indignation from Rawlins, and the grim glowering look of disappointment and disgust which settled down on Grant's usually placid countenance, when he was convinced of McClernand's duplicity, and realized its cost in dead and wounded." Grant had just about had enough, and he had the authority to do whatever he wanted. Dana had been sending regular reports of McClernand's incompetence to Washington, and these evidently resounded in the capital. On May 5, Stanton had written Dana, "General Grant has full and absolute authority to enforce his own commands, and to remove any person who, by ignorance, inaction, or any cause, interferes with or delays his operations. He has the full confidence of the Government, is expected to enforce his authority, and will be firmly and heartily supported; but he will be responsible for any failure to exert his powers. You may communicate this to him." Because of the distance, the message did not arrive until Grant was in Jackson, and he had stuck the message in his pocket to save it for later. Now that McClernand had made a major error, the only question was when to remove him.[34]

Dana reported to Washington on May 24 that "yesterday morning he [Grant] had determined to relieve General McClernand, on account of his false dispatch of the day before . . . , but he changed his mind, concluding that it would be better on the whole to leave McClernand in his present command till the siege of Vicksburg is concluded, after which he will induce McClernand to ask for leave of absence. Meanwhile he (General Grant) will especially supervise all of McClernand's operations, and will place no reliance on his reports unless otherwise corroborated." Dana could not help but add, "My own judgment is that McClernand has not the qualities necessary for a good commander, even of a regiment."[35]

The renewed fighting bothered Grant mainly because it produced so many more casualties. He later told an associate that Cold Harbor was essentially a mistake, but that "I have always regretted also allowing McClernand to continue his attack on the works at Vicksburg."[36]

By nightfall on May 22 it was obvious that assaulting the Confederate works would not provide the anticipated victory. Grant simply wrote in his report that "the assault was gallant in the extreme on the part of all the troops, but the enemy's position was too strong, both naturally and artificially, to be taken in that way. At every point assaulted, and at all of them at the same time, the enemy was able to show all the force his works would cover." Historian J. F. C. Fuller has criticized Grant for his mode of attack: "Every possible preparation was made, and it might well have succeeded, had not Grant committed the error, which he repeated the following year in the Wilderness and at Cold Harbor, of ordering a simultaneous assault all along the line, in place of overwhelming the tactical points by artillery and rifle fire, and assaulting in between and then turning by the flank." In Grant's defense, he did not assault along the entire line, and it was McClernand who actually assaulted on the widest front, leaving few reserves to exploit his "breakthrough."[37]

Still, Grant had now tried a full assault and had only casualties to show for it. While he would not launch a third assault as yet, he still could not admit that siege operations were necessary. In a note to Porter that night, he wrote that "the assault at 10 A.M. was not successful, although not an entire failure. Our troops succeeded in gaining positions close up to the enemy's batteries, which we yet hold, and, in one or two instances, getting into them." Grant now cast about trying to find anything that might work short of a siege. He added to Porter, "If the gunboats could come up and silence the upper water battery and clear the southern slope of the second range of hills from the Yazoo Bottom, it would enable Sherman to carry that position, and virtually give us the city." But soon, the realist in Grant came to realize that there was perhaps no other way to win Vicksburg short of a siege: "I now find the position of the enemy so strong that I shall be compelled to regularly besiege the city." He requested that Porter "give me all the assistance you can with the mortars and gunboats." He later added, "Let me beg that every gunboat and every mortar be brought to bear upon the city."[38]

Others had their own ideas. Porter noted that McArthur south of Vicksburg on the Warrenton Road faced no opposition at all, and "if he will assault these forts, with the aid of the gunboats, he will take them all." McClernand was also not shy in recommending what should be done, writing on May 22, "I still think that to force the enemy's works we will have to mass a strong force upon some one or two points of his defenses." He also was not shy about minutiae, even deciding where to place troops who were not in his corps. Grant of course would make up his own mind, although he did not know quite yet what to do. McClernand that night tersely noted to his division commanders that "orders from the general commanding the department are awaited, and will probably control the operations of to-morrow." There was even some talk of night maneuvers, but nothing ever materialized. Sherman, for his part, began to build fortifications and talked of building "a sap [that] may be made to reach the right bastion, and it may be we can undermine and blow it up." While Sherman and his men were much too tired from fighting all day to do more that night, it seemed that Sherman had at least resorted in his mind to siege operations. All could see the need for haste in whatever was done, however. Porter wrote Grant, "Hope you will soon finish up this Vicksburg business, or these people may get relief."[39]

Indeed, Grant was already starting to envision some of the ramifications of his failure to assault and the need for a long siege. A couple of weeks later, he wrote his father:

> I do not look upon the fall of Vicksburg as in the least doubtful. If however I could have carried the place on the 22d of last month I could by this time have made a campaign that would have made the state of Mississippi almost safe for a solitary horseman to ride over. As it is the enemy have a large Army in it and the season has so far

> advanced that water will be difficult to find for an Army marching besides the dust and heat that must be encountered. The fall of Vicksburg now will only result in the opening of the Miss. river and demoralization of the enemy. I intended more from it. I did my best however and looking back can see no blunder committed.[40]

Grant, of course, held the decision in his hands alone, and he took a couple of days to study the situation even as he corresponded with Pemberton over a truce that would allow for the burial of the dead and care for the wounded; a two-and-a-half-hour "suspension of hostilities" occurred at 6:00 P.M. on May 25 for that purpose. Dana reported that the bodies "caused his [Pemberton's] garrison great annoyance by their odor. He probably also hoped to gain information." Grant indicated some of his thinking in a note to Porter on May 23, writing, "There is no doubt of the fall of this place ultimately, but how long it will take is a matter of doubt. I intend to lose no more men, but to force the enemy from one position to another without exposing my troops." Such a policy became firm orders when he told corps commanders, "Any further assault on the enemy's works will for the present cease. Hold all the ground you have acquired; get your batteries in position, and commence regular approaches toward the city." By this time, Haynes' Bluff had become the supply depot and, although McClernand on the far left initially drew supplies from Grand Gulf and Warrenton, Grant informed him, "There are plenty of supplies at Chickasaw Bayou Landing. Direct your commissary to get up full rations for your men, and your ordnance officer full supplies of ammunition."[41]

Grant had ultimately, if slowly, come to the only conclusion he could: as he later described it, he had to "outcamp the enemy."[42]

IV

Grant had to attend to bureaucratic issues even during the major fighting. Not knowing how the news of the failed assaults would be received in Washington, he softened the blow by telling Halleck that the losses were small, rationalizing that "our troops were not repulsed from any point, but simply failed to enter the works of the enemy." He also blamed McClernand, whose "dispatches misled me as to the real state of facts, and caused much of this loss." He took the opportunity to rail against McClernand, writing Halleck that "he is entirely unfit for the position of corps commander, both on the march and on the battle-field. Looking after his corps gives me much more labor and infinitely more uneasiness than all the remainder of my department."[43]

Grant also seemed to grow increasingly worried about his rear areas and sent cavalry to "observe closely every movement of the enemy, who are reported to be assembling an army in the vicinity of Brownsville." He ordered the cavalry to destroy corn "as far as you can possibly reach" and to drive in all cattle that could be used to feed the Confederates. Of particular concern was the area east of the Big Black River in the direction of Jackson. If it could be put back into service, the city would be a staging area for a Confederate attempt to relieve Vicksburg. Grant was also concerned about the northeast corridor between the Yazoo and Big Black Rivers. At times cavalry, of which Grant had far too few, even made forays north across the Yazoo River to disperse the enemy and gather livestock. The navy helped in these efforts as well.[44]

Grant frequently asked that Grierson's cavalry be returned to him from Banks, although the latter would not oblige. Grant also called in cavalry from other areas of his department, telling Benjamin Prentiss at Helena, "The taking of Vicksburg is going to occupy time, contrary to my expectations when I first arrived near it." He thus needed cavalry to watch his rear and requested Prentiss to send all he could spare, and to include infantry with it if possible. He also asked Hurlbut in Memphis to send a heavy cavalry force toward Grenada to take some pressure off his rear.[45]

Grant's mind was occupied with the politics of his choices as well, especially after he had disregarded the order to aid Banks at Port Hudson. Grant wrote a lengthy letter on May 25 apprising Banks of the situation and sending a staff officer to fill him in. He told Banks that he was confident: "I now have Vicksburg invested, and draw my supplies from the Yazoo above Vicksburg, and from Warrenton below the city. I feel that my force is abundantly strong to hold the enemy where he is, or to whip him if he should come out." He also noted, "The greatest danger now to be apprehended is that the enemy may collect a force outside and attempt to rescue the garrison." He wrote that a force was reported nearby to the northeast but that his patrolling cavalry was far too small; he again asked that Grierson be sent back to his department. Grant concluded that Vicksburg was the key position and that "the rebels set such a value upon the possession of a foothold on the Mississippi River, however, that a desperate effort will be made to hold this point." Once again, Grant asked Banks to send any and all troops he could spare to his aid.[46]

Yet Grant still remained upbeat. To Halleck he confided, "The enemy are now undoubtedly in our grasp. The fall of Vicksburg and the capture of most of the garrison can only be a question of time."[47]

CHAPTER SEVEN

"THE WORK OF REDUCING THE ENEMY BY REGULAR APPROACHES"

"Corps commanders will immediately commence the work of reducing the enemy by regular approaches." These were Ulysses S. Grant's formal orders on May 25, although he had been thinking along those lines since the failed May 22 assault. He wrote Banks, "The place is so strongly fortified . . . that it cannot be taken without either great sacrifice of life or by a regular siege. I have determined to adopt the latter course, and save my men." Sherman had actually begun the process of creating lines and saps as early as May 23, but until Grant issued those May 25 orders, it was not formally declared a siege. Grant told his corps commanders and posterity, "It is desirable that no more loss of life shall be sustained in the reduction of Vicksburg and the capture of the garrison." He also gave some direction about the engineering aspects, adding, "Every advantage will be taken of the natural inequalities of the ground to gain positions from which to start mines, trenches, or advance batteries."[1]

This major decision was a watershed moment in the campaign, if somewhat bittersweet. Grant was supremely confident that he had Vicksburg just where he wanted and that there was no doubt of its eventual fall short of relief from the outside, what Grant termed the "greatest danger now to be apprehended." Yet if Grant could have his way, he did not want to expend weeks and perhaps months conducting a siege. He had moved quickly and decisively earlier in May, but if a siege would now provide the key ending to the campaign, he would use one. A naturally impatient person, Grant loathed wasting time on a siege, but it seemed that this is what it had come to. "The position is as strong by nature as can possibly be concieved of, and is well fortified," he wrote Halleck. That is why he stipulated that "the nature of the ground about Vicksburg is such that it can only be taken by a siege."[2]

Obviously, the other option was to continue to assault, during which many more men would be killed and wounded. While Grant has often been labeled a butcher for the manner in which he conducted the high-casualty Overland Campaign in Virginia in 1864, this is clearly not the case at Vicksburg. Grant had tried every way possible to reach the hill city short of assaulting up the western bluffs, and he had maneuvered well in the inland campaign. Yes, he had fought five battles, but he had met the enemy each time with superior numbers that allowed overwhelming force to drive away the foe. As a result, casualties were much lower than they were in more equalized battles. Maneuver had allowed Grant to save his men, and he was not inclined to begin to use them in any different fashion now.[3]

Since it was absolutely necessary, therefore, Grant resorted to siege warfare. He did not like it, but he realized he could attain the chief goal in that manner in due time. He, and the nation itself, both of whom wanted victory immediately, would have to learn more patience. He told a civilian who asked when he would capture Vicksburg, "I can't tell exactly, but I shall stay until I do, if it takes thirty years." He was in a good spot, however, writing, "My arrangements for supplies are ample, and can be expanded to meet any exigency. All I want now are men."[4]

I

Over the month-long siege of Vicksburg, Grant had a lot on his mind. The major topic, of course, was the military operations around the town itself and the threat to the rear. He would have to strategize on both fronts, with those concerns to the rear growing in importance as the weeks passed. Grant continually obsessed over his rear areas, but he also worried about a breakout attempt from inside Vicksburg itself, a matter he thought hard about, even admitting to Porter that he had put the possibility "in a light I had never thought of before." To allow for both the front and the rear to be adequately supplied and manned, Grant turned to ushering in provisions and reinforcements. And the easiest area to draw from was Hurlbut's command up the river at Memphis. "Vicksburg is going to be a siege," Hurlbut wrote in late May. "Grant demands more force from me."[5]

This "force" was represented in several ways. One was ammunition, food, supplies, and quartermaster stores, which included any number of items used by troops in the field. Ammunition was of top priority, as Hurlbut confirmed as he wrote from Memphis on May 25 that "General Grant has sent for heavy supply of ammunition." Since the army would not be moving but rather concentrated in one spot for some time, they also had to be provisioned. No longer able to feast off the land they were passing through, Grant had to bring in food for the army, horses, and mules, with Haynes' Bluff, the Federal supply depot, becoming one of the key pieces of territory gained since the crossing of the river back on April 30. Not surprisingly, Grant soon ordered the enclave at Haynes' Bluff heavily entrenched.[6]

Then there were the reinforcements, some of which were officers joining the army; Grant requested several to lead the inflow of new troops that were arriving. As early as May 25, Grant requested Hurlbut to send Brigadier General Nathan Kimball, "if he can possibly be spared, in command of the re enforcement for this place." The same day, a high-level general who was fitted for corps command, Major General Edward O. C. Ord, was also ordered to report to Grant at Vicksburg. Where Grant would put him he did not know yet, especially if he retained McClernand until the siege ended. He first considered combining many of the reinforcements into a new quasi-corps under Ord.[7]

There was also a major influx of new troops. Many of the brigades came from within Grant's own department, which was easy to organize. A few actually came from Grant's own army in the surrounding area. With the Haynes' Bluff supply depot well in hand, Grant shut down the Grand Gulf depot, ordering the attending fortifications destroyed and allowing much of that garrison to march north and rejoin the army. Others came from farther away but still within Grant's department. Informing Hurlbut that Vicksburg "must be taken by a regular siege or by starving out the garrison" and that "I have all the force necessary for this, if my rear was not threatened" (and Grant estimated the Confederate strength outside Vicksburg at nearly twenty-five thousand strong), Grant also called on Hurlbut to send all he could. "I want your district stripped to the very lowest possible standard," he wrote, giving up all but the Memphis and Charleston Railroad. Hurlbut dutifully began scraping together regiments to send down to Grant under Kimball, eventually making by early June twenty-eight regiments, or two divisions, of the Sixteenth Corps.[8]

Grant later called for more troops, and Hurlbut sent yet another division under William Sooy Smith (Grant noted that "I am looking every day for the[ir] arrival"). Hurlbut complained that his district was all but bare and talked of stripping his garrisons down first to just the Memphis and Charleston Railroad and then later to just Memphis and Corinth. Fortunately, Hurlbut had some other resources, such as arming black regiments and using what he described as a "battery car" to patrol the railroad. Fortunately, Hurlbut seemed to realize his position in the grand scheme, writing Grant that while his line was severely reduced, "nothing worse can happen than a temporary obstruction to the road." In fact, Grant so stripped Hurlbut's area that Prentiss at Helena had to ask for artillery to be sent him. With so many

Sixteenth Corps troops at Vicksburg, a full three divisions, Grant appointed a temporary corps commander. Cadwallader C. Washburn garrisoned and fortified Haynes' Bluff and took over the troops under Kimball. Evidently, Grant was not as pleased as he had imagined he would be with Kimball; he informed Washburn that Kimball had not seen to all orders, such as keeping a force of cavalry at Oak Ridge post office in the corridor between the Big Black and Yazoo Rivers. Grant ordered Washburn to open communications with Osterhaus to the south, who had similarly been sent back from the main line to cover the railroad bridge area at the Big Black River.[9]

The flow of reinforcements peaked in early June, but it was a slow process. Grant asked Porter for all the vessels he had, including those manned by the Mississippi Marine Brigade, but Porter had too few, having sent some south of Vicksburg on the various runs past the batteries. At one point, Porter ordered a foray up the Yazoo River with the intention of capturing some of the Confederate vessels, but that was not successful. "I was in hopes of presenting you with some fine transports," Porter wrote, but the enemy set fire to many of them and others were stuck aground and had to be destroyed. Porter did help by allowing Grant to use the Mississippi Marine Brigade, first to occupy Haynes' Bluff in late May and then later on a proposed expedition to Greenville. The brigade never actually went, and an expedition under Lieutenant Colonel Samuel J. Nasmith went instead.[10]

Grant also asked for other troops from outside of his department. Halleck put out the call but took yet another opportunity to remind Grant, "I hope you fully appreciate the importance of time in the reduction of Vicksburg. The large re-enforcements sent to you have opened Missouri and Kentucky to rebel raids." It was worth the risk nevertheless. Halleck told Rosecrans in middle Tennessee that as Bragg had sent at least a division and maybe more to Mississippi, Rosecrans should send troops as well: "If you can do nothing yourself, a portion of your troops must be sent to Grant's relief." Halleck also called on John Schofield in St. Louis and Ambrose Burnside in Cincinnati, telling Schofield to "send those nearest, and replace them from the interior. It is all-important that Grant have early assistance."[11]

The troops began to arrive as quickly as the limited transportation would allow. Burnside sent two divisions of his Ninth Corps of the Department of the Ohio, or about eight thousand troops under John G. Parke, in early June. He asked, "Shall I go with them? . . . I may be able to help Grant." Halleck replied that "it would be obviously improper for you to leave your department to accompany a temporary detachment of less than one-quarter of your effective force."[12]

Schofield in Missouri sent eight regiments and three batteries, a full division under Francis J. Herron. Halleck cautioned about sending any more at present since Sterling Price was making noise in Arkansas. With so many troops spilling into the Mississippi Valley, Halleck told Hurlbut he could utilize some of the troops flowing down the river if need be since his district had been all but stripped. Hurlbut also helped by keeping spies out, including one whom he described as "about as effective a scamp as the Nineteenth Illinois ever had on their rolls."[13]

Eventually so many troops came forward that Grant had upwards of seventy-seven thousand men as the siege progressed. But as the process was slow, Grant remained anxious about the speed of their movement, even as late as mid-June. "Their non-arrival causes me much uneasiness lest they may be interrupted some place by a battery of the enemy," Grant wrote Porter. He asked the admiral to send a gunboat to patrol and meet the transports so that no delay would keep these additional troops from helping him encircle Vicksburg.[14]

II

With the flow of reinforcements promising ample if delayed troop levels, Grant settled into the siege. He maintained his headquarters behind Sherman's lines to the north. "We never lacked an abundance of provisions," Charles Dana related. "There was good water, enough even for the bath, as we suffered very little from excessive heat." Sylvanus Cadwallader agreed, writing that the site "was well chosen on a pleasant elevation, in the edge of a strip of timber which afforded protection from the glaring, burning midday sun, made drainage and sanitary conditions easily secured, and was also near to a brook of running water kept from pollution." Engineers established telegraph lines from headquarters to all three corps commanders as well as to Haynes' Bluff so that Grant had instant communication. From there, he directed the siege as well as the many other duties he had to attend to, including voluminous correspondence. Obviously, he also spent much of his time on the lines, examining progress and preparations on his front as well as his rear.[15]

Grant's first task was to make Vicksburg as airtight as possible, and the troops went to work digging with a will. He reported several weeks later that "the troops being now fully awake to the necessity of this, worked diligently and cheerfully." Ultimately, the Federals created an outer ring of entrenchments just as strong as those they faced: "Our position in front of Vicksburg,"

Grant wrote, ". . . [had] been made as strong against a sortie from the enemy as his works were against an assault."[16]

Others came in and did the same. Grant already had some reinforcements on the ground before his major call for troops went out, and he immediately began to position the new men. The most notable force was Jacob Lauman's division, which had arrived about the same time as Grant and was moved to Haynes' Bluff once it was captured. Grant sent Lauman to the weakly held far-left flank, past McClernand's corps, with orders to hold the Hall's Ferry Road area. He was to connect with McClernand's corps on the right and to open roads by which he could communicate with McClernand, all while extending the lines to the south. Grant told Lauman that "every means will be resorted to in order to harass the rebels."[17]

Lauman's arrival created the problem of what to do with him administratively as he hailed from Hurlbut's Sixteenth Corps. One division was not that big of a deal (the others would come later), but the issue foreshadowed larger administrative problems when additional troops would arrive from the Ninth Corps as well as the division from Missouri. "I send you this division [Lauman's] complete," Hurlbut wrote, "and only regret that I am not there to fight it." Perhaps willing to go only that far in hinting for a transfer, if that is indeed what he was doing (Prentiss at Helena was doing it much more openly), Hurlbut was so bold as to ask where this division would be sent: "As I have a very strong interest in my old division, and know their preference, I respectfully ask of the major general commanding to attach them to General Sherman's corps, as they and I have the fullest confidence and largest acquaintance with him and his command." Hurlbut also asked for their later return: "I hope you will be able to send this division back across the country from Vicksburg. I hope they are not to be permanently separated from this command."[18]

Some of those around headquarters were not as enthusiastic about Lauman's ability as Hurlbut was. Consequently, putting him under McClernand would only complicate matters. As a result, Grant chose to oversee Lauman directly, at least for the time being, and Grant soon had to push and prod as he had feared. On June 8, he wrote a testy note: "Move your left Brigade to the right, so as to leave one Regiment, on the left of the Halls Ferry road. As you now have your troops disposed, there is great danger of having them picked up in detail."[19]

Grant continually worried about the weaker left of his line, which was not heavily reinforced until June 15 when Herron's division arrived from Missouri. These troops quickly positioned themselves on the far left so that

Vicksburg was finally completely enclosed. In ushering more and more troops to the area, Grant ordered the commanders in that area to build the regular approaches, covered ways, and parallels similar to those on other sections of the line and take extreme measures to make "the investment of the south side of the city so perfect as to prevent the possible ingress or egress of couriers of the enemy." The division therefore went into line near Lauman; Grant chose not to move Lauman's men as they had already "commenced his advances, and I do not like to move him." Perhaps Grant was trying to make it as easy as possible for the overwhelmed Lauman. To Herron he simply ordered, "You will push forward therefore as rapidly as possible towards the enemy's lines establishing your batteries on the most commanding positions as you advance."[20]

As it turned out, Grant also had to keep an eye on Herron, whom Dana related that "for ten days after he had taken his position . . . disregarded the order properly to picket the bottom between the bluff and the river on his left. He had made up his own mind that nobody could get out of the town by that way, and accordingly neglected to have the place thoroughly examined in order to render the matter clear and certain." Grant wrote with exasperation that a prisoner was brought in who had escaped Vicksburg down the river hoping to find a Federal "to give himself up to." That was in Herron's area, and he was supposed to make the line airtight, but the Confederate had traveled all the way to the Big Black River before encountering a Federal soldier. "Pickets should be run to the River bank," Grant wrote, "and as close to the enemy as possible." He also added that there should be a reconnaissance made "under the bluffs [which] might disclose a weak place, where troops can be got into the City without loss."[21]

With supplies flowing freely and the encirclement made tighter by the day, Grant began to bombard Vicksburg mercilessly; his only concern was enough ammunition. By the end of May, Grant informed his corps commanders that "two steamers have arrived loaded with ammunition. All kinds are now in great abundance except 6 pdr. Smooth bore and 12 pdr Howitzer ammunition. These will be here in a few days." He also noted that "there is also a sling cart for moving heavy artillery and all the appliances for repairing any defective pieces." With such great stashes of ammunition, Grant opted to fire on the city. "Open all your artillery on the enemy for half an hour," he wrote his corps commanders on May 31, "commencing at 3 o'clock to-morrow morning. Throw shell near to the parapets and well into the city also." Later, he ordered firing begun at 6:30 P.M., the corps to fire "ten minutes, stop twenty, and fire again for twenty minutes more." Later in the siege Grant ordered that the corps not fire indiscriminately, but that it was "desirable when there is artillery firing to have it all around the line, and continuous for certain periods of time."[22]

The navy also provided good service, despite the loss of one of its City-class ironclads, *Cincinnati*, on May 27 while trying to bombard the area in front of Sherman's corps. With a lack of siege guns, which Grant requested be sent down quickly, Porter's gunboats heavily bombarded the city, although at times the land commanders had to request a change in location for the firing. Lauman complained at one point, as Grant informed Porter, that "several shots were too far to the left, your right going into his camp." McClernand likewise wrote that although the navy was doing a stellar job, "perhaps their effect would be increased by lowering their range." Porter even offered his heavy guns to be used on land and desired to erect a naval battery commanded by Lieutenant Commander Thomas Selfridge. Sherman agreed but did not think much of the effect except that it made "the enemy suppose it is to be one of our main points of attack." The most good the navy did, however, was shelling the town from the river, especially "in direction of the cattle-pens." The navy also provided good intelligence gathered from deserters as well as slaves.[23]

All the bombardment was intended to aid the digging toward the Confederate line. Approach trenches were started at numerous places, with the heads covered by sap rollers. The closer the approaches came, the more parallels could be dug, allowing the Federal front lines to move closer and to lay down heavier fire nearer to the Confederate entrenchments. Eventually, the heads of the saps came within a few feet of the Confederate bastions. Grant himself frequently and at several points observed the progress, experiencing enemy fire in the process. In fact, many soldiers related stories about telling off an exposed soldier only to learn afterward that it was Grant. The number of anecdotes indicates that Grant frequently observed the enemy line, at one point from the famous but dangerous Coonskin's Tower, erected for a sharpshooter, where he was of course put in his place by a far junior soldier. At another point a Minnesotan, who did not realize he was speaking to Grant, told him, "Say! You old bastard, you better keep down from there or you will get shot!" The man's captain quickly informed him he was talking to the army commander himself. At another point, Grant and Alvin Hovey were observing the enemy while bullets passed around them, with Hovey cautioning Grant even while Grant was motioning for him to get down: "I'm only a general of a division and it's easy to fill my place, but with you, sir, it's different."[24]

Even while progress was being made elsewhere, Grant still had great problems with the engineering arm of his army. "There was a great scarcity of engineer officers in the beginning," he reported and later described how "we had but four engineer officers with us." Grant actually lost one engineer who was sent to communicate with Banks at Port Hudson and was retained, much like Banks kept Grierson's cavalry. Eventually more engineers arrived with the reinforcements, and two who returned from sick leave eased the burden as well. The top engineering spot underwent a change, when Frederick Prime was removed because of illness and Cyrus B. Comstock replaced him. Ultimately, Grant ordered all West Point graduates who had training in engineering to aid in the process, although not all were so disposed. Grant ordered his quartermaster and commissary to help, but the rotund commissary "begged off, however, saying that there was nothing in engineering that he was good for unless he would do for a sap roller." Weighing the need for food for the soldiers against a ready-made sap roller, Grant wrote, "I let him off." Still, because of a lack of trained engineers, Grant often gave his own personal attention to that aspect of the war, more so than was normal for an army commander.[25]

As June passed, Grant continued to move the approaches closer to the enemy line and bombard the Confederate positions, looking continually for any opening that might provide access to Vicksburg. For example, he issued orders for a major cannonading on June 20 and troops to be "ready to take advantage of any signs the enemy may show of weakness, or to repel an attack should one be made." Grant stipulated that "it is not designed to assault the enemy's works, but to be prepared. Should corps commanders believe a favorable opportunity presents itself for possessing themselves of any portion of the lines of the enemy, without a serious battle, they will avail themselves of it." For their part, the Confederates slackened their fire because of limited resources. Dana explained one surprising response on June 5: "They fired a good deal yesterday, having evidently received a new supply of caps." There was another round of major Confederate firing on June 14 and 15.[26]

Despite the increased Confederate response at times, all indications were that the siege was working. "We shell the town a little every day," Grant notified Halleck, "and keep the enemy constantly on the alert." Deserters and even association among pickets told the same story inside Vicksburg: a dwindling food supply, weariness to continue on, and at times a rumored effort to cut their way out. Grant cautioned his corps commanders to keep their men vigilant and, at times, in line during the early morning hours before dawn.

As the weeks passed, the number of deserters grew, and with them came increasingly dire reports of the worsening conditions inside Vicksburg.[27]

Yet, even while Grant had Vicksburg bottled up, he could not focus his mind solely on the siege. He also had many assets across the river, and fighting emerged there too. Scouts indicated that the Confederates were on the move in Louisiana in early June, with a force attacking a small garrison about June 1. Jeremiah Sullivan reported rumors of a proposed attack on Milliken's Bend on June 2. The Confederates were later reported moving up the Tensas River toward Milliken's Bend, where a small skirmish occurred near Richmond on June 6 before an all-out attack exploded on June 7 at Milliken's Bend. Porter notified Grant that the enemy "nearly gobbled up the whole party," but he responded with gunboats. The Federals managed to hold the area, in part with African American troops, forcing the enemy to retreat.[28]

Grant reinforced the area with a brigade under Joseph Mower on June 8. He cautioned the commander in the area, Elias S. Dennis, to protect all his supplies but to cut down on his garrisoned area. "Not being on the ground myself," Grant wrote, "I cannot say exactly how your troops should be located," but he recommended garrisoning only Milliken's Bend, Lake Providence, and some point in between. He also said that all the black troops should be drawn together as much as possible to themselves and required to fortify; he suggested sending them to Milliken's Bend. Grant later reiterated, "Negro troops should be kept aloof from white troops, especially in their camps, as much as possible," but added, "whenever the movements of the enemy require a concentration of your forces, bring them together without regard to color." In addition to the action across the river, Grant also sent patrols and raids into the delta north of Vicksburg to make sure the Confederates were not stockpiling stores there, even coordinating with Porter in the event he needed to send the Mississippi Marine Brigade.[29]

These side items notwithstanding, the main military focus was on the siege itself, and perhaps the biggest event of the operation occurred on June 25. McPherson's troops had been digging a mine under the 3rd Louisiana Redan on the Jackson Road, and after a prolonged artillery bombardment they exploded it a little after 3:00 P.M. Grant described the result: "The effect was to blow the top of the hill off and make a crater where it stood." The result was indeed a huge crater, for which Logan's division fought for possession for the next twenty-six hours. A second mine from the original crater was later blown on July 1 but with much less fighting. The Confederates fought back in similar fashion in both instances, exploding a mine in front of one of the

Union approaches in early July but doing little damage. All the piecemeal effort was soon curtailed, however, as Grant explained: "I determined to explode no more mines until we were ready to explode a number at different points and assault immediately after."[30]

Although the siege was taking much longer than Grant had anticipated and the Confederates were operating elsewhere trying to break Grant's communications, most soldiers on both sides foresaw a Union victory. Some still had reservations, such as Frank Blair, who wrote his brother Montgomery, Lincoln's postmaster general, "Tell the President to re-enforce this army, as there is great peril. General Banks declines to co-operate with General Grant," but most soldiers were more upbeat. Porter told Secretary of the Navy Gideon Welles that "General Grant's position is a safe one, though he should have all the troops that can possibly be sent to him." He forecast that Vicksburg could not hold out past June 22. For his part, Grant himself was supremely confident, writing Hurlbut, "All things are progressing here favorably. Every day pushes us a little nearer the enemy."[31]

III

If Grant was happy about the way the siege was going, he was terribly concerned about his rear. As historian Michael B. Ballard has pointed out, Grant soon became "consumed with worry." He ordered that all commands investing Vicksburg watch their rear areas, telling them to "picket all roads, respectively, in rear of their respective positions, by which their camps or the city of Vicksburg can be approached, and prohibit all persons coming into or going out of our lines without special authority." Later, Grant gave orders to "obstruct and render impassable for troops" all roads except the Jackson Road and the roads to Haynes' Bluff, by which he received his supplies. This was to be done all the way to the Big Black River. Yet the main threat, Grant believed, lay farther north.[32]

Joseph E. Johnston lurked out there, and Grant had a healthy respect for him. Sherman later noted that Grant even "told me that he was about the only general on that side whom he feared." Johnston had with him thousands of troops, and Grant continually received updates of his reinforcement from other armies such as Bragg's in Tennessee. "What his force is now is hard to tell," Grant wrote early in the siege, "but all the loose characters in the country seem to be joining his standard, besides troops coming over the railroad daily."[33]

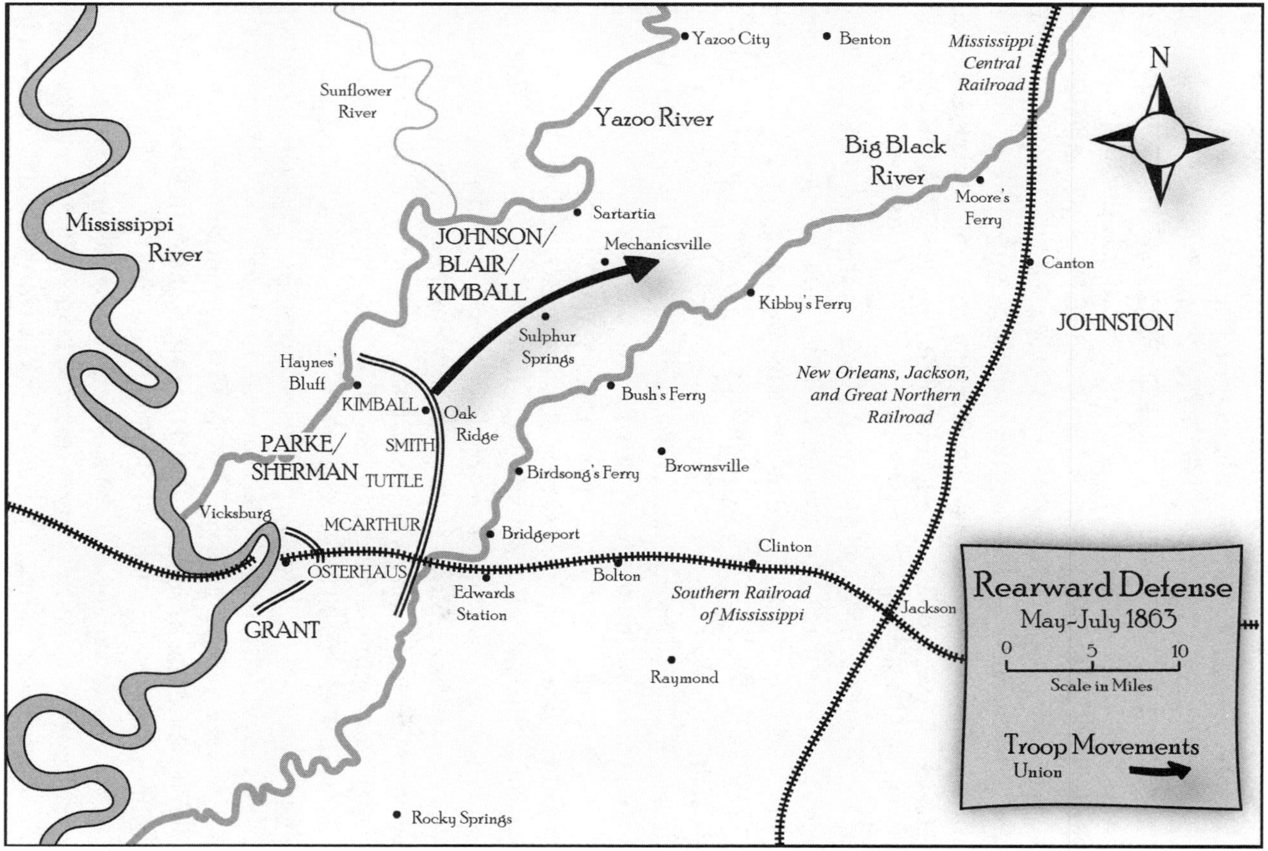
Rearward Defense
May–July 1863
0 5 10
Scale in Miles
Troop Movements
Union
N
Mississippi River
Sunflower River
Yazoo River
Big Black River
Yazoo City
Benton
Mississippi Central Railroad
Moore's Ferry
Canton
JOHNSTON
Sartartia
Mechanicsville
JOHNSON/ BLAIR/ KIMBALL
Sulphur Springs
Kibby's Ferry
Haynes' Bluff
KIMBALL
Oak Ridge
Bush's Ferry
New Orleans, Jackson, and Great Northern Railroad
PARKE/ SHERMAN
SMITH
TUTTLE
Birdsong's Ferry
Brownsville
Vicksburg
MCARTHUR
Bridgeport
Clinton
OSTERHAUS
Bolton
Edwards Station
Southern Railroad of Mississippi
Jackson
GRANT
Raymond
Rocky Springs

Although rumors of Confederate activity farther south along the Big Black River were rampant, Grant was particularly worried about two places, one of which was the normal transitory avenue between Jackson and Vicksburg along the railroad; Grant himself had utilized this approach toward Vicksburg, fighting at both Champion Hill and the Big Black River itself. The other was the northeast corridor between the Big Black and Yazoo Rivers. He expressed little concern for the area south of the railroad bridge at the various ferries, such as those at Baldwin's, Hall's, and Hankinson's, although there was periodic mention of Confederates in that area. Few thought Johnston would go that far south; Sherman insisted that "I don't think he will put his army in such a pocket." It was, of course, the very same pocket Grant had refused to enter upon his march northward from Port Gibson and Grand Gulf in early May.[34]

To cover the area around the railroad bridge at the old battlefield of May 17, Grant had sent an entire division from McClernand's corps under Peter J. Osterhaus. He ordered Osterhaus to secure the area by sending cavalry all the way to Bolton to destroy Confederate property as well as to "destroy all the railroad bridges as far out as they go beyond the Black." The cavalry was to destroy all forage in the area as well, bringing in cattle and contraband slaves. Basically, Grant ordered Osterhaus to make sure "everything [was] done to prevent an army coming this way supplying itself."[35]

Grant was less worried about the railroad approach because Confederates moving on that avenue would either have to utilize Jackson, which had been neutralized as a base and which would take months to repair, or they would have to transport arms and stores over fifty miles by wagon. The corridor between the Big Black and Yazoo Rivers gave Grant much more concern, actually tormenting him during the siege. Johnston had retreated from Jackson to that area, and all indications were that the Confederate was gathering a force around Canton to sweep down on Grant's rear to assist Pemberton and perhaps lift the siege of Vicksburg. Grant's supply and communication base was there as well, at Haynes' Bluff, and Grant quickly ordered it fortified even if contrabands had to be used. Dana wrote that by mid-June it was "a stronger defensive position even than Vicksburg."[36]

Grant also began to scout the corridor, moving a cavalry force forward as early as May 24 under Colonel Amory K. Johnson. This scout was so important that Grant stripped Haynes' Bluff of troops to send it, although he quickly sent other troops from the Vicksburg army to hold the bluff, writing to Sherman that "I deem that point [Haynes' Bluff] of so much importance that I am willing to weaken our force here rather than to leave it unoccupied."

Grant was not satisfied with just the cavalry raid, however, and two days later decided to cover the rear for good by sending infantry and artillery along as well. Hoping to "clear out any force the enemy may have between the Black and the Yazoo Rivers," Grant wrote, he sent a huge force, some twelve thousand men made up of three brigades of McPherson's corps and three more of Sherman's, all under the command of division commander Frank Blair. The cavalry under Johnson was to join them as they concentrated from their positions surrounding Vicksburg near Sulphur Springs.[37]

Blair pushed forward but found that the reports of a Confederate buildup were "greatly exaggerated." Grant did not get the word for some time, however, and actually wrote Blair on May 29: "Not hearing from you Since you left I have become some what uneasy lest the enemy should get some portion of his force in your rear. This you will have to look out for closely." Blair's report soon arrived, and Blair frequently thereafter kept Grant informed about his movements. Grant eventually offered another objective in addition to clearing out the corridor: destroy the bridge where the Mississippi Central Railroad crossed the Big Black River just north of Canton. If Blair could accomplish this, it would severely impact any Confederate concentration in the area and perhaps aid Hurlbut's defense, limiting the ability of Confederates to quickly move troops north. As time passed, Grant grew concerned about the proposed effort, telling Blair to "take no risks whatever, either of a defeat or of being cut off." He asked Porter to send a couple of gunboats up the Yazoo to support Blair and talked of holding out until he could "send out an army large enough to clean out Joe Johnston and his party."[38]

Blair held the corridor for several days but then promoted his own plan in which his recently well-armed cavalry would push forward, supported by infantry landed by the navy in rear of the Confederate forces known to be lurking around Mechanicsburg. This would, Blair hoped, drive all Confederate forces east of the Big Black and allow the cavalry to make a dash to the bridge. Grant accepted the plan on June 2, even deciding to establish a garrison at Mechanicsburg to be supplied by the navy from the Yazoo River. Grant actually called Mechanicsburg the "key point to the whole neck of land." One brigade initially moved to Mechanicsburg but was soon relieved by two small, newly arrived divisions under Kimball of the Sixteenth Corps, and Blair rejoined the main army. Grant told Kimball to take all the stores he could and to report all intelligence gathered by spies, even while Kimball was looking for an opportunity to send the cavalry on the dash to the Mississippi Central Bridge above Canton. Grant also added a note of caution to Kimball, "I do not want to run any great risk of having any portion of the army cut off or defeated. If, therefore, your judgement is against reaching Big Black River Bridge with security, and getting back again, you need not attempt it."[39]

The threat from the rear consequently weighed heavily on Grant's mind. "I am exceedingly anxious to learn the probable force of the enemy on the West side of the Black River," Grant wrote Kimball on June 5. "Keep me constantly informed of all you may be able to learn." Grant was so concerned about the rear that he went personally in early June to examine the area. He informed his corps commanders on June 6 that "I am going up to Mechanicsburg. Cannot be back before to-morrow night. Make all advance possible in approaches during my absence. Communications signaled to Haynes' Bluff will reach me."[40]

Historian Ballard has written that Grant's decision to go up the river was "a fateful move that would haunt his post-war reputation for years, right up to the present day." A story eventually emerged that Grant became drunk on the trip and slept it off overnight. Most of the embellished tales, including a fabricated story of a wild drunken ride through the infantry camps, came from later postwar memoirs of Charles Dana and Sylvanus Cadwallader. The most modern research has discredited the verity of such anecdotes, since they do not agree with one another or with the contemporary sources. Still, the problem of Grant drinking during the campaign is regularly believed, particularly because his guardian John A. Rawlins continuously warned him about any excesses. Rawlins was not afraid to challenge Grant; Dana wrote that "I have heard him curse at Grant when, according to his judgment, the general was doing something that he thought he had better not do." Moreover, Rawlins wrote Grant the famous letter in which he scolded the general for even being around alcohol: "The great solicitude I feel for the safety of this army leads me to mention what I had hoped never again to do—the subject of your drinking." Although some historians have tied this letter to Grant's trip up the river, it was actually written before the voyage. Grant no doubt had problems with alcohol, although certainly not to the extent some historians have claimed. In fact, there is no evidence of alcohol influencing any of the major decisions Grant made at Vicksburg or during the rest of the war. Nonetheless, there was apparently something to the overblown tales—staff officer Wilson wrote in his diary on June 7, "Genl. G. intoxicated."[41]

With indications that Johnston's force was growing, Grant soon developed another idea. He had numerous troops at Haynes' Bluff, in the corridor, and at the railroad bridge between Jackson and Vicksburg. Now, instead of sending out patrols and raids, he decided to wait and see what would happen and only implement a contingency plan if needed. He told Sherman that if Johnston threatened Haynes' Bluff or anywhere else in the rear, he would move him from his corps command and send him east with two of his own brigades and three of McPherson's to join those already guarding the rear. The command at Haynes' Bluff had changed hands frequently as higher-ranking generals had come in with the reinforcements, and ultimately John G. Parke, leading the Ninth Corps troops, took command of the sector. Grant wanted his own people in charge if anything developed, however, so Sherman would take overall command in the rear in the event of an emergency.[42]

News continued to filter in about Confederate movement in the corridor, such as on June 12 when a cavalry colonel reported Johnston moving out of Yazoo City with about thirty thousand troops. By June 22, when word arrived that Johnston had at long last crossed the Big Black River, Grant was convinced that he was about to be attacked "within the next twenty-four or forty-eight hours." He alerted his outlying commanders, such as Porter and Dennis across the river, that an attack would probably occur and that it might be a coordinated, simultaneous attack at several points, even perhaps including the Vicksburg garrison, which Grant knew was communicating with Johnston. Significantly, Grant felt sufficient concern that he put his contingency plan into effect, sending Sherman to take charge of the rear defenses, along with Tuttle's division of Sherman's own corps and three brigades under McArthur of McPherson's corps. If needed, Grant would also detach some of the divisions on the far left, including Herron's and even Andrew Jackson Smith's. Osterhaus at the railroad bridge was also alerted.[43]

Grant put this plan in place on June 22, and the divisions were soon moving. Wisely, he wanted to deal with Johnston as far away from Vicksburg as possible. "We want to whip Johnston at least 15 miles off, if possible," he wrote, and sent four brigades from Parke's command at Haynes' Bluff to the corridor to stop the enemy until Sherman and the rest could arrive. Grant was so concerned that he wrote Sherman to call on more troops if he needed them, which would leave the southern portion of the Vicksburg line thin, "in the same condition it was before the arrival of Lauman and Herron." Actually, Grant was so concerned about Johnston that he told Sherman he would support him with so many troops that, "should Johnston come, we want to whip him, if the siege has to be raised to do it."[44]

Intelligence placed Johnston in the corridor between the Big Black and Yazoo Rivers, with some forays south toward Bolton and Champion Hill. There were no indications of any Confederates south of the railroad, however, although Confederate cavalry were occasionally seen in the area. A slight scare occurred on July 1 when a report came in of twelve thousand

Confederates crossing at Hankinson's Ferry, but it proved to be false. Grant admitted that the possibility scared him: "My only apprehensions are that Johnston, finding us so ready [north of the railroad], may cover a movement south, and dash in at Baldwin's and south of that before troops can be got out to meet him." Sherman scouted the area and found little threat, but Grant still alerted him to be especially watchful in late June "now that the nights are light."[45]

With his massive force of some thirty thousand troops in six divisions under Parke, Kimball, Smith, Tuttle, McArthur, and Osterhaus, Sherman kept a continual lookout for Johnston in the rear. The troops were arranged from the Yazoo River northeast of Haynes' Bluff south to the railroad bridge across the Big Black River. Eventually, all learned that Johnston's advance was merely a rumor: "Sherman can find no trace of him," Dana reported to Washington, and Grant admitted, "his movements are mysterious." Although Johnston never arrived to test this line, Grant still thought it best to keep Sherman out instead of bringing him back to Vicksburg to command his corps, which was now under Frederick Steele: "I think it advisable to keep your troops out until Joe Johnston carries a design to move in some other direction."[46]

IV

Even though Grant was not on the march every day, he still had little extra time for administrative, political, and personal duties. In a letter to his father, he wrote that although he had received a letter from him and Grant's sister, "as I have to do with nineteen twentieths of those received have neglected to answer them." Sherman agreed, writing that while many had given the credit for Grant's administrative ability to Rawlins, "no commanding general of an army ever gave more of his personal attention to details, or wrote so many of his own orders, reports, and letters, as General Grant."[47]

Tenderhearted as he was, much of his concern fell on the troops themselves. Because it was the summer in the deep South, the temperature frequently rose above ninety during the day, especially after mid-June when the cool nights ended. The frequent afternoon rain showers aided somewhat, but this relief came at the expense of everything getting wet. More ominously, as the weather turned hotter and drier, the springs in the hills and ravines began to dry up, causing some to dig wells and others to haul water to the camps. Nevertheless, the overall state of the troops was very healthy, although Grant fretted when Washington sent him a new medical director. "This Department has probably suffered more than any other from frequent changes in medical

Directors, and from the incompetency of some of those serving as such," Grant complained. Now that he had a good one in Surgeon Madison Mills, whom Grant testified "has brought up his department from a low standard to a very high one," Washington wanted a change. Grant protested directly to Lorenzo Thomas, and the order was revoked.[48]

Grant also dealt with numerous administrative issues, including some that touched him personally as when he had to deal with Confederates burning leased plantations in Union-occupied areas, including one worked by Julia's brother, Lewis Dent. Another involved the discharge of men Grant had transferred to the gunboat service way back in January 1862, prior to Forts Henry and Donelson. Yet another dealt with militia recruiting in Missouri, and still another with Union prisoners from the army and even citizen prisoners from around Vicksburg. Grant also managed mounds of paperwork; Washington informed him that no copies of his general orders had reached the capital, so he promptly had them copied and sent out.[49]

Grant also dealt with the continual revolving door of staff officers, even lobbying for the appointment of Ely S. Parker, "a full blooded Indian but highly educated and very accomplished." One curious issue with which Grant had little initial compassion dealt with the arrival of a Union paymaster and nineteen subordinates with money to pay the army through April 30. Grant sent them away, with Dana explaining, "As the operations of paying men engaged as these are must prove very inconvenient and injurious to the public interest, General Grant has ordered him back to Memphis for the present." Sherman balked at the news and talked Grant into at least paying his corps, and Grant conceded to pay any others as well "whose commanders may desire it." Grant also found time to begin writing his report of the campaign.[50]

The general also had a number of visitors to deal with in addition to Dana and Lorenzo Thomas. One was the army's medical inspector John E. Summers, who arrived to look over Grant's command, most especially the wounded that had necessarily been left behind under flags of truce at Raymond, Jackson, Champion Hill, and Big Black River Bridge and were subsequently captured by the enemy. Grant later sent a surgeon into Confederate territory to remove the wounded. The letter he carried read, "I would be pleased to send and get all of my wounded at Bakers Creek, Raymond and Jackson, so that they may be sent to Northern Hospitals for care." Former United States treasurer and representative from Kentucky Samuel L. Casey also visited, bringing news of Washington's concern for Grant's campaign. Grant simply told him, "I have telegraphed to the President and to the General in chief" for reinforcements, adding that "the enemy are accumulating a force North of me, and may get more troops than I can manage with my present force." Whether Grant was really that worried about political backlash—which, according to his other correspondence, he was not—or whether he was playing a politician with clout in Washington for more help is uncertain.[51]

Grant put a humorous spin on the many visitors to his army. "As soon as the news of the arrival of the Union army behind Vicksburg reached the North," he wrote, "floods of visitors began to pour in." Some were family members, others missionaries. Grant noted that these visitors often brought with them "a dozen or two of poultry." They little knew that Federal soldiers had been living on "chickens, ducks, and turkeys without bread" for nearly a month and "the sight of poultry, if they could get bacon, almost took their appetite." He added, "But the intention was good."[52]

Grant and Nathaniel Banks carried on a frequent correspondence during this time, sometimes sending staff officers to argue their respective cases for wanting each to drop his campaign and aid the other. Banks argued that "if we hold Murfreesborough, Vicksburg, and Port Hudson at the same time, the enemy will beat us all in detail, and the campaign of the West will end like the campaigns of the East, in utter and disgraceful defeat before an inferior enemy." Yet he squarely refused to aid Grant, even keeping Grierson's cavalry. Grant also refused to send Banks aid, arguing that "concentration is essential to the success of the general campaign in the West, but Vicksburg is the vital point." Lincoln himself became involved when he sent Grant a message on June 2: "Are you in communication with General Banks? Is he coming toward you or going farther off? Is there or has there been anything to hinder his coming directly to you by water from Alexandria?" Grant simply responded that he had been in communication with Banks but that Banks refused to send any troops. Miraculously, Halleck gave Grant some political cover, writing, "I have sent dispatch after dispatch to General Banks to join you. Why he does not I cannot understand. His separate operation upon Port Hudson is in direct violation of his instructions."[53]

By far the biggest political issue Grant had to navigate concerned McClernand, who had caused Grant much grief over the course of the campaign. McClernand had been a little out of step throughout the entire operation even while performing with a fair amount of competence. During the siege McClernand had once again begun balking at Grant's orders, requesting more cavalry to watch the small threatened area to his rear and generally prompting Grant with other correspondence. At one point he asked, "Can't McPherson and Sherman send reinforcements?" At another, he complained to Grant of "what appears to be a systematic effort to destroy my usefulness and character as a commander."[54]

As per Stanton's message that arrived on May 14 while Grant was at Jackson, Grant had the authority to remove the heretofore untouchable McClernand. Grant obviously did not think the time was right in the middle of the land campaign and so retained him. But by late June he was losing his patience even as his army was growing.[55]

Grant had needed McClernand, though, first on the march south in Louisiana and then as he crossed the river and moved on Vicksburg. It is telling, of course, that Grant allowed McClernand to lead the most dangerous portions of the campaign toward Vicksburg. And, McClernand had the political ties that Grant could not afford to ignore, especially in the middle of a campaign that might not succeed. If Grant were to rid himself of McClernand and the campaign were to falter, Grant would be severely questioned, certainly by McClernand.[56]

Now that Vicksburg was secure, though, Grant could afford to cut ties with McClernand and take the political heat. Vicksburg was certainly secure; it was just a matter of time before it fell. Grant also had secured the rear, with Sherman eventually taking control there. Once all the reinforcements had come in, Grant no longer needed McClernand's ability, even if he would never admit that he depended on it, in the military operations. Consequently, Grant used a minor offense to relieve McClernand on June 19: failing to get approval before publishing army correspondence. This had been brought to Grant's attention by Sherman as well as McPherson, indicating just how disliked McClernand was by the rest of the high command. McClernand's antagonist, staff officer Wilson, delivered the note relieving McClernand in the middle of the night because he was so anxious to do so. When McClernand read it, he exclaimed, "Well, sir! I am relieved." Then, he added, "Sir, we are both relieved." Grant fortunately had Major General E. O. C. Ord on hand to take control of the Thirteenth Corps, and he wrote Lorenzo Thomas later in June, "A disposition and earnest desire on my part to do the most I could with the means at my command, without interference with the assignments to command which the President alone was authorized to make, made me tolerate General McClernand long after I thought the good of the service demanded his removal. It was only when almost the entire army under my command seemed to demand it that he was relieved."[57]

McClernand protested, claiming once again authority from the president and secretary of war to be in the fight, but he took no further action: "I might justly challenge your authority in the premises, but forbear to do so at present." McClernand did write Lincoln himself: "I have been relieved for an omission of my adjutant. Hear me." He later requested an investigation, but Grant had ample support. Dana informed Stanton of the move, noting many of the reasons in addition to McClernand's congratulatory order; it was, he said, "the occasion of McClernand's removal, [but] it is not its cause." Dana reported McClernand's "repeated disobedience of important orders, his general insubordinate disposition, and his palpable incompetence for the duties of the position." Grant also told Dana that he was concerned that if anything happened to him, McClernand would take charge of the army and "that his relations with other corps commanders rendered it impossible that the chief command of this army should devolve upon him." Dana also reported a proposed secret gathering of Thirteenth Corps officers to pass "resolutions commendatory of himself." Michael Lawler refused to attend, and he blew the whistle. For many reasons, Grant informed Halleck, "I should have relieved him long since for general unfitness for his position."[58]

Despite all this, Grant still had to deal with the enemy. His forces frequently caught Confederate deserters as well as spies or couriers trying to enter and leave Vicksburg. At one point, his forces to the south under Lauman caught four Confederates trying to enter the city with two hundred thousand percussion caps. One was a boy who had been captured doing the same thing three days prior and released. Grant also learned a great deal from the captured correspondence, including confirmation that reinforcements were on the way to Johnston from Bragg. Captured notes in cipher were especially tempting, and he sent one such note to Washington, having "no one with me who has the ingenuity to translate it." Washington broke the code and sent Grant the contents, which announced that Bragg was sending at least one division to aid Johnston. More problematic was a group of civilians sent down from St. Louis who were deemed disloyal there. Grant did not know what to do with them or how to go about "getting rid of them." He asked Porter's help, not wanting them wandering around through his lines. "Any disposition you may make of them, or any thing you can suggest for me, will [be] gladly acknowledged."[59]

Grant likewise corresponded with Confederate officials on various matters, especially Richard Taylor who commanded the area west of Vicksburg and the river. He learned that several captured white and black Union troops had been reportedly hanged after Milliken's Bend, and Grant wrote to find out about it. He told Taylor, "I feel no inclination to retaliate for the offenses of irresponsible persons" but noted that if such was Confederate policy he would reciprocate. Taylor denied any formal proceeding, which Grant accepted. In another episode, Pemberton sent Grant four "hostages" held for the alleged killing of a man in west Tennessee; Dana reckoned that their release "indicates the near surrender of Vicksburg."[60]

Other more minor political aspects also took Grant's attention. Curiously, in the middle of siege operations, Sherman asked Grant to use "your personal influence with President Lincoln" to sway the War Department toward putting new recruits into old regiments rather than organizing new ones. Grant dutifully sent Sherman's letter to Lincoln. An evidently bored Sherman, before he was sent to guard the rear on June 22, was also not bashful about asking that one of his divisions get more artillery because some of McClernand's had two batteries per brigade. He also requested that a certain regiment of Indianans be transferred to his corps.[61]

Other items such as trade regulations within his department, mail services in the area, and questions of civilians' status also took Grant's time. He announced orders for corps commanders to "issue rations to families within their respective lines who have been deprived of the means of subsistence by the Soldiery." He also allowed anyone who desired to leave "outside our lines" to do so but stipulated that "no families who voluntarily leave our lines will be permitted to return during the siege." Grant good-naturedly wrote to Sherman, who was by that time on the Big Black River covering the rear: "You need not fear, general, my tender heart getting the better of me, so as to send the secession ladies to your front; on the contrary, I rather think it advisable to send out every living being from your lines, and arrest all persons found within who are not connected with the army."[62]

Grant also caught up on his personal affairs. He thanked a woman from New York City who had sent him a cigar case, writing that he "will continue to carry and, appreciate it, long after I could have done 'smoked' any number of cigars the Express Company are capable of transmitting." He added, "I wish I could have dated my letter 'Vicksburg.' I cannot yet. My forces are very near and so far as all the 'Pemberton' forces are concerned nothing can keep me from possessing town and troops."[63]

Grant also wrote Julia on June 9, the first time in nearly a month. He explained, "I wrote you by every courier I was sending back up to the Capture of Jackson. Having written to you to start for Vicksburg as soon as you heard the place was taken, and thinking that would be before another letter would reach you, I wrote no more." He informed her that his health was still good ("I have enjoyed most excellent health during the campaign, so has Fred"), although he later had a case of dysentery that fortunately cleared up by June

15. Grant nevertheless ominously noted that "Fred has been complaining a little for a few days"; Fred explained that it was from complications from his wound at Big Black River. "Under Dr. Hewitt's expressed fears of having to amputate my leg I remained much at headquarters," Fred recalled, and later remarked that "I saw a great deal of my father's methods, his marvelous attention to detail, and his cool self-possession." Grant sent the ailing boy to spend some time with his uncle on one of the leased plantations, but Fred was back by late June, when Grant wanted to send him north: "He does not look very well but is not willing to go back until Vicksburg falls." Meanwhile, Grant wrote Julia to go ahead and start south and if Vicksburg had not surrendered by the time she arrived, she could stay on the steamer "at the landing with the prospect of my calling to see you occasionally." Those occasions would admittedly be few and far between as "my Hd Qrs. are six miles from the landing with the road always blocked with wagons bringing supplies for our immense army. My duties are such that I can scarsely leave." He also told her that Fred had "enjoyed his campaign very much" and that he kept a journal that he would not allow Grant to read "but suppose he will read to you." He also reported on the small pony he acquired for his other children; he named it "Little Rebel" and remarked that it was "the smallest horse I ever saw," noting that Fred could "ride him with one foot dragging on the ground." He asked that Julia get saddles and bridles for the children to use when they came down, although he later wrote that she need not worry about it as he had managed to obtain a set: "Some one has thought enough of him to send him [Jess] a present of a very fine set of pony equipments." He also reported that he was well fixed with clothes except for cravats; he asked her to bring him "two black ones and half a dozen light ones."[64]

Grant continued to correspond with others. June 15 must have been a slow day at headquarters, or either he decided he simply had to respond to numerous letters. Grant sent out a number of notes that day, including to Julia, his father, and another acquaintance. To Julia he inquired about whether she had leased the farm near St. Louis, noting, "I do not want White to hold it." He gave a summation of the military affairs to George G. Pride, writing that "we have our trenches pushed up so close to the enemy that we can throw Hand Grenades over into their forts. The enemy do not dare show their heads above the parapets at any point so close and so watchful are our sharpshooters. The town is completely invested." Showing his major concern for his rear, he added, "My position is so strong that I feel myself abundantly able to leave it so and go out twenty or thirty miles with force enough to whip two such garrisons. If Johnstone should come here he must do it with a larger Army than the Confederacy have now at any one place. This is what I think but do not say it boastingly nor do I want it repeated or shown."[65]

For the most part, Grant maintained all his duties amid the lengthening siege. He became sick in June, but he was not the only one; Porter around the same time had come on land and because of a horseback ride and the warmth, "the admiral got tired and overheated." Porter was also once turned away from Grant's line by a picket because he did not have the correct permit. Grant apologized for the "stupidity, of the picket in preventing you getting out to camp yesterday." He assured Porter it would not happen again and that all naval officers would heretofore be exempt from needing permits. Grant added, "I hope Admiral you will not be deterred by your experience of yesterday from making us another call."[66]

Grant consequently waited patiently as June turned into July, wishing and wondering when the siege would end. He knew it could not be long, writing Julia on June 29, "During the present week I think the fate of Vicksburg will be decided." Again showing his major concern for the rear, he wrote that "Johnston is still hovering beyond the Black river and will attack before you receive this or never. After accumulating so large an army as he has, at such risk of loosing other points in the Confederacy by doing it, he cannot back out without giving battle or loosing prestige. I expect a fight by Wednsday or Thursday. There may be much loss of life but I feel but little doubt as to the result." As far as Grant was concerned, that would just about do it for the campaign. In fact, he added in his June 29 letter to Julia, "Saturday or Sunday next I set for the fall of Vicksburg."[67]

That next Saturday was July 4.

CHAPTER EIGHT

"VICKSBURG HAS SURRENDERED"

Ulysses S. Grant knew that time was short, but he did not know how short. Admiral Porter had passed along some intelligence, gained from two deserters, on June 28 that indicated the Confederates would "surrender on the 4th of July, after the rebels fire a salute." Independence Day seemed too ironic and therefore unlikely, but all indications in late June pointed to a swift submission.[1]

Grant's commanders forwarded on to him the growing tales of misery emanating from Vicksburg, allowing headquarters to create a clear picture of what was happening from a myriad of sources. For instance, some deserters reported that "mules were killed this morning and the meat distributed to the troops." Others described "six days' of quarter rations left yesterday." Still others indicated additional news such as Confederate brigade commander Martin E. Green being killed on June 27 "by a musket ball." Even outlying commanders were hearing the same thing; Hurlbut in Memphis, who kept a firm watch on northern Mississippi, told Grant that "the feeling throughout Mississippi is despondent, and they all talk of the line of the Tombigbee River as the next last ditch."[2]

Grant had actually thought Vicksburg was nearing its end for a while now. "I confidently expected that Vicksburg would be in our possession before this," he wrote Banks on June 30, and he also expressed his continued concern for his rear: "I have a very large force here—much more than can be used in the investment of the rebel works—but Johnston still hovers east of [Big] Black River." Nevertheless, he added as he did frequently to his correspondence (perhaps in sensitivity to the issue), "The troops of this command are in excellent health and spirits. There is not the slightest indication of despondency either among officers or men."[3]

Just because Grant was confident did not mean he would let up. In fact, he tightened his hold on Vicksburg and continued his bombardment. One of his division commanders reported that the navy mortar fire had been "exceedingly well directed," prompting Grant to send along the report to Porter and ask, "Please have them continue firing in the same direction and elevation."[4]

By mid-June, Grant was preparing for a final showdown on land as well, although a "council of war," according to Charles Dana, on June 30 revealed that most officers wanted to starve the enemy out a little longer. Certainly, the May 19 and 22 assaults had failed due to stiff Confederate resistance, but now the depleted Confederates could be counted on to show less heart in the defense. Moreover, the Federals were correspondingly stronger, certainly in numbers but also in body. The troops that assaulted in late May had been on campaign for nearly a month and had not had fully adequate provisions, sometimes stretching a few rations over several days and only being augmented by what they could forage as they passed through the Mississippi countryside. Now, Grant had fresh troops to add to those hardy campaigners, and all were on ample rations. Probing to see if any weakness existed, Grant instituted a major bombardment on June 20, but it offered little information.[5]

Perhaps the biggest factor in Grant's decision to launch a new assault was that the Federal lines were now at places within only a few feet of the enemy fortifications. Whereas the troops had needed to traverse hundreds of yards of open territory to get to the Confederate lines in May, with the approaches now dug it would only take a quick leap forward, thereby reducing the time they would be under fire. The only problem was that McClernand's (Ord's) parallels were farther out than McPherson's and Sherman's—the latter had both graduated from West Point, with its engineering-heavy curriculum, and had pushed their work along better than the political general. Dana reported to Washington that while a competent engineer was on McClernand's staff, "the corps commanders and generals of divisions were not willing to follow his directions, either as to the manner of opening the lines of advance or the positions of the batteries to protect those lines." Grant wanted McClernand's lines, now that Ord was in charge, pushed forward rapidly for another assault. Ord pushed hard, and in several days the works were more professionally developed.[6]

Grant ordered preparations for an assault to begin in early July. He commanded that the approaches be widened "to 8 feet, so that a column of four (by the flank) can march therein." One engineer gave more detail of Grant's orders, writing that the approaches were to be "placed at once in such condition as to allow the most rapid movements of troops by fours along them, and the equally rapid *debouch* of troops. . . . The heads of trenches, for 60 feet, should be cut with gentle steps, so that troops can leave the trenches rapidly and in order." Grant wanted all the work done by July 5, because he planned to attack at daylight on July 6 and end this siege for good.[7]

Other elements factored in to the situation before then, however, most notably Confederate commander John C. Pemberton. White flags began to appear on the Confederate works on July 3, and "it was a glorious sight to officers and soldiers on the line where these white flags were visible. The news soon spread to all parts of the command," Grant later wrote. He then received a quick note from the Confederate commander, stating in part, "I have the honor to propose to you an armistice . . . , with a view to arranging terms for the capitulation of Vicksburg."[8]

I

At last Grant was on the cusp of victory, but it had to be done right. And Grant already noticed complications in Pemberton's desires. Whether he was stalling or being difficult, or just complicating a simple situation, Pemberton advised that he would appoint three Confederate commissioners to meet with three commissioners sent by Grant to work out the details. In order to punctuate his case, Pemberton added language such as "save the further effusion of blood" and posited that he was able to hold "indefinitely" if Grant did not agree. Pemberton sent the message by one of his generals, John S. Bowen, and Grant had to quickly formulate a response.[9]

At first Grant did not quite know what to make of the situation. He sent Porter a quick note that "there is a cessation of hostilities. You will please cease firing till you hear from me." Then he followed with more information that betrayed his confusion: "The enemy have asked armistice to arrange terms of capitulation. Will you please cease firing until notified, or hear our batteries open? I shall fire a national salute into the city at daylight if they do not surrender." Indeed, Grant already had plans for "a national salute of thirty-four guns from each battery (not from each gun) they may have in position on tomorrow, the eighty-seventh anniversary of American Independence, at 5 A.M." He continued, "After which they will only fire at living objects or batteries until such times as they may receive special directions from these headquarters." Grant now allowed a caveat in case Pemberton was serious: "Should white flags be displayed upon the enemy's lines and forts in their immediate fronts, they will move up and take possession of such lines, and hold them until further orders." Obviously, Grant was not convinced that Pemberton was being genuine.[10]

Grant had to think quickly and pondered various possibilities. The main question confronting him was not whether to accept the surrender but what to do with the Confederate garrison once he had captured it. In his only prior experience with this type of situation, Grant had sent north all fourteen thousand prisoners from Fort Donelson; it was a Herculean effort, and many Confederates escaped in the attempt. The Vicksburg garrison was evidently twice as large and had more than twice as far to travel. If he sent the soldiers to prison camps, they would severely tax the transportation, logistical, and prison systems in the west. Despite that, Grant actually favored sending the prisoners north, but most of his commanders argued for paroling them and letting them go home until duly exchanged. Grant so informed Porter, who backed the parole plan. Porter wrote, "I congratulate you in getting Vicksburg on any honorable terms. You would find it a troublesome job to transport so many men, and I think that you will be left so free to act it will counterbalance any little concession you may seem to make to the garrison."[11]

Because surrender was not the issue and the other details could be worked out later, Grant sent back his most basic terms: "The useless effusion of blood you propose stopping by this course can be ended at any time you may choose, by an unconditional surrender of the city and garrison." He added a bit of compassion, saying, "Men who have shown so much endurance and courage as those now in Vicksburg will always challenge the respect of an adversary, and I can assure you will be treated with all the respect due to prisoners of war." He nevertheless remained firm: "I do not favor the proposition of appointing commissioners to arrange terms of capitulation, because I have no terms other than those indicated above."[12]

Grant also bought some time to settle the prison/parole issue by agreeing to meet Pemberton himself. Bowen, whom Grant knew well from his Missouri days, had wanted to see Grant when he brought the note, but Grant would not admit a junior officer, although he did agree to meet Pemberton himself. Andrew Jackson Smith carried the news back to Bowen, who stated he was sure Pemberton would meet with Grant and even went so far as to name the place, near the Great Redoubt in front of McPherson's lines, and the time, at 3:00 P.M., although Ord noted that "the rebel time is forty-eight minutes faster than mine." The meeting eventually happened around 3:00 P.M. between the lines, although Pemberton arrived a little later than Grant. With Grant were Ord, McPherson, Logan, and Smith; Bowen and a staff officer accompanied Pemberton.[13]

Grant met Pemberton under a stunted oak tree in front of the Confederate works. He later humorously wrote that "it was but a short time before the last vestige of its body, root and limb had disappeared, the fragments taken as trophies. Since then the same tree has furnished as many cords of wood, in the shape of trophies, as 'The True Cross.'" Grant and Pemberton, who knew each other from Mexico, thus met, but neither seemed to want to bring up the topic of surrender. Apparently, each thought the other had requested the meeting and accordingly should start the dialogue. Pemberton finally broached the subject, saying he understood Grant wanted to meet, to which Grant replied in the negative. It turned out that Bowen had fibbed to get the two together, telling Pemberton that Grant had requested the meeting. Despite the rocky start, the two generals met for an hour and a half, with Pemberton pushing for marching his paroled troops out of Vicksburg but Grant objecting. Even if he decided to parole the Confederates, Grant wanted a firm process by which each Confederate signed a parole, which was to be countersigned by a Union officer. That process, of course, would take days. At points, the meeting was tense; "He was much excited, and was impatient in his answer to Grant," Dana noted, and Grant later related that Pemberton responded "rather snappishly" when he would not budge on his terms. "The conference might as well end," Pemberton snapped, to which Grant responded, "Very well." Bowen recommended that he and one of Grant's officers work out the details, to which both agreed and they continued to talk while Bowen and A. J. Smith worked out terms. Grant "promptly and unceremoniously rejected" the terms recommended by them as well, however, and, without coming to any conclusion, ended the conversation by saying he would send his final terms by courier later on and Pemberton could react. Grant wrote Sherman of his concerns: "Pemberton wants conditions to march out paroled, &c. The conditions wanted are such as I cannot give; I am to submit my propositions at 10 o'clock to-night."[14]

To get advice, Grant called in his commanders ("the nearest approach to a 'council of war' I ever had," Grant wrote) but told them he held "the power of deciding entirely in my own hands." Fred described the result as "the largest assemblage of general officers which I had ever seen." Although Grant later changed his story in his memoirs, saying that he always wanted the Confederates paroled, all except Steele and Grant supported the parole plan. Even so, Grant eventually agreed to the idea and sent the final terms to Pemberton: "On your accepting the terms proposed, I will march in one division as a guard, and take possession at 8 A.M. tomorrow. As soon as rolls can be made out, and paroles signed by officers and men, you will be allowed to march out of our lines." Grant allowed officers to keep side arms and horses and the men to keep their clothing but nothing else, except "any amount of rations you may deem necessary . . . from the stores you now have, and also the necessary cooking utensils for preparing them." Grant also allowed a certain number of wagons, but stipulated once more that "the paroles . . .

must be signed, however, while officers are present authorized to sign the roll of prisoners."[15]

Grant's reasons for ultimately agreeing to the parole of the Confederates were myriad. He realized it would cost a great deal to ship the prisoners north and then to Virginia to be paroled. The Confederates would have to be paroled later or imprisoned because the south had no such lot of Union prisoners to exchange. So, paroling them outright at Vicksburg would require much less expense than moving them and then paroling them elsewhere. Grant also hoped that many would just go home if left alone.[16]

With the negotiations so close, Grant canceled the 5:00 A.M. national salute he had planned for July 4. He also wrote Porter explaining his situation and that he would not send the Confederates north, which was obviously an important issue with Porter, who would have to do the hauling. "I have given the rebels a few hours to consider the proposition of surrendering," he wrote, "all to be paroled here." Grant admitted that "my own feelings are against this, but all my officers think the advantage gained by having our forces and transports for immediate purposes more than counterbalance the effect of sending them north." He also alerted his corps commanders to "permit some discreet persons to communicate to their pickets" that Grant was offering to parole the Confederates "here and let them proceed to their homes." The hope was that if Pemberton and the Confederate high command balked, then a grassroots effort by the rank and file would demand surrender now.[17]

Pemberton countered with an amendment around daylight the next morning, July 4, admitting that "in the main, your terms are accepted." He desired to march out of the works at 10:00 A.M. and stack arms, at which time the Federals would march in. Grant responded in as clear a fashion as he could: "The amendment proposed by you cannot be acceded to in full. It will be necessary to furnish every officer and man with a parole signed by himself, which, with the completion of the rolls of prisoners, will necessarily take some time." To make sure all were thinking the same, he added, "If you mean by your proposition for each brigade to march to the front of the lines now occupied by it, and stack arms at 10 A.M. and then return to the inside, and there remain as prisoners until properly paroled, I will make no objection to it." Grant also dealt with another issue Pemberton raised, the fair treatment of civilians. He added firmly, "Again, I can make no stipulations with regard to the treatment of citizens and their private property. While I do not propose to cause them any undue annoyance or loss, I cannot consent to leave myself under any restraint by stipulations." Perhaps tiring of the back-and-forth negotiations, which he had not experienced at Fort Donelson where his unconditional and immediate surrender terms were accepted outright (perhaps because he had added the caveat, "I propose to move immediately upon your works"), Grant once more added a firm ending to aid his efforts to sway the Confederates. "Should no notification be received of your acceptance of my terms by 9 A.M., I shall regard them as having been rejected, and shall act accordingly. Should these terms be accepted, white flags should be displayed along your lines to prevent such of my troops as may not have been notified from firing upon your men."[18]

Perhaps this threat got Pemberton's attention, and he responded with a simple, "I have the honor to acknowledge the receipt of your communication of this day, and in reply to say that the terms proposed by you are accepted." Grant was busy writing orders when the orderly came in with the note. Fred, restless as usual, was in Grant's tent when the message arrived, and he remembered, "He opened it, gave a sigh of relief, and said calmly, 'Vicksburg has surrendered.'"[19]

II

The Federal rank and file knew something had happened, but official confirmation only came when Grant sent out a circular early on July 4. "Should white flags be displayed upon the enemy's works at 10 o'clock this morning," Grant wrote, "it will be to signify the acceptance of the terms of capitulation." He then laid out the process: "The enemy will be permitted to move to the front of his works, and, after stacking flags and arms, will then return to their camps." Grant stipulated that "the works will be occupied only by such [Federal] troops as may afterward be selected. Those troops not designated for the purpose will not occupy the enemy's line, but remain in their present camps." It seemed simple, but it would turn out to be much more complicated.[20]

The Union army was thrilled, but there was much work still to be done, in fact too much to celebrate. As Grant moved toward Vicksburg, he heard a booming cannon and became agitated, saying that the commander of those troops "ought to know better than to allow any triumphing over conquered countrymen." Steele rode up at that exact moment, and it was determined that the firing actually came from the left. Grant had it stopped anyway. Still, Grant's officers wanted the men to look their best during the climactic entrance and occupation. Commanding the force that would enter and occupy Vicksburg, McPherson wrote on July 3, "As it is very probable we will take possession of the place this afternoon, have the men who are in camp clean up and put their arms, clothes, &c., in good trim, so as to present a good soldierly appearance when we march in." He also noted, "The brigade bands will have their instruments in readiness, so that they can take their proper position when the orders arrive. Field music will, of course, accompany the regiments." Unfortunately, not every Federal soldier obeyed, and Ord reported to Grant, "[I] am of opinion many men broke by the guards and went into town."[21]

Grant was certainly less interested in the pomp and circumstance of the event and more focused on the reality of getting the job done. There was still some desultory firing around dawn on July 4, which Grant informed Porter "arises from misapprehension." He was nevertheless so convinced of the timing that he wrote, "The enemy has accepted in the main my terms of capitulation, and will surrender the city, works, and garrison at 10 A.M." They did so, and to facilitate the surrender and occupation, Grant ordered Herron's division in the south and McPherson's corps elsewhere, primarily Logan's division, to enter and occupy the works. They were supposed to block off any transportation routes "to prevent all persons, soldiers or citizens, from entering or leaving the city." Other orders facilitated the actual process of surrender once the Confederates marched out of the works and stacked arms and colors to their front and then returned inside the defenses. Grant told his officers to "collect together all the arms, accouterments, and colors on your front, and hold them for the ordnance officer to get when he calls." He reminded them, "None of the colors are to be taken by any individual; they are all to be sent to Washington."[22]

Grant himself rode into town around 11:00 A.M., heading down to the landing to meet Porter and the navy. He first came to Pemberton's headquarters, where he was treated rudely. Pemberton and staff did not even acknowledge him despite sitting on the porch when he rode up. When Grant came onto the porch, no one offered him a seat. When he asked for water, they told him to get it himself, but a black servant charitably gave the general water from inside. Grant remained for a while but then moved on to the river. His staff expressed anger at the treatment, but he told them, "Well, if Pemberton can stand it, under the circumstances, I can." And those circumstances were very favorable. A proud Charles Dana related that "I rode into Vicksburg at the side of the conqueror." Quite a conquest it was; Grant ultimately reported around 30,000 prisoners, 128 field guns, and many siege cannon. To his father Grant admitted, "I found I had continuously underestimated the force of the enemy both in men and Artillery." The Federals also found "a large number of very rudely constructed boats," which verified rumors that the enemy was building small boats to escape across the river. Grant was glad they had not tried, writing that they "would have been drowned, or [been] made prisoners on the Louisiana side." Grant soon returned to his headquarters outside the lines before moving into Vicksburg itself the next day, residing at a widow Lum's house; there he began to organize the occupation.[23]

McPherson became the point man for the surrender, and Grant had special instructions for him regarding the parole process. He wanted it done quickly to relieve the burden he felt about the Confederate army, but he also wanted it done right. He told McPherson to "take immediate charge of the paroling of the capitulated Confederate States forces, and hurry the same forward with all possible dispatch." To do so, Grant authorized McPherson to obtain all the printing presses in the city "for the printing of the necessary blanks." He reminded McPherson of the details, writing, "Not one of the capitulated garrison must be allowed to escape, but all must be paroled, and duplicate lists, certified by the proper officers, retained."[24]

While Pemberton did not want to delay the process any more than Grant did, he raised a few issues that took time for Grant to rule upon. Pemberton broached the subject of "what course is intended to be pursued with regard to our servants." The Confederate argued that many wanted to go with their owners, "and it was like severing families to part them." Grant responded that while no blacks would be enlisted as of now, they were needed as laborers for the Union army. He thus flatly refused to allow Confederates to force their slaves to go with them, but said that as they were now free, the Federals could not keep them and would not keep blacks from following their masters if they so chose. This halfway solution soon proved troublesome, however, as Logan registered a protest that Confederate officers were intimidating the freed slaves. Grant promptly canceled all passes out of the city but still allowed for free choice within limits: "If there is any indication that a suspicious number of blacks are going to accompany the troops out, then all should be turned back except such as are voluntarily accompanying families, not more than one to each family."[25]

Pemberton also asked if Confederate general officers could retain mounted couriers to help facilitate the march toward the parole camps in east Mississippi and west Alabama. Grant flatly refused, and added that he could not yet allow Pemberton himself to "send a courier with dispatches to your Government to-day," although he hoped to be able to allow that in the near future. Grant was certainly doing things differently than he had at Fort Donelson just a little over a year earlier.[26]

Complicating the process, some Confederates would not sign paroles. Grant ordered that they be put under guard and sent north to prison camps, but they would not leave until the paroled garrison left the city. Most signed, but some did not, including many of the artillerymen who had manned the river batteries, perhaps as many as seventeen hundred of them. Trans-Mississippi Confederates also caused a problem. Once they signed paroles, they began to cross the river on skiffs, returning to their homes instead of reporting to parole camps. Pemberton complained; he wanted to take his entire paroled garrison to a designated camp. Grant went over the orders again with McPherson: "There apparently being some misunderstanding between Lieutenant-General Pemberton and the paroling officers as to the method of conducting the paroling of prisoners." Grant again insisted that all who would not sign a parole be confined in a steamer in the river while all who signed would be dismissed out of Union lines as soon as Pemberton approved the rolls. He also reminded Pemberton that their agreement stated that all who were inside the garrison on July 4 were required to be exchanged before they could reenter service.[27]

For the "large number of our sick and wounded, and still greater of Confederate sick and wounded," Grant ordered the quartermaster to provide anything needed by the medical corps. Pemberton also requested leaving division commander M. L. Smith in Vicksburg as liaison with the Federals for the purpose of paroling sick and wounded and granting furloughs; Grant again obliged. Less important but still time consuming, an issue also emerged regarding nurses and stewards leaving Vicksburg, as well as rumors that Confederates would leave Vicksburg with powder hidden in their canteens. A question about Confederate officers' families leaving in their own carriages also came up. It was all so detailed that it was almost impossible to see to everything. Grant wrote his father, "The process of paroling is so tedious . . . that many who are desirous of getting to their homes will escape before the paroling officers get around to them."[28]

Tiring of the situation, Grant tried to speed the process. "I would be pleased if those already paroled be moved out as early as possible to-morrow," Grant informed McPherson on July 8. Pemberton was only ready on July 10 and informed McPherson that he would march early the next morning, giving him the roads by which each division would move east. Grant approved the move, only requiring that officers be on every road to call rolls and thereby document who left with their commands and who did not to "avoid leaving the same man subject to exchange twice." Grant wanted officers present "to witness and compare rolls of absentees with the officers appointed by General Pemberton."[29]

Despite such details, Grant was soon rid of the Confederate garrison. Now, he could turn his attention elsewhere, continuing the war he had just taken such a large step toward winning.

III

"If you are in Vicksburg, glory, hallelujah!," Sherman wrote from the Big Black River on July 3. "The best fourth of July since 1776. Of course we must not rest idle, only don't let us brag too soon." Grant was of course not inside Vicksburg at that point, but the final negotiations were taking place and he would be there the next day. Still, the actual capture of Vicksburg and the subsequent days of administrative work were only part of what Grant had to do in those busy days of early July. The sheer amount of correspondence, which picked up dramatically around July 3 and 4, illustrated how much Grant had to juggle, and while his mind was certainly on finishing the business at Vicksburg itself, he also had numerous other tasks to deal with.[30]

Among his duties were those of an administrative nature. He corresponded with Secretary of the Treasury Salmon P. Chase about agents in the area as well as oversaw a situation involving loyal civilians in Louisiana. The Duncan family were Unionists, yet their slaves had been taken away. With a prompt from Washington, Grant ordered a full investigation. He also had to care for other leased plantations in Louisiana; he admitted that "the location of these leased plantations was most unfortunate, and against my judgment. I wanted them put north of the White River."[31]

Military operations were nonetheless at the forefront of Grant's attention. He realized that there was another bastion on the Mississippi River at Port Hudson but knew that it could not hold out after Vicksburg fell, if indeed it was even still holding out. Grant nevertheless wanted the entire river open as quickly as possible and began to make plans to send Banks the troops he had always talked about sending. Still, Grant did not want to break up corps if he could help it and so chose to send Herron's independent division south to aid Banks "as soon as the prisoners of war are turned out of our lines." Port Hudson, of course, surrendered on July 9 before Herron could finish up his work in Vicksburg. With the entire river opened, Grant canceled Herron's move, although the division was already on transports. He informed Banks of the situation, and in perhaps an attempt to justify to himself that he had done the right thing concerning the surrender, he informed Banks, "I regard the terms really more favorably than an unconditional surrender. It leaves the transports and troops for immediate use. At the present junction of affairs in the East and on the river above here, this may prove of vast importance." Finally, Grant reiterated his desire to have Grierson back in his department.[32]

Grant responded to and managed other military activities as well. In a classic case of too little too late, Confederates under Sterling Price attacked one of Grant's garrisons at Helena, Arkansas, on July 4, the day of Vicksburg's surrender. In an attempt to cut off the river somewhere other than Vicksburg, they planned to hit the isolated garrison that had actually been calling for reinforcements while all troops went south. Benjamin Prentiss was able to parry the attacks, resulting in yet another Union victory on Independence Day, though minor in comparison to the big victory at Vicksburg.[33]

Grant sent troops elsewhere as well in the immediate days after the surrender. Hearing the Confederates were crossing a large cattle herd at Natchez, he sent troops south to garrison the town and capture the cattle. He also sent Herron up the Yazoo River with Porter to capture Yazoo City, including any defenses and steamers. The expedition was successful despite the loss of one of the City-class ironclads, the *Baron De Kalb*, which was sunk in the Yazoo River just south of the town.[34]

By far the most important military action for Grant now that Vicksburg had surrendered was Sherman's confrontation of Joseph E. Johnston. Immediately upon word of negotiations for surrender, Grant had notified Sherman to be ready to go after Johnston. "The news is so good I can hardly believe it," Sherman responded, but added that he was confused by the continued firing on July 3, to which Grant responded, "Flag of truce only covered bearer of dispatches; firing was continued by balance of the line." Still, Sherman had anticipated Grant's desires and asked that two corps be sent to him, Ord's and his own now under Frederick Steele. He wanted to leave McPherson's to clean up at Vicksburg. "I have directed Steele and Ord to be in readiness to move, as you suggested, the moment Vicksburg is surrendered," Grant wrote Sherman. "I want Johnston broken up as effectually as possible, and roads destroyed." At another time he wrote, "When we go in, I want you to drive Johnston from the Mississippi Central Railroad." Later on July 3, Grant frequently updated Sherman: "There is but little doubt but that the enemy will surrender to-night or in the morning; make your calculations to attack Johnston." Early the next morning he reported, "Propositions have been sent in for the surrender of Vicksburg. Pemberton's reply is momentarily expected."[35]

Grant had every confidence in Sherman, writing Banks, "His force is so large I think it cannot fail." He had perhaps less faith in Ord simply because Ord had not traversed the territory between Jackson and Vicksburg as Sherman had, and as McClernand had for that matter. Grant informed Ord as he was preparing to leave the Vicksburg lines to join Sherman that "the route traveled by your corps on coming to Vicksburg is exactly the route they will travel back. That is the route they came—by Big Black River Bridge, Edwards Station, and Champion's Hill. That is the route they now go. If they leave that route after passing Champion's Hill, all will be equally ignorant of the route, none of our troops having been north of that road." Of course, Alvin Hovey, Eugene Carr, and Andrew Jackson Smith had all been in the area. Grant added as well, "[Peter C.] Hains [chief engineer of the Thirteenth Corps] can tell you all about the route."[36]

When Vicksburg finally fell, Grant immediately sent word to Sherman, the latter admitting that "I can hardly contain myself." He also termed it "this most glorious anniversary of the birth of a nation, whose sire and father was a Washington." And Sherman took some time to caution Grant that

> did I not know the honesty, modesty, and purity of your nature, I would be tempted to follow the examples of my standard enemies of the press in indulging in wanton flattery; but as a man and a soldier, and ardent friend of yours, I warn you against the insence of flattery that will fill our land from one extreme to the other. Be natural and yourself, and this glittering flattery will be as the passing breeze of the sea on a warm summer day. To me the delicacy with which you have treated a brave but deluded enemy is more eloquent than the most gorgeous oratory of an [Edward] Everett.[37]

After the mild lecture, Sherman turned to business, writing that although he would "like to hear the shout of my old and patient troops," he was moving forward. "Already are my orders out to give one big huzza and sling the knapsack for new fields," Sherman informed Grant. He was going after "the unseen Johnston," as Sherman termed him, and Grant could not have been happier. "I have no suggestions or orders to give," Grant wrote Sherman. "I want you to drive Johnston out in your own way, and inflict on the enemy all the punishment you can. I will support you to the last man that can be spared."[38]

Sherman did just that, moving quickly eastward and laying siege to Jackson in mid-July. He finally forced Johnston east of the Pearl River. Sherman once again reduced Jackson's role as a transportation and Confederate supply center. Then he turned back west to join Grant around Vicksburg, ready for future operations.[39]

IV

Those future operations were on everybody's mind, not just Grant's. With active campaigning over for the moment, Henry Halleck began to correspond more often with his victorious general. At first he questioned Grant's paroling of the Confederate troops, writing, "I fear your paroling the garrison at Vicksburg without actual delivery to a proper agent, as required by the fourteenth article of the [Dix-Hill] cartel, may be construed into an absolute release, and that the men will be immediately placed in the ranks of the enemy. . . . If these prisoners have not been allowed to depart, you will retain them till further orders." Fortunately, Halleck wrote again two days later, "On full examination of the question, it is decided that you, as the commander of an army, were authorized to agree upon the parole and release of the garrison of Vicksburg with the general commanding the place."[40]

A more welcome piece of correspondence was dated on July 7, when Halleck wrote that Grant had been promoted to major general in the regular army, to date from July 4, 1863. More good news arrived in a telegram on July 10 stating that "Meade had whipped Lee badly, and that the latter was retreating and Meade in full pursuit." Looking to the future, Halleck also noted there were two brigadier general positions open at the time, with three more hopefully to be opened soon by retiring officers. He asked Grant to forward Sherman and McPherson's names for the posts, which Grant later did—directly to Lincoln. Halleck also expressed his desire to be back in the Mississippi Valley. "I sincerely wish I was with you again in the West," he wrote. "I am utterly sick of this political hell."[41]

Halleck also included something that he had held back from Grant for a long time: praise. He had notably sent no congratulations after Forts Henry and Donelson, and he had not been happy with Grant after Shiloh. Now, Halleck sent fulsome praise when notifying Grant of the reception of his official report: "Your narrative of this campaign, like the operations themselves, is brief, soldierly, and in every respect credible and satisfactory. In boldness of plan, rapidity of execution, and brilliancy of results, these operations will compare most favorably with those of Napoleon about Ulm. You and your army have well deserved the gratitude of your country, and it will be the boast of your children that their fathers were of the heroic army which reopened the Mississippi River." Napoleon at Ulm: high praise indeed.[42]

Perhaps most importantly, at least to Grant, Halleck began to think of what to do next, sending his thoughts on July 11. He nixed following Johnston into Alabama if he retreated or if he held "the line of the Tombigbee, even after he has been driven east of that river." Halleck stated again that "the Mississippi should be the base of future operations east and west." Halleck had no further suggestions except to use black troops to garrison posts while the white army continued to campaign. "What is to be done with the forces available for the field?" Halleck asked. "This is an important question, which should be carefully considered."[43]

The ever-active Grant was already doing that. It was not long before he was writing that "my troops were not allowed one hours idle time after the surrender but were at once started after other game." He also replied to Halleck about future operations: "It seems to me now that Mobile should be captured, the expedition starting from some point on Lake Pontchartrain." That expedition never took place, but the aggressive Grant was nonetheless ready to keep pressing forward.[44]

EPILOGUE: "I DO NOT EXPECT TO BE STILL"

"It is great, Mr. Welles, it is great!," Lincoln nearly shouted when Secretary of the Navy Gideon Welles brought him the news of Vicksburg's fall. "I cannot, in words, tell you my joy over this result." Lincoln had constantly favored Grant, holding on to him amid calls for his removal and even his own doubts. This confirmed that he had made the right choice, and now Lincoln made another. Speaking to a visitor after the news reached the capital, Lincoln simply noted, "Grant is my man, and I am his, for the rest of the war."[1]

Lincoln did not stop there. Illustrating his humility that no doubt drew the president to the similarly humble Grant, Lincoln wrote one of the most extraordinary letters ever to come from an American president:

> To Major-General Grant:
>
> My dear general: I do not remember that you and I ever met personally. I write this now as a grateful acknowledgment for the almost inestimable service you have done the country. I wish to say a word further. When you first reached the vicinity of Vicksburg, I thought you should do what you finally did—march the troops across the neck, run the batteries with the transports, and thus go below; and I never had any faith, except a general hope that you knew better than I, that the Yazoo Pass expedition and the like could succeed. When you got below and took Port Gibson, Grand Gulf, and vicinity, I thought you should go down the river and join General Banks; and when you turned northward east of the Big Black, I feared it was a mistake. I now wish to make the personal acknowledgment that you were right and I was wrong.
>
> Yours very truly,
> A. Lincoln[2]

Certainly Grant cherished such a wonderful letter, but more so the heartfelt congratulation it represented and Grant deserved. Grant had defied normal military customs and the odds and had succeeded in one of the most brilliant campaigns of any war. He had done it by taking risks, and Grant later expounded on the lessons he had learned from them: "If the Vicksburg campaign meant anything, in a military point of view, it was that there are now fixed laws of war which are not subject to the conditions of the country, the climate, and the habits of the people. The laws of successful war in one generation would ensure defeat in another. I was well served in the Vicksburg campaign."[3]

Others picked up on the risk-taking as well and Grant's lack of modern allegiance to the common-held Jominian laws of war that almost everyone, including Sherman, had recommended. One of Grant's staff officers and earliest biographers, Adam Badeau, described the difference between the Clausewitzian Grant and the foremost Jominian authority in America, Henry Halleck:

> General Halleck's strategy was always based on a great appreciation of the value of places, while Grant, as has been seen, made armies rather than places the objects of his campaigns. The minds of the two soldiers were differently constituted; they looked at most military matters with different eyes. Halleck set so high a value on what had already been obtained, especially after sacrifice, that he seemed unwilling to risk the actual prize for the sake of securing another. Grant believed that, in war, what is won is only a fulcrum on which to rest the lever for another effort. One was essentially a defensive, the other an offensive general; one always prepared for defeat, the other always expected to win.[4]

Grant was extraordinarily Clausewitzian, but at a time when Clausewitz was not read in America. That Grant determined the major principles of the philosophy on his own with no training and without reading the writer's works is amazing in itself, but it also illustrates just what a marvelous military mind Grant had. Of course, the humble Grant would never say as much, preferring simply to mumble, "Taking it all in all, I see fewer mistakes in the Vicksburg campaign than in any other. Others, no doubt, see many; but I am speaking now as a critic of myself."[5]

The record was clear for all to see, and Grant laid it out matter-of-factly in his report of the campaign:

> The result of this campaign has been the defeat of the enemy in five battles outside of Vicksburg; the occupation of Jackson, the capital of the State of Mississippi, and the capture of Vicksburg and its garrison

> and munitions of war; a loss to the enemy of 37,000 prisoners, among whom were 15 general officers; at least 10,000 killed and wounded, and among the killed Generals Tracy, Tilghman, and Green [also Garrott], and hundreds and perhaps thousands of stragglers, who can never be collected and reorganized. Arms and munitions of war for an army of 60,000 men have fallen into our hands, besides a large amount of other public property, consisting of railroads, locomotives, cars, steamboats, cotton, &c., and much was destroyed to prevent our capturing it.[6]

Grant was, of course, not above giving others the credit, especially the soldiers he had led to ultimate victory through the wilds of Mississippi. He also gave heartfelt credit to Porter and the navy: "Admiral Porter and the very efficient officers under him have ever shown the greatest readiness in their co-operation, no matter what was to be done or what risk to be taken, either by their men or their vessels. Without this prompt and cordial support, my movements would have been much embarrassed, if not wholly defeated." Grant also had a certain feeling of providential aid, even if he was not an especially religious person. In describing the five major battles of the maneuver campaign, he simply related, "We were fortunate, to say the least, in meeting them in detail." At other times he expanded on the meaning of that fortune, writing of the early failures that "all this may have been providential in driving us ultimately to a line of operations which has proven eminently successful." Grant certainly thought that was what happened once it was all said and done. He wrote, "It looks now as though Providence had directed the course of the campaign while the Army of the Tennessee executed the decree."[7]

Obviously, there were others that Grant did not credit with the victory, mainly his old and now conquered foe, John A. McClernand. When McClernand's report came through, Grant endorsed it by writing, "This report contains so many inaccuracies that to correct it, to make it a fair report to be handed down as historical, would require the rewriting of most of it. It is pretentious and egotistical." McClernand tried to get a court of inquiry to clear his name and reinstate him, but Lincoln would not have it. Lincoln had erred earlier when he had hitched his wagon to McClernand's star; doing so had actually hampered Grant's efforts. Now, he was totally and unashamedly a Grant man, which would produce additional important results.[8]

Efforts were already under way to realize those aspirations. Grant knew he could not stay idle; he had begun to think even before the siege was over about what to do with Julia and the children when the scene of conflict moved on. He had always wanted them to come down to Vicksburg for a time, but he reminded Julia, "We will have to make some arrangements for them to go to school as soon as schools open after vacation. You will have to stay with them as a general thing." He related that they could perhaps visit him if the correct place was chosen: "When I am still." He then added significantly, "I do not expect to be still much however whilst the war lasts."[9]

In fact, Grant was not still even now. He was so busy that Charles Dana sent word to Washington: "General Grant, being himself intensely occupied, desires me to say that he would like to receive from General Halleck as soon as practicable either general or specific instructions as to the future conduct of the war in his department. He has no idea of going into summer quarters, nor does he doubt the ability to employ his army so as to make its blows tell toward the great result; but he would like to be informed whether the Government wishes him to follow his own judgment or co-operate in some particular scheme of operations."[10]

Grant was ready to move on, but the major blow had already been landed. There would be hard fighting in the next year and a half, but the war was all but decided. Many historians have said as much, including Bruce Catton who wrote of Gettysburg, "Yet the real pull of fate was at Vicksburg. Lee took the eye but the pivot of the war was down here by the great river."[11]

Those were the words of a historian writing long after the fact, not contemporary participants in the conflict who had a direct stake in how it all turned out. In that sense, perhaps Ulysses S. Grant himself deserves the final word: "The fate of the Confederacy was sealed when Vicksburg fell."[12]

NOTES

BIBLIOGRAPHIC ESSAY

INDEX

NOTES

Preface

1. John Russell Young, *Around the World with General Grant: A Narrative of the Visit of General U. S. Grant, Ex-President of the United States, to Various Countries in Europe, Asia, and Africa, in 1877, 1878, 1879. To Which Are Added Certain Conversations with General Grant on Questions Connected with American Politics and History* (New York: American News Company 1879), 2:306.

2. George W. Bush, *Decision Points* (New York: Crown Publishers, 2010).

Prologue: The Military Education of Ulysses S. Grant

1. Allen R. Millett, Peter Maslowski, and William B. Feis, *For the Common Defense: A Military History of the United States from 1607 to 2012* (New York: Free Press, 2012), 117–19, 292–95.

2. Ulysses S. Grant, *Personal Memoirs of U. S. Grant*, 2 vols. (New York: Charles L. Webster and Company, 1892), 1:30–31.

3. Grant, *Personal Memoirs*, 1:38–39; John F. Marszalek, ed., *The Best Writings of Ulysses S. Grant* (Carbondale: Southern Illinois University Press, 2015), 3–4.

4. Grant, *Personal Memoirs*, 1:167; Ronald F. Lee, *The Origin and Evolution of the National Military Park Idea* (Washington, DC: National Park Service, 1973), 35–36.

5. Grant, *Personal Memoirs*, 1:250.

6. Grant, *Personal Memoirs*, 1:377, 385.

7. Grant, *Personal Memoirs*, 1:573.

8. Grant, *Personal Memoirs*, 2:115.

9. Paul L. Schmelzer, "A Strong Mind: A Clausewitzian Biography of U. S. Grant" (PhD diss., Texas Christian University, 2010).

1. "I Go Forward with the Advance"

1. *War of the Rebellion: A Compilation of the Official Records of the Union and Confederate Armies* (Washington, DC: U.S. Government Printing Office, 1880–1901), vol. 17(part 2): 294. Hereafter cited as *OR* with volume and part afterward; all references are to series 1.

2. *OR*, 17(2): 278, 294.

3. *OR*, 17(2): 101–2; Ulysses S. Grant, *Personal Memoirs of U. S. Grant*, 2 vols. (New York: Charles L. Webster and Company, 1892), 1:393.

4. *OR*, 17(2): 279.

5. *OR*, 17(2): 296; Grant, *Personal Memoirs*, 1:421.

6. For Jomini, see Carol Reardon, *With a Sword in One Hand and Jomini in the Other* (Chapel Hill: University of North Carolina Press, 2012).

7. *OR*, 17(2): 279, 297.

8. *OR*, 17(2): 296.

9. Grant, *Personal Memoirs*, 1:422.

10. For Vicksburg's geographical details, see Warren E. Grabau, *Ninety-Eight Days: A Geographer's View of the Vicksburg Campaign* (Knoxville: University of Tennessee Press, 2000).

11. John Y. Simon and John F. Marszalek, eds., *The Papers of Ulysses S. Grant*, 32 vols. to date (Carbondale: Southern Illinois University Press, 1967–present.), 6:320. Hereafter cited as Simon, *PUSG*, followed by volume and page number.

12. *OR*, 17(2): 296, 302, 307; Simon, *PUSG*, 6:320; *OR*, 52(1): 314; John Y. Simon, ed., *The Personal Memoirs of Julia Dent Grant [Mrs. Ulysses S. Grant]* (New York: G. P. Putnam's Sons, 1975), 105; Tamara A. Smith, "A Matter of Trust: Grant and James B. McPherson," in *Grant's Lieutenants: From Cairo to Vicksburg*, ed. Steven E. Woodworth (Lawrence: University Press of Kansas, 2001), 159–60.

13. *OR*, 17(2): 296, 302, 307; Simon, *PUSG*, 6:194, 197, 234, 256; Grant, *Personal Memoirs*, 1:422.

14. *OR*, 17(2): 298, 303, 307–8, 314; *OR*, 17(1): 467; Sylvanus Cadwallader, *Three Years with Grant*, ed. Benjamin P. Thomas (Lincoln: University of Nebraska Press, 1996), 16.

15. *OR*, 17(2): 315; *OR*, 17(1): 467.

16. Grant, *Personal Memoirs*, 1:427; William T. Sherman, *Memoirs of General William T. Sherman: Written by Himself*, 2 vols. (New York: D. Appleton and Company, 1875), 1:179–280.

17. *OR*, 17(2): 316, 322, 380; Simon, *PUSG*, 6:340; Grant, *Personal Memoirs*, 1:428.

18. *OR*, 17(2): 311–12, 317, 320; Simon, *PUSG*, 6:285; Grant, *Personal Memoirs*, 1:423; Cadwallader, *Three Years with Grant*, 18, 21.

19. *OR*, 17(2): 322; Simon, *PUSG*, 7:43.

20. *OR*, 17(2): 322, 328, 335–36, 348; *OR*, 17(1): 470.

21. *OR*, 17(2): 362, 367; *OR*, 17(1): 471; Simon, *PUSG*, 6:320, 353, 354.

22. Grant, *Personal Memoirs*, 1:428.

23. *OR*, 17(2): 374, 393; *OR*, 17(1): 471–72; Simon, *PUSG*, 6:400; Sherman, *Memoirs*, 1:280; Grant, *Personal Memoirs*, 1:428.

24. *OR*, 17(2): 374, 380, 385, 387, 389, 398, 422–23; *OR*, 17(1): 472, 475; Simon, *PUSG*, 6:398; Grant, *Personal Memoirs*, 1:427; David G. Sansing, *The University of Mississippi: A Sesquicentennial History* (Jackson: University Press of Mississippi, 1999), 111; Cadwallader, *Three Years with Grant*, 27.

25. Simon, *PUSG*, 6:397–98; *OR*, 52(1): 331; Sansing, *University of Mississippi*, 34.

26. *OR*, 17(2): 393; Simon, *PUSG*, 6:404; Simon, *PUSG*, 7:23; Grant, *Personal Memoirs*, 1:428; T. Harry Williams, *Lincoln and His Generals* (New York: Alfred A. Knopf, 1952), 191.

27. Simon, *PUSG*, 6:345–46; Grant, *Personal Memoirs*, 1:429.

28. Simon, *PUSG*, 7:44.

29. *OR*, 17(2): 347, 392; Grant, *Personal Memoirs*, 1:426.

30. Sherman, *Memoirs*, 1:281–82; Sansing, *University of Mississippi*, 112–13, 115; James Pickett Jones, *Black Jack: John A. Logan and Southern Illinois in the Civil War Era* (Carbondale: Southern Illinois University Press, 1967), 148; Cadwallader, *Three Years with Grant*, 27.

31. *OR*, 17(2): 393, 407; *OR*, 17(1): 472, 474–75, 601; Simon, *PUSG*, 6:406; Grant, *Personal Memoirs*, 1:430; David Dixon Porter, *Incidents and Anecdotes of the Civil War* (New York: D. Appleton and Company, 1885), 125; Brooks D. Simpson, *Triumph Over Adversity, 1822–1865* (Boston: Houghton Mifflin Company, 2000), 160; Michael B. Ballard, *Grant at Vicksburg: The General and the Siege* (Carbondale: Southern Illinois University Press, 2013), 91; *The Official Records of the Union and Confederate Navies in the War of the Rebellion*, 30 vols. (Washington, DC: Government Printing Office, 1894–1922), 23:497. Hereafter cited as *ORN* with volume number afterward; all references are to series 1.

32. Simon, ed., *Personal Memoirs of Julia Dent Grant*, 109.

33. *OR*, 17(2): 434; *OR*, 17(1): 468; *OR*, 10(1): 89; *ORN*, 23:633; Sherman, *Memoirs*, 1:284–85; Grant, *Personal Memoirs*, 1:431; John F. Marszalek, *Sherman: A Soldier's Passion for Order* (New York: Free Press, 1993), 203.

34. Simon, *PUSG*, 6:184.

35. Simon, *PUSG*, 6:154–55, 256, 359; Simon, *PUSG*, 7:44.

36. Simon, *PUSG*, 6:344–45; Simon, *PUSG*, 7:24, 396.

37. Simon, *PUSG*, 6:186, 188, 203, 244, 273, 275, 294–95, 318–19, 355; Simon, *PUSG*, 7:11, 19, 28–32; *OR*, 52(1): 293, 297, 313.

38. Simon, *PUSG*, 6:164–65, 188, 221, 229, 341; *OR*, 17(2): 307, 312; *OR*, 17(1): 468; Simon, *PUSG*, 7:24–25, 39–40, 45; Simon, ed., *Personal Memoirs of Julia Dent Grant*, 104.

39. Simon, *PUSG*, 6:164–65, 188, 221, 229, 341; *OR*, 17(2): 307, 312; *OR*, 17(1): 468; Simon, *PUSG*, 7:24–25, 39–40, 45; Simon, ed., *Personal Memoirs of Julia Dent Grant*, 104.

40. *OR*, 17(2): 370, 379, 386; Simon, *PUSG*, 6:240, 337.

41. *OR*, 17(2): 296–97.

42. *OR*, 17(1): 468–69, 471; *OR*, 17(2): 399; Simon, *PUSG*, 6:242, 245, 314, 328.

43. *OR*, 17(2): 309, 319, 326, 331, 349–50, 405; Simon, *PUSG*, 6:195–96, 354.

44. Simon, *PUSG*, 6:192.

45. Simon, *PUSG*, 6:349.

46. Simon, *PUSG*, 7:3–4.

47. *OR*, 17(2): 335, 354, 396, 400, 405; 393–94; Simon, *PUSG*, 7:44.

48. *OR*, 17(2): 396, 400; Simon, *PUSG*, 7:8.

49. *OR*, 52(1): 314.

50. *OR*, 17(2): 354, 396; *OR*, 17(1): 470–71; Simon, *PUSG*, 6:329, Simon, *PUSG*, 8:342; *OR*, 52(1): 301, 323; Grant, *Personal Memoirs*, 1:424–25; Bruce Catton, *Grant Moves South* (Boston: Little, Brown, and Company, 1960), 359, 361. For Dodge, see Stanley P. Hirshson, *Grenville M. Dodge: Soldier, Politician, Railroad Pioneer* (Bloomington: Indiana University Press, 1967).

51. *OR*, 17(2): 337, 421; *OR*, 52(1): 302–3; Sansing, *University of Mississippi*, 113.

52. *OR*, 17(2): 424, 506, 530, 544; *Congressional Globe*, 37th Congress, 3rd Session, 184, 222, 245–46; H. W. Brands, *The Man Who Saved the Union: Ulysses S. Grant in War and Peace* (New York: Doubleday, 2012), 214–20. For a full examination of this episode, see Jonathan D. Sarna, *When General Grant Expelled the Jews* (New York: Schocken, 2012).

53. *OR*, 24(1): 9.

54. *OR*, 17(1): 469.

55. *OR*, 17(2): 282.

56. *OR*, 17(2): 300, 302, 332–35, 345, 371–72, 401, 413, 415.

57. *OR*, 17(2): 420.

58. *OR*, 17(2): 420.

59. *OR*, 17(2): 425, 436, 441, 461–62, 480; *OR*, 17(1): 476; Simpson, *Triumph Over Adversity*, 167.

2. *"To Command the Expedition down the River in Person"*

1. John Y. Simon and John F. Marszalek, eds., *The Papers of Ulysses S. Grant*, 32 vols. to date (Carbondale: Southern Illinois University Press, 1967–present), 7:43–44. Hereafter cited as Simon, *PUSG*, followed by volume and page number.

2. *War of the Rebellion: A Compilation of the Official Records of the Union and Confederate Armies* (Washington, DC: U.S. Government Printing Office, 1880–1901), vol. 17(part 2): 415. Hereafter cited as *OR* with volume and part afterward; all references are to series 1; Simon, *PUSG*, 7:47.

3. *OR*, 17(2): 415.

4. *OR*, 17(2): 426–28; Simon, *PUSG*, 7:57.

5. *OR*, 17(2): 435.

6. *OR*, 17(2): 437–38.

7. *OR*, 17(2): 447; *OR*, 17(1): 477; Simon, *PUSG*, 7:137, 225; Ulysses S. Grant, *Personal Memoirs of U. S. Grant*, 2 vols. (New York: Charles L. Webster and Company, 1892), 1:423, 432, 434; John Y. Simon, ed., *The Personal Memoirs of Julia Dent Grant [Mrs. Ulysses S. Grant]* (New York: G. P. Putnam's Sons, 1975),

107; Sylvanus Cadwallader, *Three Years with Grant,* ed. Benjamin P. Thomas (Lincoln: University of Nebraska Press, 1996), 35. For Van Dorn's Raid, see Thomas E. Parson, "Thwarting Grant's First Drive on Vicksburg: Van Dorn's Holly Springs Raid," *Blue and Gray Magazine* 27, no. 3 (2010): 6–24, 26–27, 29–50.

8. *OR,* 17(2): 439–40.

9. *OR,* 17(2): 447; *OR,* 17(1): 477; Simon, *PUSG,* 7:137, 225; Grant, *Personal Memoirs,* 1:423, 432, 434; Simon, ed., *Personal Memoirs of Julia Dent Grant,* 107; Cadwallader, *Three Years with Grant,* 35.

10. *OR,* 17(2): 447; *OR,* 17(1): 477; Simon, *PUSG,* 7:137, 225; Grant, *Personal Memoirs,* 1:423, 432, 434.

11. Simon, *PUSG,* 7:24, 43, 95; Thomas E. Parson, "Where Was Julia Grant during the Raid?," *Blue and Gray Magazine* 27, no. 3 (2010): 24–25.

12. *OR,* 17(2): 442–43.

13. *OR,* 17(2): 442, 445, 448; *OR,* 17(1): 478; Cadwallader, *Three Years with Grant,* 38.

14. *The Official Records of the Union and Confederate Navies in the War of the Rebellion,* 30 vols. (Washington, DC: Government Printing Office, 1894–1922), 23:626. Hereafter cited as *ORN* with volume number afterward; all references are to series 1. For Forrest's Raid, see Lonnie E. Maness, *Lightning Warfare: Forrest's First West Tennessee Campaign—December 1862* (Jackson, TN: Main Street Publishing, 2007) and Edwin C. Bearss, "Forrest's West Tennessee Campaign of 1862 and the Battle of Parker's Cross-Roads," *Blue and Gray Magazine* 20, no. 6 (Fall 2003): 6–22, 43–50.

15. *OR,* 17(2): 443, 445, 449–51, 455; *OR,* 17(1): 478; Simon, *PUSG,* 7:81, 184.

16. *OR,* 17(2): 452, 463, 488; Simon, *PUSG,* 7:81, 139.

17. *OR,* 17(2): 465, 490, 518; *OR,* 17(1): 478; Grant, *Personal Memoirs,* 1:424, 435.

18. Grant, *Personal Memoirs,* 1:435–36.

19. *OR,* 17(2): 504, 518; Simon, *PUSG,* 7:116, 213.

20. *OR,* 17(2): 524–25.

21. *OR,* 17(2): 504, 523; Simon, *PUSG,* 7:141, 251.

22. *OR,* 17(2): 502, 528; Grant, *Personal Memoirs,* 1:437.

23. *OR,* 17(2): 511.

24. *OR,* 17(2): 511.

25. William T. Sherman, *Memoirs of General William T. Sherman: Written by Himself,* 2 vols. (New York: D. Appleton and Company, 1875), 1:293; Edwin C. Bearss, *The Vicksburg Campaign,* 3 vols. (Dayton, OH: Morningside, 1985), 1:223.

26. *OR,* 17(1): 613; Sherman, *Memoirs,* 1:295.

27. *OR,* 17(2): 526, 531; Simon, *PUSG,* 7:140, 156, 163.

28. Simon, *PUSG,* 7:171, 196. For Banks, see James G. Hollandsworth Jr., *Pretense of Glory: The Life of General Nathaniel P. Banks* (Baton Rouge: Louisiana State University Press, 1998).

29. *OR*, 17(2): 528; Simon, *PUSG*, 7:135; Richard L. Kiper, *Major General John Alexander McClernand: Politician in Uniform* (Kent, OH: Kent State University Press, 1999), 156.

30. *OR*, 17(2): 528–29.

31. *OR*, 17(2): 534–35.

32. *OR*, 17(2): 535–36, 560, 564; Simon, *PUSG*, 7:188.

33. *OR*, 17(2): 537, 546, 552; Sherman, *Memoirs*, 1:296–97.

34. *OR*, 17(2): 552–54, 559; Simon, *PUSG*, 7:224; Sherman, *Memoirs*, 1:302; Grant, *Personal Memoirs*, 1:441.

35. *OR*, 17(2): 562, 567.

36. *OR*, 17(2): 566–67; Kiper, *Major General John Alexander McClernand*, 196.

37. *OR*, 17(2): 555, 579; Kiper, *Major General John Alexander McClernand*, 182.

38. Simon, *PUSG*, 7:150, 155.

39. Simon, *PUSG*, 7:147, 181–82.

40. *OR*, 17(2): 566, 569, 575–76, 586–87; Simon, *PUSG*, 7:183, 188–89, 194, 199, 203, 212.

41. *OR*, 17(2): 566, 569, 575–76, 586–87; Simon, *PUSG*, 7:183, 188–89, 194, 199, 203, 212.

42. *OR*, 17(1): 481.

43. *OR*, 17(2): 569–70; *OR*, 17(1): 475; Simon, *PUSG*, 7:60, 132; Grant, *Personal Memoirs*, 1:432, 440. For Hurlbut, see Jeffrey N. Lash, *A Politician Turned General: The Civil War Career of Stephen Augustus Hurlbut* (Kent, OH: Kent State University Press, 2003).

44. Grant, *Personal Memoirs*, 1:440.

45. *OR*, 24(3): 5; *OR*, 17(2): 553, 555; Grant, *Personal Memoirs*, 1:432, 440; Kiper, *Major General John Alexander McClernand*, 180.

46. *OR*, 17(2): 555; Grant, *Personal Memoirs*, 1:432.

47. Grant, *Personal Memoirs*, 1:433, 438. For the Tennessee River Campaign, see the trilogy by Timothy B. Smith, *Grant Invades Tennessee: The 1862 Battles of Forts Henry and Donelson* (Lawrence: University Press of Kansas, 2016); *Shiloh: Conquer or Perish* (Lawrence: University Press of Kansas, 2014); *Corinth 1862: Siege, Battle, Occupation* (Lawrence: University Press of Kansas, 2012).

48. *OR*, 17(2): 549, 551, 557; *OR*, 24(3): 6; Simon, *PUSG*, 7:191, 204.

49. Grant, *Personal Memoirs*, 1:443, 446.

50. *OR*, 24(1): 8–9, 11; *ORN*, 24:165, 179; Grant, *Personal Memoirs*, 1:440–41.

51. *OR*, 17(2): 574; *OR*, 17(1): 481; *OR*, 24(1): 12; Simon, *PUSG*, 7:202; Sherman, *Memoirs*, 1:305; Grant, *Personal Memoirs*, 1:441.

52. *OR*, 17(2): 574; *OR*, 17(1): 481; *OR*, 24(1): 12; Simon, *PUSG*, 7:202; Sherman, *Memoirs*, 1:305; Grant, *Personal Memoirs*, 1:441; *ORN*, 24:165.

53. *OR*, 24(1): 8; Albert D. Richardson, *A Personal History of Ulysses S. Grant* (Hartford, CT: American Publishing Company, 1868), 284.

54. Simon, *PUSG,* 7:225; Adam Badeau, *Military History of Ulysses S. Grant, from April, 1861, to April, 1865,* 2 vols. (New York: D. Appleton and Company, 1881), 1:151; James H. Wilson to Adam Badeau, March 9, 1867, James H. Wilson Papers, Library of Congress, copy in Vicksburg file, Ulysses S. Grant Presidential Library, hereafter cited as USGPL.

3. *"The Problem Is a Difficult One, but I Shall Certainly Solve It"*

1. *War of the Rebellion: A Compilation of the Official Records of the Union and Confederate Armies* (Washington, DC: U.S. Government Printing Office, 1880–1901), vol. 17(part 1): 470, 473. Hereafter cited as *OR* with volume and part afterward; all references are to series 1; *OR,* 24(3): 6; John Y. Simon and John F. Marszalek, eds., *The Papers of Ulysses S. Grant,* 32 vols. to date (Carbondale: Southern Illinois University Press, 1967–present), 7:231, 253. Hereafter cited as Simon, *PUSG,* followed by volume and page number; Ulysses S. Grant, *Personal Memoirs of U. S. Grant,* 2 vols. (New York: Charles L. Webster and Company, 1892), 1:442.

2. *OR,* 17(1): 470, 473; *OR,* 24(3): 6; Simon, *PUSG,* 7:231, 253; Grant, *Personal Memoirs,* 1:442; Bruce Catton, *Grant Moves South* (Boston: Little, Brown, and Company, 1960), 374.

3. *OR,* 24(1): 44; William T. Sherman, *Memoirs of General William T. Sherman: Written by Himself,* 2 vols. (New York: D. Appleton and Company, 1875), 1:305.

4. *OR,* 17(2): 571; *OR,* 24(1): 8.

5. *OR,* 24(1): 8; Simon, *PUSG,* 7:249, 260, 491.

6. *The Official Records of the Union and Confederate Navies in the War of the Rebellion,* 30 vols. (Washington, DC: Government Printing Office, 1894–1922), 24:324–25. Hereafter cited as *ORN* with volume number afterward; all references are to series 1.

7. *OR,* 24(1): 8; Grant, *Personal Memoirs,* 1:446.

8. *OR,* 24(1): 67; *OR,* 24(3): 288; Charles A. Dana, *Recollections of the Civil War* (New York: D. Appleton and Company, 1898), 30; J. F. C. Fuller, *The Generalship of Ulysses S. Grant* (Bloomington: Indiana University Press, 1958), 136; Grant, *Personal Memoirs,* 1:458; Richard L. Kiper, *Major General John Alexander McClernand: Politician in Uniform* (Kent, OH: Kent State University Press, 1999), 207.

9. *OR,* 24(1): 67; *OR,* 24(3): 288; Grant, *Personal Memoirs,* 1:458; Dana, *Recollections of the Civil War,* 30; Fuller, *Generalship of Ulysses S. Grant,* 136.

10. *OR,* 17(2): 541; *OR,* 24(3): 49; *OR,* 24(1): 65; Simon, *PUSG,* 7:253; Dana, *Recollections of the Civil War,* 21.

11. For Vicksburg's geography, see Warren E. Grabau, *Ninety-Eight Days: A Geographer's View of the Vicksburg Campaign* (Knoxville: University of Tennessee Press, 2000).

12. *OR,* 24(1): 10.

13. *OR*, 24(3): 126; *OR*, 17(2): 551–52; *OR*, 24(1): 8; *ORN*, 24:149.

14. *OR*, 24(3): 9, 12; *OR*, 24(1): 10; Simon, *PUSG*, 7:311, 366, 383–84; Grant, *Personal Memoirs*, 1:446.

15. *OR*, 24(3): 38, 65, 126; *OR*, 24(1): 44; Simon, *PUSG*, 7:402; Sylvanus Cadwallader, *Three Years with Grant*, ed. Benjamin P. Thomas (Lincoln: University of Nebraska Press, 1996), 46, 48, 54; Albert D. Richardson, *A Personal History of Ulysses S. Grant* (Hartford, CT: American Publishing Company, 1868), 284; Earl J. Hess, "Grant's Ethnic General: Peter J. Osterhaus," in *Grant's Lieutenants: From Cairo to Vicksburg*, ed. Steven E. Woodworth (Lawrence: University Press of Kansas, 2001), 206. For a biography of Osterhaus, see Mary Bobbitt Townsend, *Yankee Warhorse: A Biography of Major General Peter Osterhaus* (Columbia: University of Missouri Press, 2010).

16. *OR*, 24(3): 38, 65, 126; *OR*, 24(1): 17, 44; Fuller, *Generalship of Ulysses S. Grant*, 135–36.

17. *OR*, 24(3): 17.

18. *OR*, 24(3): 18, 32.

19. *OR*, 24(3): 33, 38.

20. *OR*, 24(3): 43–44, 120; Grant, *Personal Memoirs*, 1:448.

21. *OR*, 24(3): 131; Grant, *Personal Memoirs*, 1:449.

22. *OR*, 24(1): 45.

23. *OR*, 24(3): 6; *OR*, 24(1): 14, 45; Simon, *PUSG*, 7:409, 463.

24. *OR*, 24(3): 26.

25. Simon, *PUSG*, 7:323; Grant, *Personal Memoirs*, 1:450.

26. *OR*, 24(3): 36, 56; Simon, *PUSG*, 7:256.

27. *OR*, 24(3): 62; Simon, *PUSG*, 7:289–90, 411.

28. *OR*, 24(3): 86, 126; *OR*, 24(1): 20; Simon, *PUSG*, 7:369.

29. *OR*, 24(3): 112, 119; *OR*, 24(1): 19.

30. *OR*, 24(3): 112, 119; *OR*, 24(1): 21; Grant, *Personal Memoirs*, 1:452.

31. *OR*, 24(3): 112–13, 126; Simon, *PUSG*, 7:423; Grant, *Personal Memoirs*, 1:453.

32. *OR*, 24(3): 118, 126; *OR*, 24(1): 46; Simon, *PUSG*, 7:420; Sherman, *Memoirs*, 1:307.

33. Simon, *PUSG*, 7:421; Sherman, *Memoirs*, 1:308; R. Blake Dunnavent, "'We Had Lively Times up the Yazoo': Admiral David Dixon Porter," in *Grant's Lieutenants: From Cairo to Vicksburg*, ed. Steven E. Woodworth (Lawrence: University Press of Kansas, 2001), 177.

34. Simon, *PUSG*, 7:268, 270, 276, 357–58, 411, 489.

35. *OR*, 24(3): 15, 83, 86, 153; Simon, *PUSG*, 7:247, 250, 261.

36. *OR*, 24(3): 116, 122, 126, 166; Simon, *PUSG*, 7:230, 232, 238, 312–14, 327, 337, 442, 492; Simon, *PUSG*, 8:24.

37. *OR*, 24(3): 116, 122, 126, 166; Simon, *PUSG*, 7:230, 232, 238, 312–14, 327, 337, 442, 492; Simon, *PUSG*, 8:24.

38. *OR*, 24(3): 65–66, 118–19; *ORN*, 24:183–84, 435–36; Simon, *PUSG*, 7:245, 336, 352, 368, 382, 411, 414–15.

39. *OR*, 24(3): 46–47, 105, 157; Simon, *PUSG*, 7:278.

40. *OR*, 24(3): 66; Simon, *PUSG*, 7:370–72, 489; *OR*, 10(1): 174–89.

41. Simon, *PUSG*, 7:253, 309, 311, 321–22, 324–25, 330, 397, 490–91.

42. Simon, *PUSG*, 7:397, 490–91; Frederick D. Grant, "A Boy's Experience at Vicksburg," *Personal Recollections of the War of the Rebellion: Addresses Delivered before the Commandery of the State of New York, Military Order of the Loyal Legion of the United States*, ed. A. Noel Blakeman (New York: G. P. Putnam's Sons, 1907), 86; Fred Grant, "A Boy's Experience at Vicksburg," manuscript in Vicksburg files, USGPL, 2; Richardson, *Personal History of Ulysses S. Grant*, 284; Cadwallader, *Three Years with Grant*, 54.

43. Grant, "A Boy's Experience at Vicksburg," 4–5. Ed Bearss states that the "machine gun" must have been a Gatling gun; personal discussion with author, October 28, 2016.

44. *OR*, 24(3): 75; Simon, *PUSG*, 7:409–10; Brooks D. Simpson, *Triumph Over Adversity, 1822–1865* (Boston: Houghton Mifflin Company, 2000), 178; Catton, *Grant Moves South*, 387.

45. Simon, *PUSG*, 7:311.

46. Simon, *PUSG*, 7:246, 248, 297, 301–2, 309, 333, 347, 359, 392, 398, 403, 419, 483; *ORN*, 24:341–42.

47. *OR*, 24(3): 137–41, 147, 151; *OR*, 52(1): 345; Catton, *Grant Moves South*, 395.

48. *OR*, 24(3): 19; Simon, *PUSG*, 7:259.

49. *OR*, 24(1): 11–13; Simon, *PUSG*, 7:264.

50. *OR*, 24(3): 57.

51. *OR*, 24(3): 73, 164.

52. Simon, *PUSG*, 7:452–53.

53. *OR*, 24(1): 8–9.

54. *OR*, 24(3): 151.

55. *OR*, 24(3): 127; Jane Turner Censer, ed., *The Papers of Frederick Law Olmsted*, 12 vols. (Baltimore: Johns Hopkins University Press, 1977–present), 4:581.

56. *OR*, 24(3): 126–27.

57. *OR*, 24(3): 151; *OR*, 24(1): 18; Simon, *PUSG*, 7:293, 343–44, 351, 381, 391–92, 413.

58. Simon, *PUSG*, 7:325, 331, 368, 396.

59. Richardson, *Personal History of Ulysses S. Grant*, 292–93; Catton, *Grant Moves South*, 400; Mary A. Livermore, *My Story of the War: A Woman's Narrative of Four Years' Personal Experience as Nurse in the Union Army, and in Relief Work at Home, in Hospitals, Camps, and at the Front during the War of the Rebellion. With Anecdotes, Pathetic Incidents, and Thrilling Reminiscences*

Portraying the Lights and Shadows of Hospital Life and the Sanitary Service of the War (Hartford, CT: A. D. Worthington and Company, 1890), 308–17.

60. *OR*, 24(1): 14, 22, 24–25, 69; Simon, *PUSG*, 7:278.

61. *OR*, 24(1): 14, 22, 24–25, 69; Simon, *PUSG*, 7:278.

62. *OR*, 24(1): 25, 29; Simon, *PUSG*, 7:342–43.

63. Adam Badeau, *Military History of Ulysses S. Grant, from April, 1861, to April, 1865*, 2 vols. (New York: D. Appleton and Company, 1881), 1:180; Richardson, *Personal History of Ulysses S. Grant*, 290, 299.

4. *"I Thought That War Anyhow Was a Risk"*

1. *War of the Rebellion: A Compilation of the Official Records of the Union and Confederate Armies* (Washington, DC: U.S. Government Printing Office, 1880–1901), vol. 24(part 3): 134. Hereafter cited as *OR* with volume and part afterward; all references are to series 1; *OR*, 24(1): 28; John Y. Simon and John F. Marszalek, eds., *The Papers of Ulysses S. Grant*, 32 vols. to date (Carbondale: Southern Illinois University Press, 1967–present), 7:463, 480. Hereafter cited as Simon, *PUSG*, followed by volume and page number.

2. *OR*, 24(3): 168; *OR*, 24(1): 24; Simon, *PUSG*, 7:489; Simon, *PUSG*, 8:110.

3. *OR*, 24(1): 70–71; Simon, *PUSG*, 7:480; Bruce Catton, *U. S. Grant and the American Military Tradition* (Boston: Little, Brown, and Company, 1954), 98; John Russell Young, *Around the World with General Grant: A Narrative of the Visit of General U. S. Grant, Ex-President of the United States, to Various Countries in Europe, Asia, and Africa, in 1877, 1878, 1879. To Which Are Added Certain Conversations with General Grant on Questions Connected with American Politics and History* (New York: American News Company, 1879), 2:616.

4. *OR*, 24(1): 70; Simon, *PUSG*, 7:471; Ulysses S. Grant, *Personal Memoirs of U. S. Grant*, 2 vols. (New York: Charles L. Webster and Company, 1892), 1:460–61; Adam Badeau, *Military History of Ulysses S. Grant, from April, 1861, to April, 1865*, 2 vols. (New York: D. Appleton and Company, 1881), 1:182; Bruce Catton, *Grant Moves South* (Boston: Little, Brown, and Company, 1960), 407.

5. *OR*, 24(3): 123, 131, 133, 136; Simon, *PUSG*, 7:475.

6. *OR*, 24(3): 104, 131–32, 135; *OR*, 24(1): 73, 75, 78.

7. *OR*, 24(3): 151–52; *The Official Records of the Union and Confederate Navies in the War of the Rebellion*, 30 vols. (Washington, DC: Government Printing Office, 1894–1922), 24:517. Hereafter cited as *ORN* with volume number afterward; all references are to series 1; Simon, *PUSG*, 7:354, 360, 367, 463, 476; Grant, *Personal Memoirs*, 1:461; Frederick D. Grant, "A Boy's Experience at Vicksburg," *Personal Recollections of the War of the Rebellion: Addresses Delivered before the Commandery of the State of New York, Military Order of the Loyal Legion of the United States*, ed. A. Noel Blakeman (New York: G. P. Putnam's Sons, 1907), 86–87.

8. *OR*, 24(3): 168; *OR*, 24(1): 29, 47; Simon, *PUSG*, 8:5, 19, 87; Grant, *Personal Memoirs*, 1:466. For detail on the march south in Louisiana, see Terrence J. Winschel, *Triumph and Defeat: The Vicksburg Campaign* (Mason City, IA: Savas Publishing Company, 1999), 17–32.

9. *OR*, 24(3): 179–80, 201; William T. Sherman, *Memoirs of General William T. Sherman: Written by Himself*, 2 vols. (New York: D. Appleton and Company, 1875), 1:315; Grant, *Personal Memoirs*, 1:542–43; Brooks D. Simpson, *Triumph Over Adversity, 1822–1865* (Boston: Houghton Mifflin Company, 2000), 174.

10. Sherman, *Memoirs*, 1:317.

11. Grant, *Personal Memoirs*, 1:462.

12. *OR*, 24(3): 181–82; *OR*, 24(1): 72, Simon, *PUSG*, 8:25; Catton, *Grant Moves South*, 420.

13. Simon, *PUSG*, 8:29, 9–10, 133.

14. Simon, *PUSG*, 8:30, 52.

15. Simon, *PUSG*, 8:9, 30, 101.

16. Simon, *PUSG*, 8:100–101, 110.

17. Simon, *PUSG*, 8:3.

18. Simon, *PUSG*, 8:8, 109.

19. Simon, *PUSG*, 8:23, 28, 30–31, 33, 35, 58, 66–69, 83, 112.

20. Simon, *PUSG*, 8:164; William E. Parrish, *Frank Blair: Lincoln's Conservative* (Columbia: University of Missouri Press, 1998), 162, 164; Grant, *Personal Memoirs*, 1:573–74.

21. Simon, *PUSG*, 8:38–39.

22. Simon, *PUSG*, 8:63, 65, 79, 99, 105, 113–14, 119.

23. Simon, *PUSG*, 8:63, 65, 79, 99, 105, 113–14, 119.

24. *OR*, 24(3): 188; *OR*, 24(1): 26, 71.

25. *OR*, 24(3): 188; *OR*, 24(1): 26, 71.

26. *OR*, 24(1): 74; Grant, *Personal Memoirs*, 1:465; Charles A. Dana, *Recollections of the Civil War* (New York: D. Appleton and Company, 1898), 32–33.

27. *OR*, 24(3): 186, 194, 200–201; *OR*, 24(1): 76; Simon, *PUSG*, 8:15–16, 47; Grant, *Personal Memoirs*, 1:464; Dana, *Recollections of the Civil War*, 36, 38; Badeau, *Military History of Ulysses S. Grant*, 1:195.

28. *OR*, 24(3): 186, 194, 200–201; *OR*, 24(1): 76; Simon, *PUSG*, 8:15–16, 47; John Y. Simon, ed., *The Personal Memoirs of Julia Dent Grant [Mrs. Ulysses S. Grant]* (New York: G. P. Putnam's Sons, 1975), 111–12; Grant, *Personal Memoirs*, 1:464; Dana, *Recollections of the Civil War*, 36, 38; Grant, "A Boy's Experience at Vicksburg," 87–88; Badeau, *Military History of Ulysses S. Grant*, 1:195; James Harrison Wilson, *Under the Old Flag: Recollections of Military Operations in the War for the Union, the Spanish War, the Boxer Rebellion, Etc.*, 2 vols. (New York: D. Appleton and Company, 1912), 163–64.

29. *OR*, 24(3): 186, 194, 200–201; *OR*, 24(1): 76; Simon, *PUSG*, 8:15–16, 47; Simon, ed., *Personal Memoirs of Julia Dent Grant*, 111–12; Grant, *Personal Memoirs*, 1:464; Dana, *Recollections of the Civil War*, 36, 38; Grant, "A Boy's Experience at Vicksburg," 87–88; Badeau, *Military History of Ulysses S. Grant*, 1:195; Wilson, *Under the Old Flag*, 163–64; Fred Grant, "A Boy's Experience at Vicksburg," manuscript in Vicksburg files, USGPL, 8.

30. *OR*, 24(3): 211, 217, 222, 227; *OR*, 24(1): 81; Simon, *PUSG*, 8:134; Simon, ed., *Personal Memoirs of Julia Dent Grant*, 112.

31. *OR*, 23(2): 214; *OR*, 24(3): 197, 202, 215; *OR*, 24(1): 33, 79; Simon, *PUSG*, 7:307.

32. *OR*, 24(3): 212, 231, 234, 240, 242–45; Sherman, *Memoirs*, 1:319; John F. Marszalek, "'A Full Share of All the Credit': Sherman and Grant to the Fall of Vicksburg," in *Grant's Lieutenants: From Cairo to Vicksburg*, ed. Steven E. Woodworth (Lawrence: University Press of Kansas, 2001), 18.

33. *OR*, 24(3): 222.

34. *OR*, 24(3): 189–90, 198, 207.

35. *OR*, 24(3): 186–87, 208.

36. *OR*, 24(3): 187, 220; *OR*, 52(1): 352.

37. *OR*, 24(3): 188, 192, 205; *OR*, 24(1): 80; Simon, *PUSG*, 8:36.

38. James H. Wilson to Adam Badeau, March 18, 1867, James H. Wilson Papers, Library of Congress, copy in Vicksburg file, USGPL; Wilson, *Under the Old Flag*, 167–68.

39. *OR*, 24(3): 213.

40. *OR*, 24(3): 229–31, 235–36; *OR*, 24(1): 80; Wilson, *Under the Old Flag*, 169.

41. *OR*, 24(1): 80–81; Simon, *PUSG*, 8:122–23, 132; Dana, *Recollections of the Civil War*, 41.

42. *OR*, 24(3): 222, 226, 237, 246; *OR*, 24(1): 47–48, 82 Simon, *PUSG*, 8:109; Grant, *Personal Memoirs*, 1:476; Grant, "A Boy's Experience at Vicksburg," 88; Earl J. Hess, "Grant's Ethnic General: Peter J. Osterhaus," in *Grant's Lieutenants: From Cairo to Vicksburg*, ed. Steven E. Woodworth (Lawrence: University Press of Kansas, 2001), 204–5.

43. *OR*, 24(1): 32, 47–48, 82; *OR*, 24(3): 222, 226, 237, 246; Simon, *PUSG*, 8:109; Grant, *Personal Memoirs*, 1:476–77; Grant, "A Boy's Experience at Vicksburg," 88; Dana, *Recollections of the Civil War*, 43; Catton, *Grant Moves South*, 424–25.

44. Simon, *PUSG*, 8:132; *OR*, 24(1): 83; Grant, *Personal Memoirs*, 1:477–78, 481; Dana, *Recollections of the Civil War*, 43–44.

45. Dana, *Recollections of the Civil War*, 43–44.

46. Simon, *PUSG*, 8:132; *OR*, 24(1): 83; Grant, *Personal Memoirs*, 1:477–78, 481; Dana, *Recollections of the Civil War*, 43–44; Kenneth P. Williams, *Grant Rises in the West: From Iuka to Vicksburg, 1862–1863* (Lincoln: University of

Nebraska Press, 1997), 344; Grant, "A Boy's Experience at Vicksburg," manuscript in Vicksburg files, USGPL, 11.

47. *OR*, 24(1): 33, 48.

48. *OR*, 24(1): 32; Simon, *PUSG*, 8:79; Grant, *Personal Memoirs*, 1:480–81; James Pickett Jones, *Black Jack: John A. Logan and Southern Illinois in the Civil War Era* (Carbondale: Southern Illinois University Press, 1967), 157.

49. *OR*, 24(3): 248.

50. Grant, *Personal Memoirs*, 1:488.

51. *OR*, 24(3): 260, 268–69; *OR*, 24(1): 32.

52. Albert D. Richardson, *A Personal History of Ulysses S. Grant* (Hartford, CT: American Publishing Company, 1868), 305; Grant, "A Boy's Experience at Vicksburg," 89; J. H. Wilson, "A Staff Officer's Journal of the Vicksburg Campaign, April 30 to July 4, 1863," *Journal of the Military Service Institution of the United States* 43, no. 154 (July–August 1908): 93; Sylvanus Cadwallader, *Three Years with Grant*, ed. Benjamin P. Thomas (Lincoln: University of Nebraska Press, 1996), 63.

53. *OR*, 24(3): 260, 268–69; *OR*, 24(1): 32, 49; Simon, *PUSG*, 8:138; Grant, *Personal Memoirs*, 1:483, 487; Dana, *Recollections of the Civil War*, 45; Richardson, *Personal History of Ulysses S. Grant*, 306; Badeau, *Military History of Ulysses S. Grant*, 1:209; Jane Turner Censer, ed., *The Papers of Frederick Law Olmsted*, 12 vols. (Baltimore: Johns Hopkins University Press, 1977–present), 4:583. For detail on the battle at Port Gibson, see Winschel, *Triumph and Defeat*, 57–88.

54. Grant, *Personal Memoirs*, 1:486–87; Dana, *Recollections of the Civil War*, 46; Grant, "A Boy's Experience at Vicksburg," 89–90.

55. *OR*, 24(3): 269; Simon, *PUSG*, 8:139; Grant, *Personal Memoirs*, 1:485; Dana, *Recollections of the Civil War*, 47; Wilson, "A Staff Officer's Journal of the Vicksburg Campaign," 93; Edwin C. Bearss, *The Vicksburg Campaign*, 3 vols. (Dayton, OH: Morningside, 1985), 2:410; Grant, "A Boy's Experience at Vicksburg," manuscript in Vicksburg files, USGPL, 13.

56. *OR*, 24(3): 263; *OR*, 24(1): 49; Simon, *PUSG*, 8:141.

57. *OR*, 24(3): 262, 265; *OR*, 24(1): 32; Simon, *PUSG*, 8:142; Grant, *Personal Memoirs*, 1:485, 490; Grant, "A Boy's Experience at Vicksburg," 90; Badeau, *Military History of Ulysses S. Grant*, 1:213.

58. *OR*, 24(3): 266; Simon, *PUSG*, 8:132, 142.

59. *OR*, 24(3): 265; *OR*, 24(1): 33, 38–39, 50; Simon, *PUSG*, 8:150.

60. Grant, "A Boy's Experience at Vicksburg," 90–91.

61. *OR*, 24(3): 267, 269; *OR*, 24(1): 33, 49; Simon, *PUSG*, 8:155–56; Grant, *Personal Memoirs*, 1:473; Wilson, *Under the Old Flag*, 194, 196; Cadwallader, *Three Years with Grant*, 60; Wilson, "A Staff Officer's Journal of the Vicksburg Campaign," 95; David Dixon Porter, *Incidents and Anecdotes of the Civil War* (New

York: D. Appleton and Company, 1885), 182; Simon, ed., *Personal Memoirs of Julia Dent Grant,* 111.

62. *OR,* 24(3): 267, 269; *OR,* 24(1): 33, 49; Simon, *PUSG,* 8:155–56; Cadwallader, *Three Years with Grant,* 60; Porter, *Incidents and Anecdotes of the Civil War,* 182; Simon, ed., *Personal Memoirs of Julia Dent Grant,* 111.

63. Grant, *Personal Memoirs,* 1:490–91; Dana, *Recollections of the Civil War,* 47–48.

64. Simon, *PUSG,* 8:155; Dana, *Recollections of the Civil War,* 49; Grant, "A Boy's Experience at Vicksburg," 91; Young, *Around the World with General Grant,* 2:99; Badeau, *Military History of Ulysses S. Grant,* 1:226.

65. *OR,* 24(3): 267, 269; *OR,* 24(1): 33, 49; Simon, *PUSG,* 8:156; Dana, *Recollections of the Civil War,* 48; Grant, "A Boy's Experience at Vicksburg," 91.

66. *OR,* 24(3): 263, 272, 273–75; Simon, *PUSG,* 8:156, 158.

67. *OR,* 24(3): 261; Simon, *PUSG,* 8:159.

68. *OR,* 24(3): 271, 274; Simon, *PUSG,* 8:174; Sherman, *Memoirs,* 1:321.

69. *OR,* 24(3): 268; Simon, *PUSG,* 8:162.

70. *OR,* 24(3): 271–72, 275; Simon, *PUSG,* 8:107, 120, 167–68.

71. *OR,* 24(3): 266, 270; Simon, *PUSG,* 8:168, 174.

72. Wilson, *Under the Old Flag,* 175.

73. *OR,* 24(3): 270, 277, 279; Simon, *PUSG,* 8:162, 165, 169, 174–75.

5. *"You Can Do a Great Deal in Eight Days"*

1. Mary Amelia (Boomer) Stone, *Memoir of George Boardman Boomer* (Boston: Press of George C. Rand and Avery, 1864), 244–46, 250.

2. *War of the Rebellion: A Compilation of the Official Records of the Union and Confederate Armies* (Washington, DC: U.S. Government Printing Office, 1880–1901), vol. 24(part 1): 35. Hereafter cited as *OR* with volume and part afterward; all references are to series 1; John Y. Simon and John F. Marszalek, eds., *The Papers of Ulysses S. Grant,* 32 vols. to date (Carbondale: Southern Illinois University Press, 1967–present), 7:491. Hereafter cited as Simon, *PUSG,* followed by volume and page number.

3. *OR,* 24(1): 33.

4. Ulysses S. Grant, *Personal Memoirs of U. S. Grant,* 2 vols. (New York: Charles L. Webster and Company, 1892), 1:491.

5. *OR,* 24(3): 225, 265, 281, 288–89, 298; Simon, *PUSG,* 8:196; Grant, *Personal Memoirs,* 1:491–92, 500.

6. *OR,* 24(3): 225, 265, 281, 288–89, 298; Simon, *PUSG,* 8:196; Grant, *Personal Memoirs,* 1:491–92, 500.

7. Grant, *Personal Memoirs,* 1:492; John Russell Young, *Around the World with General Grant: A Narrative of the Visit of General U. S. Grant, Ex-President*

of the United States, to Various Countries in Europe, Asia, and Africa, in 1877, 1878, 1879. To Which Are Added Certain Conversations with General Grant on Questions Connected with American Politics and History (New York: American News Company, 1879), 2:621.

8. Young, *Around the World with General Grant*, 2:621.

9. *OR*, 24(1): 35; Grant, *Personal Memoirs*, 1:493.

10. *OR*, 24(1): 83; Grant, *Personal Memoirs*, 1:493, 495.

11. *OR*, 24(3): 273, 290; *OR*, 24(1): 84.

12. J. H. Wilson, "A Staff Officer's Journal of the Vicksburg Campaign, April 30 to July 4, 1863," *Journal of the Military Service Institution of the United States* 43, no. 154 (July–August 1908): 96–99, 101.

13. Grant, *Personal Memoirs*, 1:496; J. F. C. Fuller, *The Generalship of Ulysses S. Grant* (Bloomington: Indiana University Press, 1958), 142–43.

14. *OR*, 24(3): 278–79; Simon, *PUSG*, 8:189.

15. *OR*, 24(3): 280, 284, 287–89; *OR*, 24(1): 50, 85; Simon, *PUSG*, 8:176, 181–82.

16. *OR*, 24(3): 279, 282.

17. *OR*, 24(3): 280, 284–85; Simon, *PUSG*, 8:184.

18. *OR*, 24(3): 285–86; *OR*, 24(1): 84; Grant, *Personal Memoirs*, 1:434–35; Fuller, *Generalship of Ulysses S. Grant*, 145.

19. Simon, *PUSG*, 8:178–79, 181, 186.

20. Simon, *PUSG*, 8:186–87.

21. *OR*, 24(3): 286, 290, 293, 296.

22. James Harrison Wilson, *Under the Old Flag: Recollections of Military Operations in the War for the Union, the Spanish War, the Boxer Rebellion, Etc.*, 2 vols. (New York: D. Appleton and Company, 1912), 182–83, 198.

23. *OR*, 24(3): 289, 295; Simon, *PUSG*, 8:40.

24. *OR*, 24(3): 282, 287, 292–93, 296; *OR*, 24(1): 49, 84.

25. Frederick D. Grant, "A Boy's Experience at Vicksburg," *Personal Recollections of the War of the Rebellion: Addresses Delivered before the Commandery of the State of New York, Military Order of the Loyal Legion of the United States*, ed. A. Noel Blakeman (New York: G. P. Putnam's Sons, 1907), 92.

26. *OR*, 24(3): 286–87.

27. *OR*, 24(3): 286, 296; William T. Sherman, *Memoirs of General William T. Sherman: Written by Himself*, 2 vols. (New York: D. Appleton and Company, 1875), 1:321; Terrence J. Winschel, *Triumph and Defeat: The Vicksburg Campaign*, vol. 2 (New York: Savas Beatie, 2006), 13.

28. *OR*, 24(3): 292.

29. *OR*, 24(3): 293, 295, 299, 301.

30. *OR*, 24(3): 286, 295–97, 299–300.

31. *OR*, 24(3): 290; *OR*, 24(1): 50, 701. For detail on Raymond, see J. Parker

Hills, "Roads to Raymond," in *The Vicksburg Campaign: March 29–May 18, 1863*, eds. Steven E. Woodworth and Charles D. Grear (Carbondale: Southern Illinois University Press, 2013), 65–95.

32. *OR*, 24(3): 299; *OR*, 24(1): 50.

33. *OR*, 24(3): 268, 280–81, 301.

34. *OR*, 24(3): 300; *OR*, 24(1): 50; Grant, *Personal Memoirs*, 1:499–500; Albert D. Richardson, *A Personal History of Ulysses S. Grant* (Hartford, CT: American Publishing Company, 1868), 313; Edwin C. Bearss, *The Vicksburg Campaign*, 3 vols. (Dayton, OH: Morningside, 1985), 2:480.

35. *OR*, 24(3): 300, 305, 307; Grant, *Personal Memoirs*, 1:500, 503.

36. *OR*, 24(3): 305–6; Grant, *Personal Memoirs*, 1:501.

37. *OR*, 24(3): 307–8; *OR*, 24(1): 50; Simon, *PUSG*, 8:217; Grant, *Personal Memoirs*, 1:503.

38. *OR*, 24(3): 309.

39. *OR*, 24(3): 311; Grant, *Personal Memoirs*, 1:505; Grant, "A Boy's Experience at Vicksburg," 92. For detail on the fighting at Jackson, see Winschel, *Triumph and Defeat*, 2:31–48, and Steven E. Woodworth, "The First Capture and Occupation of Jackson, Mississippi," in *The Vicksburg Campaign: March 29–May 18, 1863*, eds. Steven E. Woodworth and Charles D. Grear (Carbondale: Southern Illinois University Press, 2013), 96–115.

40. Grant, "A Boy's Experience at Vicksburg," 93.

41. *OR*, 24(3): 312; Sherman, *Memoirs*, 1:321.

42. *OR*, 24(3): 310–11.

43. *OR*, 24(3): 311–12.

44. Simon, *PUSG*, 8:184–85.

45. Simon, *PUSG*, 8:230, 233–34, 244.

46. Simon, *PUSG*, 8:189; Grant, *Personal Memoirs*, 1:506; Grant, "A Boy's Experience at Vicksburg," 93.

47. Simon, *PUSG*, 8:189; Sylvanus Cadwallader, *Three Years with Grant*, ed. Benjamin P. Thomas (Lincoln: University of Nebraska Press, 1996), 64–65, 74.

48. Grant, *Personal Memoirs*, 1:507; Timothy B. Smith, *Mississippi in the Civil War: The Home Front* (Jackson: University Press of Mississippi, 2010), 38–40.

49. *OR*, 24(3): 313; Grant, *Personal Memoirs*, 1:503.

50. *OR*, 24(3): 319.

51. *OR*, 24(3): 314–15; Simon, *PUSG*, 8:222; Grant, *Personal Memoirs*, 1:510.

52. *OR*, 24(3): 313–14, 317; Simon, *PUSG*, 8:224.

53. *OR*, 24(3): 314, 316–17.

54. *OR*, 24(3): 317–18, 320; *OR*, 24(1): 51–52; Grant, *Personal Memoirs*, 1:508, 510–11, 513; Richard L. Kiper, *Major General John Alexander McClernand: Politician in Uniform* (Kent, OH: Kent State University Press, 1999), 243.

55. *OR*, 24(3): 318; *OR*, 24(1): 53; Grant, *Personal Memoirs*, 1:498, 513.

56. Grant, *Personal Memoirs*, 1:517, 519–20; Grant, "A Boy's Experience at Vicksburg," 93–94; Timothy B. Smith, *Champion Hill: Decisive Battle for Vicksburg* (New York: Savas Beatie, 2004), 212. While laying much blame on Grant, McClernand's biographer still held some fault for McClernand at Champion Hill. See Kiper, *Major General John Alexander McClernand*, 247.

57. *OR*, 24(1): 53; Simon, *PUSG*, 8:228. For detail on Champion Hill, see Smith, *Champion Hill*.

58. *OR*, 24(3): 322; *OR*, 24(1): 53; Simon, *PUSG*, 8:228–29; Sherman, *Memoirs*, 1:322–23; Grant, *Personal Memoirs*, 1:519, 521.

59. Grant, "A Boy's Experience at Vicksburg," 94.

60. *OR*, 24(3): 322; *OR*, 24(1): 53; Simon, *PUSG*, 8:228–29; Sherman, *Memoirs*, 1:322–23; Grant, *Personal Memoirs*, 1:519.

61. *OR*, 24(3): 321–22; *OR*, 24(1): 54; Simon, *PUSG*, 8:231; Grant, *Personal Memoirs*, 1:526; Wilson, "A Staff Officer's Journal of the Vicksburg Campaign," 109. For detail on the battle at Big Black River, see Timothy B. Smith, "'A Victory Could Hardly Have Been More Complete': The Battle of Big Black River Bridge," in *The Vicksburg Campaign: March 29–May 18, 1863*, eds. Steven E. Woodworth and Charles D. Grear (Carbondale: Southern Illinois University Press, 2013), 173–93.

62. Grant, *Personal Memoirs*, 1:487, 525–26; *OR*, 24(1): 36; Grant, "A Boy's Experience at Vicksburg," 94–95.

63. John F. Marszalek, *Commander of All Lincoln's Armies: A Life of General Henry W. Halleck* (Cambridge: Harvard University Press, 2004), 177; Young, *Around the World with General Grant*, 2: 623; Bruce Catton, *Grant Moves South* (Boston: Little, Brown, and Company, 1960), 447–48.

64. *OR*, 24(3): 322; Sherman, *Memoirs*, 1:323–24; J. H. Wilson, "A Staff Officer's Journal of the Vicksburg Campaign, April 30 to July 4, 1863," *Journal of the Military Service Institution of the United States* 43, no. 155 (September–October 1908): 261; Cadwallader, *Three Years with Grant*, 83.

6. "To Carry Vicksburg by Assault"

1. *War of the Rebellion: A Compilation of the Official Records of the Union and Confederate Armies* (Washington, DC: U.S. Government Printing Office, 1880–1901), vol. 24(part 3): 325, 333. Hereafter cited as *OR* with volume and part afterward; all references are to series 1.

2. *OR*, 24(3): 325, 336, 342.

3. *OR*, 24(3): 325, 336, 342, 350.

4. *OR*, 24(3): 327; Ulysses S. Grant, *Personal Memoirs of U. S. Grant*, 2 vols. (New York: Charles L. Webster and Company, 1892), 1:527–28; J. H. Wilson, "A Staff Officer's Journal of the Vicksburg Campaign, April 30 to July 4, 1863,"

Journal of the Military Service Institution of the United States 43, no. 154 (July–August 1908): 261.

5. *OR*, 24(3): 328; Grant, *Personal Memoirs*, 1:528, 541–42.

6. Special Orders, May 20, 1863, Series 3, USGPL; John Y. Simon and John F. Marszalek, eds., *The Papers of Ulysses S. Grant*, 32 vols. to date (Carbondale: Southern Illinois University Press, 1967–present), 8:240–41. Hereafter cited as Simon, *PUSG*, followed by volume and page number; Grant, *Personal Memoirs*, 1:530.

7. *OR*, 24(3): 324, 327; *OR*, 24(1): 54; William T. Sherman, *Memoirs of General William T. Sherman: Written by Himself*, 2 vols. (New York: D. Appleton and Company, 1875), 1:324–25; Grant, *Personal Memoirs*, 1:526–27; Wilson, "A Staff Officer's Journal of the Vicksburg Campaign," 263.

8. *OR*, 24(3): 324, 327; *OR*, 24(1): 54; Sherman, *Memoirs*, 1:324–25; Grant, *Personal Memoirs*, 1:526–27; Wilson, "A Staff Officer's Journal of the Vicksburg Campaign," 263.

9. Albert D. Richardson, *A Personal History of Ulysses S. Grant* (Hartford, CT: American Publishing Company, 1868), 322; Fred Grant, "A Boy's Experience at Vicksburg," manuscript in Vicksburg files, USGPL, 28–29.

10. *OR*, 24(3): 327–28, 334; Simon, *PUSG*, 8:218, 256, 259; John A. Rawlins to Commanding Officer, Grand Gulf, May 20, 1863, Series 3, USGPL.

11. *OR*, 24(3): 326, 329; *OR*, 24(1): 54; Simon, *PUSG*, 8:243.

12. *OR*, 24(1): 54; Simon, *PUSG*, 8:243; Frederick D. Grant, "A Boy's Experience at Vicksburg," *Personal Recollections of the War of the Rebellion: Addresses Delivered before the Commandery of the State of New York, Military Order of the Loyal Legion of the United States*, ed. A. Noel Blakeman (New York: G. P. Putnam's Sons, 1907), 95.

13. *OR*, 24(3): 329; Grant, *Personal Memoirs*, 1:529.

14. *OR*, 24(3): 329.

15. Timothy B. Smith, *Grant Invades Tennessee: The 1862 Battles of Forts Henry and Donelson* (Lawrence: University Press of Kansas, 2016), 154–61.

16. *OR*, 24(1): 54.

17. Warren E. Grabau, *Ninety-Eight Days: A Geographer's View of the Vicksburg Campaign* (Knoxville: University of Tennessee Press, 2000), 354–55.

18. Edwin C. Bearss, *The Vicksburg Campaign*, 3 vols. (Dayton, OH: Morningside, 1985), 3:754, 763–64.

19. W. T. Duff to John A. McClernand, May 19, 1863, Series 3, USGPL; Grabau, *Ninety-Eight Days*, 354–66.

20. *OR*, 24(1): 38, 54; Grant, *Personal Memoirs*, 1:530, 535.

21. Bearss, *Vicksburg Campaign*, 3:787–88.

22. *OR*, 24(3): 324, 331–32.

23. *OR*, 24(3): 331; *OR*, 24(1): 86.

24. *OR*, 24(3): 332.

25. *OR*, 24(3): 333; Simon, *PUSG*, 8:247.

26. *OR*, 24(1): 54–55; J. F. C. Fuller, *The Generalship of Ulysses S. Grant* (Bloomington: Indiana University Press, 1958), 154.

27. *OR*, 24(1): 55; *OR*, 24(3): 333–34; Sherman, *Memoirs*, 1:325; Grant, *Personal Memoirs*, 1:531.

28. *OR*, 24(3): 335.

29. *OR*, 24(1): 55; Grant, "A Boy's Experience at Vicksburg," 95; Grant, "A Boy's Experience at Vicksburg," manuscript in Vicksburg files, USGPL, 30.

30. *OR*, 24(1): 55; *In Memoriam: Charles Ewing* (Philadelphia: J. P. Lippincott Company, 1888), 52–53.

31. *OR*, 24(3): 320.

32. Bearss, *Vicksburg Campaign*, 3:813–33.

33. *OR*, 24(1): 55–56, 86; Sherman, *Memoirs*, 1:326–27; Terrence J. Winschel, "Fighting Politician: John A. McClernand," in *Grant's Lieutenants: From Cairo to Vicksburg*, ed. Steven E. Woodworth (Lawrence: University Press of Kansas, 2001), 140.

34. *OR*, 24(1): 84; Sylvanus Cadwallader, *Three Years with Grant*, ed. Benjamin P. Thomas (Lincoln: University of Nebraska Press, 1996), 92.

35. *OR*, 24(1): 87.

36. John Russell Young, *Around the World with General Grant: A Narrative of the Visit of General U. S. Grant, Ex-President of the United States, to Various Countries in Europe, Asia, and Africa, in 1877, 1878, 1879. To Which Are Added Certain Conversations with General Grant on Questions Connected with American Politics and History* (New York: American News Company, 1879), 2:304; Grant, "A Boy's Experience at Vicksburg," 95–96.

37. *OR*, 24(1): 55; Fuller, *Generalship of Ulysses S. Grant*, 155.

38. *OR*, 24(3): 337–38; Simon, *PUSG*, 8:263.

39. *OR*, 24(3): 338–45.

40. Simon, *PUSG*, 8:376.

41. *OR*, 24(3): 342–43, 348; *OR*, 24(1): 89; Simon, *PUSG*, 8:264; *The Official Records of the Union and Confederate Navies in the War of the Rebellion*, 30 vols. (Washington, DC: Government Printing Office, 1894–1922), 25:33. Hereafter cited as *ORN* with volume number afterward; all references are to series 1.

42. Grant, *Personal Memoirs*, 1:532.

43. *OR*, 24(1): 37.

44. *OR*, 24(3): 335–36, 346.

45. *OR*, 24(3): 349–50.

46. *OR*, 24(3): 346–47.

47. *OR*, 24(1): 37.

7. "The Work of Reducing the Enemy by Regular Approaches"

1. *War of the Rebellion: A Compilation of the Official Records of the Union and Confederate Armies* (Washington, DC: U.S. Government Printing Office, 1880–1901), vol. 24(part 3): 346, 348. Hereafter cited as *OR* with volume and part afterward; all references are to series 1; John Y. Simon and John F. Marszalek, eds., *The Papers of Ulysses S. Grant*, 32 vols. to date (Carbondale: Southern Illinois University Press, 1967–present), 8:255, 387. Hereafter cited as Simon, *PUSG*, followed by volume and page number.

2. *OR*, 24(3): 346; *OR*, 24(1): 37.

3. For an examination of the butcher idea, see Edward H. Bonekemper III, *Ulysses S. Grant: A Victor, Not a Butcher: The Military Genius of the Man Who Won the Civil War* (Washington, DC: Regnery History, 2004).

4. *OR*, 24(3): 367; Albert D. Richardson, *A Personal History of Ulysses S. Grant* (Hartford, CT: American Publishing Company, 1868), 328.

5. *OR*, 24(3): 358; Simon, *PUSG*, 8:389.

6. *OR*, 24(3): 350.

7. *OR*, 24(3): 350–51; *OR*, 24(1): 97.

8. *OR*, 24(3): 358, 368–69, 379, 381.

9. *OR*, 24(3): 365, 382, 386, 391, 394, 396, 444; Simon, *PUSG*, 8:336, 359.

10. *OR*, 24(3): 361, 368, 378; *The Official Records of the Union and Confederate Navies in the War of the Rebellion*, 30 vols. (Washington, DC: Government Printing Office, 1894–1922), 25:53. Hereafter cited as *ORN* with volume number afterward; all references are to series 1; *ORN*, 25:199–200; Simon, *PUSG*, 8:424–25.

11. *OR*, 24(3): 376–77; *OR*, 24(1): 42.

12. *OR*, 24(3): 383–84.

13. *OR*, 24(3): 384, 386–87, 389, 404–5.

14. *OR*, 24(3): 396; Ulysses S. Grant, *Personal Memoirs of U. S. Grant*, 2 vols. (New York: Charles L. Webster and Company, 1892), 1:546.

15. *OR*, 24(3): 395; Charles A. Dana, *Recollections of the Civil War* (New York: D. Appleton and Company, 1898), 79; Sylvanus Cadwallader, *Three Years with Grant*, ed. Benjamin P. Thomas (Lincoln: University of Nebraska Press, 1996), 100.

16. *OR*, 24(1): 57.

17. *OR*, 24(3): 356; *OR*, 24(1): 56; Simon, *PUSG*, 8:351.

18. *OR*, 24(3): 288, 291, 363.

19. Simon, *PUSG*, 8:330–31, 451–52; Dana, *Recollections of the Civil War*, 67.

20. *OR*, 24(3): 380, 401, 409; *OR*, 24(2): 319; Simon, *PUSG*, 8:358, 383, 439.

21. *OR*, 24(3): 380, 401, 409; *OR*, 24(2): 319; Simon, *PUSG*, 8:358, 383, 439; Dana, *Recollections of the Civil War*, 70.

22. *OR*, 24(3): 368, 375, 401, 411; Simon, *PUSG*, 8:281.

23. *OR*, 24(3): 372, 378; *OR*, 24(1): 90; *ORN*, 25:37, 50; Simon, *PUSG*, 8:276, 281; S. C. Lyford to Benjamin Prentiss, May 25, 1863, Series 3, USGPL.

24. Bruce Catton, *Grant Moves South* (Boston: Little, Brown, and Company, 1960), 459–60; Cadwallader, *Three Years with Grant*, 95; Charles Bracelen Flood, *Grant and Sherman: The Friendship That Won the Civil War* (New York: Farrar, Straus, and Giroux, 2005), 171; William L. Shea and Terrence J. Winschel, *Vicksburg Is the Key: The Struggle for the Mississippi River* (Lincoln: University of Nebraska Press, 2003), 156–57.

25. *OR*, 24(1): 56, 93, 99, 111; Grant, *Personal Memoirs*, 1:537; Adam Badeau, *Military History of Ulysses S. Grant, from April, 1861, to April, 1865*, 2 vols. (New York: D. Appleton and Company, 1881), 1:338. For detail on the Union siege operations, see Justin S. Solonick, *Engineering Victory: The Union Siege of Vicksburg* (Carbondale: Southern Illinois University Press, 2015).

26. *OR*, 24(3): 419, 422; *OR*, 24(1): 94, 99–100; Simon, *PUSG*, 8:409.

27. *OR*, 24(3): 378, 380, 407, 423, 426, 439; *OR*, 24(1): 41.

28. *OR*, 24(3): 375, 388; *ORN*, 25:164.

29. *OR*, 24(3): 390, 404, 411–12, 435, 437–38; Simon, *PUSG*, 8:326.

30. *OR*, 24(3): 438, 440–41, 444, 456–57; *OR*, 24(1): 113; Grant, *Personal Memoirs*, 1:551, 553; John A. Rawlins to S. C. Lyford, May 23, 1863, Series 3, USGPL.

31. *OR*, 24(3): 380, 390, 409.

32. *OR*, 24(3): 356, 363; Michael B. Ballard, *Grant at Vicksburg: The General and the Siege* (Carbondale: Southern Illinois University Press, 2013), 33.

33. *OR*, 24(3): 380; William T. Sherman, *Memoirs of General William T. Sherman: Written by Himself*, 2 vols. (New York: D. Appleton and Company, 1875), 1:328.

34. *OR*, 24(3): 359, 458; Simon, *PUSG*, 8:307, 397.

35. *OR*, 24(3): 351, 362; Simon, *PUSG*, 8:303.

36. *OR*, 24(3): 351–52, 361; *OR*, 24(1): 38, 98; Simon, *PUSG*, 8:275, 317–18.

37. *OR*, 24(3): 351–52, 361; *OR*, 24(1): 38, 98; Simon, *PUSG*, 8:275, 317–18.

38. *OR*, 24(3): 354, 361–62; Simon, *PUSG*, 8:287–88.

39. *OR*, 24(3): 373–75, 379, 380, 384; Simon, *PUSG*, 8:316.

40. *OR*, 24(3): 387, 316; Simon, *PUSG*, 8:321–25; Dana, *Recollections of the Civil War*, 62, 82–84.

41. *OR*, 24(3): 387, 316; Simon, *PUSG*, 8:321–25; Dana, *Recollections of the Civil War*, 62, 82–84; Brooks D. Simpson, *Triumph Over Adversity, 1822–1865* (Boston: Houghton Mifflin Company, 2000), 208; Ballard, *Grant at Vicksburg*, 42. For an in-depth examination that accepts the popular memory of Grant's drunkenness, see William S. McFeely, *Grant: A Biography* (New York: Norton, 1981), 132–35. For an exceptionally detailed examination of the evidence that does not accept the drunken theory, see Ballard, *Grant at Vicksburg*, 43–63.

42. *OR*, 24(3): 402–3, 410, 418; Orville E. Babcock Diary, June 15–July 4, 1863, USGPL.

43. *OR*, 24(3): 405, 427, 429–30, 444; *OR*, 24(1): 105; Simon, *PUSG*, 8:403; Grant, *Personal Memoirs*, 1:548; Dana, *Recollections of the Civil War*, 84; Ballard, *Grant at Vicksburg*, 125.

44. *OR*, 24(3): 428, 430–31.

45. *OR*, 24(3): 440, 449, 457–58; *OR*, 24(2): 208–9; Simon, *PUSG*, 8:440, 447, 449, 452.

46. *OR*, 24(3): 439, 442–43, 449–50; *OR*, 24(1): 43, 107–8.

47. *OR*, 24(1): 101, 104; Simon, *PUSG*, 8:356–57, 375; Sherman, *Memoirs*, 1:334.

48. *OR*, 24(1): 101, 104; Simon, *PUSG*, 8:356–57, 375; Sherman, *Memoirs*, 1:334.

49. *OR*, 24(1): 98, 100; Simon, *PUSG*, 8:361–62, 380, 388, 414, 432–33, 449, 454, 483–524.

50. *OR*, 24(1): 98, 100; Simon, *PUSG*, 8:361–62, 380, 388, 414, 432–33, 449, 454, 483–524.

51. *OR*, 24(3): 357, 419; Simon, *PUSG*, 8:314, 331.

52. Grant, *Personal Memoirs*, 1:541.

53. *OR*, 24(3): 360, 366–67, 385–86; *OR*, 24(1): 40–41.

54. *OR*, 24(3): 393; *OR*, 24(1): 165.

55. *OR*, 24(1): 84.

56. Catton, *Grant Moves South*, 466.

57. *OR*, 24(3): 419; *OR*, 24(1): 159, 162; James Harrison Wilson, *Under the Old Flag: Recollections of Military Operations in the War for the Union, the Spanish War, the Boxer Rebellion, Etc.*, 2 vols. (New York: D. Appleton and Company, 1912), 185–86; Catton, *Grant Moves South*, 466.

58. *OR*, 24(1): 102–3, 105; *OR*, 24(1): 43, 158.

59. *OR*, 24(1): 39–40; *OR*, 24(3): 365; Simon, *PUSG*, 8:347.

60. *OR*, 24(3): 425–26, 469; *OR*, 24(1): 108.

61. *OR*, 24(3): 372–73, 402; Simon, *PUSG*, 8:395.

62. Special Orders, May 25, 1863, Series 3, USGPL *OR*, 24(3): 412–13, 449.

63. Simon, *PUSG*, 8:319.

64. Simon, *PUSG*, 8:332, 376–77, 453, 445; Frederick D. Grant, "A Boy's Experience at Vicksburg," *Personal Recollections of the War of the Rebellion: Addresses Delivered before the Commandery of the State of New York, Military Order of the Loyal Legion of the United States*, ed. A. Noel Blakeman (New York: G. P. Putnam's Sons, 1907), 96; Fred Grant, "A Boy's Experience at Vicksburg," manuscript in Vicksburg files, USGPL, 31, 44.

65. Simon, *PUSG*, 8:375–79, 445; Grant, *Personal Memoirs*, 1:540.

66. *OR*, 24(3): 372; Simon, *PUSG*, 8:389–90.

67. Simon, *PUSG*, 8:445.

8. "Vicksburg Has Surrendered"

1. *War of the Rebellion: A Compilation of the Official Records of the Union and Confederate Armies* (Washington, DC: U.S. Government Printing Office, 1880–1901), vol. 24(part 3): 447, 452, 457. Hereafter cited as *OR* with volume and part afterward; all references are to series; *OR*, 24(1): 112.

2. *OR*, 24(3): 439, 447–48, 452, 457.

3. *OR*, 24(3): 452.

4. *OR*, 24(3): 458.

5. *OR*, 24(1): 112; Charles A. Dana, *Recollections of the Civil War* (New York: D. Appleton and Company, 1898), 91, 94.

6. *OR*, 24(1): 101, 107.

7. *OR*, 24(3): 458–59; *OR*, 24(1): 58.

8. *OR*, 24(1): 59; Ulysses S. Grant, *Personal Memoirs of U. S. Grant*, 2 vols. (New York: Charles L. Webster and Company, 1892), 1:557.

9. *OR*, 24(1): 59.

10. *OR*, 24(3): 459–60, 467; Grant, *Personal Memoirs*, 1:557–58.

11. *OR*, 24(3): 460, 470.

12. *OR*, 24(1): 60.

13. *OR*, 24(3): 460; *OR*, 24(1): 114; Grant, *Personal Memoirs*, 1:557–58.

14. *OR*, 24(3): 460; *OR*, 24(1): 115; Grant, *Personal Memoirs*, 1:559; Dana, *Recollections of the Civil War*, 97; Edwin C. Bearss, *The Vicksburg Campaign*, 3 vols. (Dayton, OH: Morningside, 1985), 3:1286.

15. *OR*, 24(1): 60, 115; Grant, *Personal Memoirs*, 1:559–60; Dana, *Recollections of the Civil War*, 97; Frederick D. Grant, "A Boy's Experience at Vicksburg," *Personal Recollections of the War of the Rebellion: Addresses Delivered before the Commandery of the State of New York, Military Order of the Loyal Legion of the United States*, ed. A. Noel Blakeman (New York: G. P. Putnam's Sons, 1907), 98; Bruce Catton, *Grant Moves South* (Boston: Little, Brown, and Company, 1960), 474–75.

16. Grant, *Personal Memoirs*, 1:561.

17. *OR*, 24(3): 460, 467.

18. *OR*, 24(1): 60–61, 115.

19. *OR*, 24(1): 60–61, 115; Grant, "A Boy's Experience at Vicksburg," 98.

20. *OR*, 24(3): 472.

21. Grant, "A Boy's Experience at Vicksburg," 99; *OR*, 24(3): 466–67, 471.

22. *OR*, 24(3): 470, 474, 477–78; *OR*, 24(1): 62; John Y. Simon and John F. Marszalek, eds., *The Papers of Ulysses S. Grant*, 32 vols. to date (Carbondale: Southern Illinois University Press, 1967–present), 8:524. Hereafter cited as Simon, *PUSG*, followed by volume and page number; Grant, *Personal Memoirs*, 1:554, 566–67;

Dana, *Recollections of the Civil War*, 99; Grant, "A Boy's Experience at Vicksburg," 99; Albert D. Richardson, *A Personal History of Ulysses S. Grant* (Hartford, CT: American Publishing Company, 1868), 334; Adam Badeau, *Military History of Ulysses S. Grant, from April, 1861, to April, 1865*, 2 vols. (New York: D. Appleton and Company, 1881), 1:387.

23. *OR*, 24(3): 470, 474, 477–78; *OR*, 24(1): 62; Simon, *PUSG*, 8:524; Grant, *Personal Memoirs*, 1:554, 566–67; Dana, *Recollections of the Civil War*, 99; Grant, "A Boy's Experience at Vicksburg," 99; Richardson, *Personal History of Ulysses S. Grant*, 334; Badeau, *Military History of Ulysses S. Grant*, 1:387; Sylvanus Cadwallader, *Three Years with Grant*, ed. Benjamin P. Thomas (Lincoln: University of Nebraska Press, 1996), 123.

24. *OR*, 24(3): 478.

25. *OR*, 24(3): 478–79, 483.

26. *OR*, 24(3): 481.

27. *OR*, 24(3): 484, 488–89; Grant, *Personal Memoirs*, 1:569.

28. *OR*, 24(3): 489, 493–94; Simon, *PUSG*, 8:482, 524.

29. *OR*, 24(3): 489, 493, 495.

30. *OR*, 24(3): 461.

31. *OR*, 24(3): 469, 500; *OR*, 24(1): 44.

32. *OR*, 24(3): 470, 491, 493, 499; *OR*, 24(1): 44; 57.

33. *OR*, 24(3): 480.

34. *OR*, 24(3): 500.

35. *OR*, 24(3): 460–63, 469; Simon, *PUSG*, 8:474.

36. *OR*, 24(3): 470–71.

37. *OR*, 24(3): 472.

38. *OR*, 24(3): 472–73.

39. For Jackson, see Jim Woodrick, *The Civil War Siege of Jackson, Mississippi* (Mount Pleasant, SC: Arcadia Publishing, 2016).

40. *OR*, 24(1): 62.

41. *OR*, 24(3): 483, 492, 498, 540–42.

42. *OR*, 24(1): 63.

43. *OR*, 24(3): 497.

44. *OR*, 24(3): 530; Simon, *PUSG*, 8:525.

Epilogue: "I Do Not Expect to Be Still"

1. John F. Marszalek, *Lincoln and the Military* (Carbondale: Southern Illinois University Press, 2014), 58; Charles Bracelen Flood, *Grant and Sherman: The Friendship That Won the Civil War* (New York: Farrar, Straus, and Giroux, 2005), 188.

2. Adam Badeau, *Military History of Ulysses S. Grant, from April, 1861, to April, 1865*, 2 vols. (New York: D. Appleton and Company, 1881), 1:399–400; Albert D.

Richardson, *A Personal History of Ulysses S. Grant* (Hartford, CT: American Publishing Company, 1868), 337.

3. John Russell Young, *Around the World with General Grant: A Narrative of the Visit of General U. S. Grant, Ex-President of the United States, to Various Countries in Europe, Asia, and Africa, in 1877, 1878, 1879. To Which Are Added Certain Conversations with General Grant on Questions Connected with American Politics and History* (New York: American News Company, 1879), 2:625.

4. Badeau, *Military History of Ulysses S. Grant,* 1:126–27.

5. Young, *Around the World with General Grant,* 2:626; Paul L. Schmelzer, "A Strong Mind: A Clausewitzian Biography of U. S. Grant" (PhD diss., Texas Christian University, 2010).

6. *War of the Rebellion: A Compilation of the Official Records of the Union and Confederate Armies* (Washington, DC: U.S. Government Printing Office, 1880–1901), vol. 24(part 1): 58–59. Hereafter cited as *OR* with volume and part afterward; all references are to series.

7. Ulysses S. Grant, *Personal Memoirs of U. S. Grant,* 2 vols. (New York: Charles L. Webster and Company, 1892), 1:533, 575; *OR,* 24(1): 46, 58.

8. *OR,* 24(1): 157, 165–86.

9. John Y. Simon and John F. Marszalek, eds., *The Papers of Ulysses S. Grant,* 32 vols. to date (Carbondale: Southern Illinois University Press, 1967–present), 8:445. Hereafter cited as Simon, *PUSG,* followed by volume and page number.

10. Charles A. Dana, *Recollections of the Civil War* (New York: D. Appleton and Company, 1898), 102.

11. Bruce Catton, *Grant Moves South* (Boston: Little, Brown, and Company, 1960), 104.

12. Grant, *Personal Memoirs,* 1:567.

BIBLIOGRAPHIC ESSAY

There is no lack of resources dealing with Ulysses S. Grant at Vicksburg, but the major primary sources from which this book was principally written are relatively few. The vast majority of Grant's correspondence is unsurprisingly found in *War of the Rebellion: A Compilation of the Official Records of the Union and Confederate Armies* (Washington, DC: U.S. Government Printing Office, 1880–1901). Thousands and thousands of Grant's official orders, letters, and notes are contained therein, and the Vicksburg entries (volume 24 in three parts) are, as would be expected, especially rich in Grant material. Similarly, *The Official Records of the Union and Confederate Navies in the War of the Rebellion* (Washington, DC: Government Printing Office, 1894–1922) also contains many Grant items, although some were cross-published from the army records. The thirty-two volumes of Grant papers published under the auspices of the Ulysses S. Grant Association were another major source of Grant letters: John Y. Simon and John F. Marszalek, eds., *The Papers of Ulysses S. Grant*, 32 vols. to date (Carbondale: Southern Illinois University Press, 1967–present). Volumes 6, 7, and 8 contain a wide array of Grant material, including much of what is in the *Official Records* but also including a vast amount of Grant's nonofficial letters, particularly to his family. His letters to Julia contained therein are particularly rich in determining Grant's mindset and inner thoughts. Finally, the Ulysses S. Grant Presidential Library at Mississippi State University contains a wealth of material, including unpublished Grant letters and contextual items.

Postwar primary sources are also abundant, although these have to be cross-checked against the contemporary records to weed out any errors of fact or interpretation that crept in during the intervening years following the war. The most notable, of course, is Ulysses S. Grant, *Personal Memoirs of U. S. Grant*, 2 vols. (New York: Charles L. Webster and Company, 1892). A wonderful new annotated edition has just appeared: John F. Marszalek et al., eds., *The Personal Memoirs of Ulysses S. Grant: The Complete Annotated Edition* (Cambridge: Harvard University Belknap Press, 2017). Grant also gave a wealth of information during his world tour after his presidency, and much of that material is found in John Russell Young, *Around the World with General Grant: A Narrative of the Visit of General U. S. Grant, Ex-President of the United States, to Various Countries in Europe, Asia, and Africa, in 1877, 1878, 1879. To Which Are Added*

Certain Conversations with General Grant on Questions Connected with American Politics and History (New York: American News Company, 1879). Members of Grant's immediate family also left memoirs and remembrances, including John Y. Simon, ed., *The Personal Memoirs of Julia Dent Grant [Mrs. Ulysses S. Grant]* (New York: G. P. Putnam's Sons, 1975) and Frederick D. Grant, "A Boy's Experience at Vicksburg," in *Personal Recollections of the War of the Rebellion: Addresses Delivered before the Commandery of the State of New York, Military Order of the Loyal Legion of the United States*, ed. A. Noel Blakeman (New York: G. P. Putnam's Sons, 1907). The Grant Presidential Library at Starkville, Mississippi, contains a lengthier version of Fred's essay, in which more detail of his time with his father during the campaign is given.

Grant's subordinates and associates during the campaign also left letters and memoirs, although much of their contemporary correspondence can also be found in the *Official Records*. Several friends left postwar memoirs as well, although these also have to be fact-checked against more accurate contemporary records. The most notable is William T. Sherman, *Memoirs of General William T. Sherman: Written by Himself*, 2 vols. (New York: D. Appleton and Company, 1875). Grant's naval counterpart also wrote a memoir in which Grant figured largely, David Dixon Porter, *Incidents and Anecdotes of the Civil War* (New York: D. Appleton and Company, 1885). One of Grant's staff officers similarly left a diary and memoir, James Harrison Wilson, *Under the Old Flag: Recollections of Military Operations in the War for the Union, the Spanish War, the Boxer Rebellion, Etc.*, 2 vols. (New York: D. Appleton and Company, 1912). Two of Grant's headquarters associates provided reminiscences, although they were written decades later and sometimes contain obvious errors where they do not agree with each other or the contemporary record. Nevertheless, Sylvanus Cadwallader, *Three Years with Grant*, ed. Benjamin P. Thomas (Lincoln: University of Nebraska Press, 1996) and Charles A. Dana, *Recollections of the Civil War* (New York: D. Appleton and Company, 1898) offer an inside look at Grant's activities during the campaign.

Secondary biographies of Grant are legion, although earlier ones such as Adam Badeau, *Military History of Ulysses S. Grant, from April, 1861, to April, 1865*, 2 vols. (New York: D. Appleton and Company, 1881) contain some of Grant's own imprint. Another early biography full of anecdotal material is Albert D. Richardson, *A Personal History of Ulysses S. Grant* (Hartford, CT: American Publishing Company, 1868). More modern biographies include the brand new Ron Chernow, *Grant* (New York: Penguin, 2017), and Ronald C. White, *American Ulysses: A Life of Ulysses S. Grant* (New York: Random House, 2016); William S. McFeely, *Grant: A Biography* (New York: Norton, 1981); H. W. Brands, *The Man Who Saved the Union: Ulysses S. Grant in War and Peace* (New York: Doubleday, 2012), and Brooks D. Simpson, *Triumph Over Adversity, 1822–1865* (Boston: Houghton Mifflin Company, 2000). A convenient overview of Grant's life told largely in his own words is John F. Marszalek, ed., *The Best Writings of Ulysses S. Grant* (Carbondale: Southern Illinois University Press, 2015).

Several historians have examined Grant's military life in particular, including T. Harry Williams, *Lincoln and His Generals* (New York: Alfred A. Knopf, 1952); Bruce Catton, *Grant Moves South* (Boston: Little, Brown, and Company, 1960); J. F. C. Fuller, *The Generalship of Ulysses S. Grant* (Bloomington: Indiana University Press, 1958); Bruce Catton, *U. S. Grant and the American Military Tradition* (Boston: Little, Brown, and Company, 1954); Kenneth P. Williams, *Grant Rises in the West: From Iuka to Vicksburg, 1862–1863* (Lincoln: University of Nebraska Press, 1997); Michael B. Ballard, *U. S. Grant: The Making of a General* (Lanham, MD: Rowman and Littlefield, 2005); and Harry S. Laver, *A General Who Will Fight: The Leadership of Ulysses S. Grant* (Lexington: University Press of Kentucky, 2012).

Several historians have examined Grant's military career in specific ways or focused on specific events, including Paul L. Schmelzer, "A Strong Mind: A Clausewitzian Biography of U. S. Grant" (PhD diss., Texas Christian University, 2010); Edward H. Bonekemper III, *Ulysses S. Grant: A Victor, Not a Butcher: The Military Genius of the Man Who Won the Civil War* (Washington, DC: Regnery History, 2004); and Jonathan D. Sarna, *When General Grant Expelled the Jews* (New York: Schocken, 2012).

Much information can also be gleaned from biographies of Grant's superiors and subordinates. His relationship with Halleck is treated in John F. Marszalek, *Commander of All Lincoln's Armies: A Life of General Henry W. Halleck* (Cambridge: Harvard University Press, 2004). Grant's army counterpart working in the Mississippi Valley can be seen in James G. Hollandsworth Jr., *Pretense of Glory: The Life of General Nathaniel P. Banks* (Baton Rouge: Louisiana State University Press, 1998), while Chester G. Hearn, *Admiral David Dixon Porter: The Civil War Years* (Annapolis, MD: Naval Institute Press, 1996) covers Grant's naval equivalent.

Grant's corps commanders mostly have good biographies, including a joint biography of Grant and his favored subordinate, Sherman: Charles Bracelen Flood, *Grant and Sherman: The Friendship That Won the Civil War* (New York: Farrar, Straus, and Giroux, 2005). The standard biography of Sherman is John F. Marszalek, *Sherman: A Soldier's Passion for Order* (New York: Free Press, 1993). Grant's disjointed relationship with McClernand is covered in Richard L. Kiper, *Major General John Alexander McClernand: Politician in Uniform* (Kent, OH: Kent State University Press, 1999). See Bernarr Cresap, *Appomattox Commander: The Story of General E. O. C. Ord* (San Diego, CA: A. S. Barnes and Company, 1981) for McClernand's successor. Jeffrey N. Lash, *A Politician Turned General: The Civil War Career of Stephen Augustus Hurlbut* (Kent, OH: Kent State University Press, 2003) deals with Grant's rearward corps commander. The lack of a modern biography of James B. McPherson is amazing and marks one of the great historiographical needs in Civil War scholarship.

Lower-level commanders have fewer biographies, but some do exist, including Stanley P. Hirshson, *Grenville M. Dodge: Soldier, Politician, Railroad Pioneer* (Bloomington: Indiana University Press, 1967); James Pickett Jones, *Black Jack: John A. Logan and Southern Illinois in the Civil War Era* (Carbondale: Southern Illinois University Press, 1967); William E. Parrish, *Frank Blair: Lincoln's Conservative* (Columbia: University of Missouri Press, 1998); and Mary Bobbitt Townsend, *Yankee Warhorse: A Biography of Major General Peter Osterhaus* (Columbia: University of Missouri Press, 2010). The relationship between Grant and many of his commanders is explored in essay form in Steven E. Woodworth, ed., *Grant's Lieutenants: From Cairo to Vicksburg* (Lawrence: University Press of Kansas, 2001).

The literature on the Vicksburg campaign is also legion. The starting point among secondary works is obviously Edwin C. Bearss, *The Vicksburg Campaign*, 3 vols. (Dayton: Morningside, 1985). The standard one-volume history is Michael B. Ballard, *Vicksburg: The Campaign That Opened the Mississippi* (Chapel Hill: University of North Carolina Press, 2004). A unique geographical investigation of the land campaign is Warren E. Grabau, *Ninety-Eight Days: A Geographer's View of the Vicksburg Campaign* (Knoxville: University of Tennessee Press, 2000). Other standard works include William L. Shea and Terrence J. Winschel, *Vicksburg Is the Key: The Struggle for the Mississippi River* (Lincoln: University of Nebraska Press, 2003); Terrence J. Winschel, *Triumph and Defeat: The Vicksburg Campaign* (Mason City, IA: Savas Publishing Company, 1999); Terrence J. Winschel, *Triumph and Defeat: The Vicksburg Campaign*, vol. 2 (New York: Savas Beatie, 2006); and Steven E. Woodworth and Charles D. Grear, eds., *The Vicksburg Campaign: March 29–May 18, 1863* (Carbondale: Southern Illinois University Press, 2013).

Individual battle and siege studies are fewer, but include Timothy B. Smith, *Champion Hill: Decisive Battle for Vicksburg* (New York: Savas Beatie, 2004) and Justin S. Solonick, *Engineering Victory: The Union Siege of Vicksburg* (Carbondale: Southern Illinois University Press, 2015). Smaller essays on Port Gibson, Raymond, Jackson, and Big Black River Bridge can be found in Woodworth and Grear, *The Vicksburg Campaign*. Smaller treatments of earlier bayou operations and raids can be found in numerous magazine and journal articles.

While the amount of literature on Grant is large, as is that on the Vicksburg Campaign, few historians prior to this book have combined the two and examined Grant at Vicksburg in depth. The standard treatment is the antiquated Earl S. Miers, *The Web of Victory: Grant at Vicksburg* (New York: Knopf, 1955). More recently, Michael B. Ballard, *Grant at Vicksburg: The General and the Siege* (Carbondale: Southern Illinois University Press, 2013) dealt with Grant during the siege but by definition only covered the period from late May to July 1863.

INDEX

Italicized page numbers indicate figures.

Timothy B. Smith teaches history at the University of Tennessee at Martin. He has published numerous books on the Civil War, including *Grant Invades Tennessee: The 1862 Battles for Forts Henry and Donelson* and *Shiloh: Conquer or Perish*.

THE WORLD OF ULYSSES S. GRANT

Edited by John F. Marszalek & Timothy B. Smith

After the assassination of Abraham Lincoln, Ulysses S. Grant became the most popular American alive. He symbolized the Federal victory, the destruction of slavery, and the preservation of the Union. Grant remained a popular topic among historians who have written about those years, but over time scholars and the public removed Grant from his place in the pantheon of leading Americans. As the decades passed and attitudes toward the Civil War and war itself changed, the public's perception of Grant devolved: no longer a national idol, Grant was instead written off as a heartless general and corrupt president. In the early twenty-first century, however, Grant's place in history is being reinterpreted. Now he is increasingly seen as a success on the battlefield, a leading proponent of African American civil rights, and the first of the modern American presidents.

To further an understanding of Ulysses S. Grant through a close analysis of his life and work, this innovative book series provides a thorough examination of particular events and periods of Grant's life in order to present important insights into his generalship, presidency, influence, and reputation. Books in the series explore Grant's character as well as his role in American history. By delving into the deeper detail and context of what Grant did and saw, this series aims to break new ground and provide the historical profession and the general reading public with accurate, readable perspectives showing Grant's significant contributions to the world he lived in and to the years that followed.

OTHER BOOKS IN
The World of Ulysses S. Grant

Citizen of a Wider Commonwealth: Ulysses S. Grant's Postpresidential Diplomacy
Edwina S. Campbell

The Best Writings of Ulysses S. Grant
Edited by John F. Marszalek